From the
Outside in

Other Lake Hickory Resources

James H. Royston, Executive Editor
George W. Bullard Jr., Senior Editor
SeniorEditor@LakeHickoryResources.org

Operation Inasmuch:
Mobilizing Believers beyond the Walls of the Church
David W. Crocker

Spiritual Leadership in a Secular Age:
Building Bridges Instead of Barriers
Edward H. Hammett

Pursuing the Full Kingdom Potential of Your Congregation
George W. Bullard Jr.

Seeds for the Future:
Growing Organic Leaders for Living Churches
Robert D. Dale

Christ-Centered Coaching:
7 Benefits for Ministry Leaders
Jane Creswell

Available at
www.lakehickoryresources.com

From the Outside in

Connecting to the Community around You

RONALD W. JOHNSON

Lake Hickory
RESOURCES
ST. LOUIS, MISSOURI

Cover art: FotoSearch
Cover and interior design: Elizabeth Wright

See more Lake Hickory resources at
www.lakehickoryresources.com or www.cbp21.com

10 9 8 7 6 5 4 3 2 1   06 07 08 09 10 11

Library of Congress Cataloging-in-Publication Data

Johnson, Ronald W., 1949-
    From the outside in : connecting to the community around you / Ronald W. Johnson.
        p. cm.
    Includes bibliographical references.
    ISBN-13: 978-0-827242-53-1 (pbk.)
    ISBN-10: 0-827242-53-0 (pbk.)
    1. Community–Religious aspects–Christianity. 2. Church attendance. 3. Evangelistic work. I. Title.
BV625.J64 2006
253–dc22

                                                2005037496

Printed in the United States of America

*To my students at the McAfee School of Theology,
who have dared to dream along with me.*

Contents

Editors' Foreword

Inspiration and Wisdom for Twenty-First–Century Christian Leaders

You have chosen wisely in deciding to study and learn from a **Lake Hickory Resources** book. Lake Hickory Resources publishes for

- congregational leaders who desire to serve effectively
- Christian ministers who pursue excellence in service
- members of a congregation that desires to reach its full Kingdom potential
- denominational leaders who want to come alongside affiliated congregations in a servant leadership role

Lake Hickory Resources is an inspiration- and wisdom-sharing vehicle of Lake Hickory Learning Communities. LHLC is the web of relationships developing from the base of Hollifield Leadership Center (www.Hollifield.org) near Hickory, North Carolina. LHLC addresses emerging strategic issues of leadership development for congregations, denominations, and parachurch organizations.

The mission of **Lake Hickory Resources** currently is being expressed through two meaningful avenues. First, George Bullard, executive coach for Lake Hickory Learning Communities, also is senior editor for *Net Results* magazine (www.NetResults.org), a national, transdenominational publication that appears monthly in print and electronic form.

Second, **Lake Hickory Resources** publishes books in partnership with Christian Board of Publication. Once this partnership is in full production it will produce eight to twelve new books each year.

We welcome your comments on these books, and we welcome your suggestions for new subject areas and authors we ought to consider.

James H. Royston, Executive Editor
George W. Bullard Jr., Senior Editor
SeniorEditor@LakeHickoryResources.org

Lake Hickory Learning Communities is a ministry of
www.NorthCarolinaBaptists.org

Introduction

Each summer my students travel with me to a different country in the world to be immersed in the culture of that country and to learn how Christians there cope with the challenges that are unique to their culture. It is a meaningful experience for the students and a significant way to understand the dynamics of mission and evangelism from a different perspective. We were in Belgium during the summer of 2004. We interviewed Christians and church leaders across the country. We learned how difficult it has become to reach people there with the gospel. It is a secular state where the majority of the population simply does not attend church at all. We spoke with Catholic priests in large cathedrals who seemed to all agree that the culture viewed the church as a place to be married or buried, but not critical to everyday life. One priest told us that mass is generally poorly attended, even at Easter.

Protestant churches have an even harder time, since the majority of Christians in Belgium are Catholic. One pastor who has been working for more than twenty-five years has fewer than fifty members in his church congregation. He summed up the situation by saying to me, "In America there is religious noise in the culture. Everywhere in America you hear people talking about faith. Not here. It is strangely quiet." I understood his meaning.

In America, we bemoan the fact that so many of our churches are less than full. Research has shown that the largest group of persons who say they believe in Jesus Christ are those who actually do not attend church. We have religious programs on the television and radio, religious slogans on bumper stickers, and almost every media figure or politician evokes the name of God at some point in speeches. We are a people who talk a lot about God in everyday conversation. There is indeed much religious noise in our culture. One would think that this interest ought to be found at a heightened level on Sundays. The truth is that many of our churches feel like the message that is preached is just not being heard in America today. Radio talk show hosts and groups in the culture often negatively characterize Christians because they see their beliefs as a threat. The political "Religious Right" has not helped the cause of the church's appeal to the larger public. Many in the culture have been turned away by the political overtones and debates over arguments such as the display of the Ten Commandments in government buildings and schools, pro-choice/pro-life issues, and positions related to alternate lifestyles. It is indeed clear that many have turned a deaf ear to what the churches are saying about faith.

This book attempts to address that issue from a missional perspective. Why is it that communities that surround our churches seem not to hear the message that is being proclaimed within the walls of the churches? Why do so many people stereotype Christians as being legalistic, narrow-minded people? Why is it that we do not seem to see communities or individuals in the larger culture changed by the message we proclaim every Sunday?

Jesus came preaching the kingdom of God. It was good news. The culture was buzzing with the message he proclaimed. Have the cultures around our churches just grown weary of hearing the message, or have they not really heard it at all? Has it been deadened by religious language that just does not connect, or by ritual that has little meaning to "post-moderns" today? It is clear from most of the research that has been done that Americans are indeed interested in spiritual things. But they seem deaf—or at least indifferent—to the way many churches speak about faith.

The time may have come when we Christians need to learn—or at least relearn—a different language: the language and actions of the kingdom of God. Rather than speaking in church-ese or in religious platitudes, maybe we need to take seriously the kind of language that Jesus spoke when he talked about the kingdom of God. We need to learn to listen with the heart of God to what people around us are telling us about their search for meaning. Then we need to respond in ways that are sensitive to what they are saying.

Many people have written about the kingdom of God. There are those who are uncomfortable with such language. I fully respect their concern that words like *kingdom* suggest negative images in the minds of many. I believe that we can redefine concepts, however, in ways that help Christians understand the fullness of images, and at the same time discover ways to communicate those images that will be attractive to the culture around us. Even so, my purpose is not to argue with that conversation or scholarship as it pertains to God's kingdom. Rather, I hope to focus the subject in a manner that will suggest some ways that churches can better interface with the culture around them.

When we meet a person who is hearing-impaired, we cannot communicate by merely shouting. Yet, I am afraid many feel that is what we are doing. We need instead to learn a different language. I want to suggest that we take seriously the language of the kingdom of God, and not only the language but the mind-set and actions related to living a life focused on what Jesus taught the kingdom of God to be. It may just be that this is a language that some who have given up on organized religion can understand.

Over my years of teaching, I have had to modify my language and illustrations to enable my students to understand me. Many of these students have no idea what I talk about when I illustrate events that seem recent in my memory, but happened before they were born. I have had to leave the 1960s behind. The events, the music, and the feel of my student days make no sense to them. I have had to learn their language, which, at times, I have to admit, makes little to no sense to me. But it makes sense to them and it defines how they look at life. Why do we think that the way we communicate the gospel is exempt from changes in language, action, music, ministry, or application? This, in many ways, suggests what it will take to become a church for the twenty-first century. I am convinced that the cultures around our churches need not turn a deaf ear to us. But they will never hear us or the gospel we proclaim if we do not listen to them.

I have tried to write this book in a way that speaks to churches in general. However, much of my experience in ministry has been in the Baptist context, and many of my examples in this work reflect that. I have worked in churches of other traditions on many occasions, and have found that the propositions I offer in this book do translate across denominational lines. I offer these ideas with the belief that the grains of truth can be taken and applied in each tradition in a way that fits most appropriately.

As is always the case, one does not write a text without the influence of many others. My friends in the academy, churches I have served, and ordinary Christians have all contributed. I have had ongoing conversations with several people that have encouraged me and challenged my thinking. Colleagues in the Academy for Evangelism in Theological Education have been most supportive. My good friend Hal Poe and I have been conversation partners for over twenty years and each time we get together the ideas we bounce off one another soon wind up in print. I am also grateful to Zihna Edwards, my teaching assistant, who read and reread the manuscript, and to my students who over the course of years have heard me lecture on this issue and have encouraged me along the way. And thanks be to God for the McAfee School of Theology, whose faculty feels to me like family. We laugh together, we debate issues, we teach together, and in the end we stir up enough ideas in each other's offices and in the hallways to spend a lifetime writing about them.

Ronald W. Johnson, Th.D.
McAfee School of Theology,
Mercer University
Atlanta, Georgia, May 2005

1

Becoming a Church for the Twenty-first Century

My children have reached the age at which what they seem to enjoy most in family conversations is listening to my father recall what it was like when he was a young boy. On those occasions when we can gather all the family together for a Sunday meal or special occasion, they will often invite him to "tell us what it was like when you were growing up." I must admit that I enjoy hearing my father reminisce. Not long ago, in a conversation with him about the world's problems, he paused and said with a sigh, "This is not the world I was born into." He was right. It is not the same world. The cultures around us seem to sense that fact. Governments recognize the fact. Schools, industry, technology, all recognize the fact that it is a different world.

The burning question on my mind is whether our churches recognize just how different the world is today. For example, Martin Luther King Jr. once said that Sunday morning is the most segregated hour in America. It still seems to be that way. There are exceptions, of course, but the plurality of our daily lives seems to hold no significant counterpart in many houses of worship. There is still resistance not only to the integration of different racial and language groups, but also significant prejudice toward women as faith leaders, although many of those same women hold important leadership positions in industry. This is but one example of how the world around us has changed, and yet many churches have not. Other indicators are there. Gender-inclusive language is growing in use in the public, but hardly in many churches. There are laws that respect and enable those who are physically challenged, and yet many of our churches lack access for people with physical needs. Many people work hours that include weekends, yet worship services are still structured around "milking time" or the agricultural lifestyle. There are a host of other examples we could mention in conversation together.

The most graphic indicator of the need for the church to rethink its mission in the world has become evident to me as I have ministered there. Let me explain. I had always dreamed of being pastor of a church somewhere, but when I finished seminary my ministerial career seemed to go in a different direction. I worked for my denomination for nearly twenty-five years, and for the last ten years I have taught Mission and Evangelism at the masters and doctoral levels at the McAfee School of Theology of Mercer University in Atlanta, Georgia.

During this time, though, I have also had the great privilege of serving as interim pastor in sixteen different churches. The last two churches I served have been the inspiration for this book and have brought the issue of the mission of the church into sharper focus for me. These two congregations are a study in contrasts: one church unclear about its mission in the world, the other growing in its understanding.[1]

One of the churches is a dying congregation. Right now, it is still large enough to give the members the sense that all is well, but it is not. It is a congregation of older persons, largely monocultural. It is all white, upper class, and formal in its worship. The city in which it is located is growing with many young families and increasing ethnic diversity. The members of the church seem to live under the impression that because they have been the historic "First Church" downtown, their future is secure. Worship has changed little in the last fifty years. Other ministries of the church are all focused inward.

The other church is smaller, but growing. It is full of young families, is multicultural, ministers directly to its community, and seems to have a future. One member explained to me that the church seems to be always rediscovering itself and reinventing itself.[2] Each time they discover a need in the community around them, they respond, sometimes with success and at other times with an increased awareness of the depth of the opportunity. But they are not afraid to launch out and try new approaches. My guess is that in fifty years, the former church, if they continue in their present path, will be out of business, or at least much more marginalized in the community. The latter church, if they continue to discover what God is doing around them, may very well continue to grow and thrive as they touch lives.

Why is there such a sharp contrast? What causes some congregations to thrive while others die a slow death? Very often church consultants are asked this question by the leadership of congregations. Almost monthly I receive a phone call from some pastor or church leader wanting me to come and diagnose their situation. They hope that I will bring them some word that will spark the flame and release them from the doldrums, or solve whatever ills they perceive they have at the time. More often than not, an underlying motivation for such consultation occurs when someone in the church leadership believes that the church may be losing or has already lost effectiveness in the community. They are often correct. Some congregants may not address the uneasiness openly, but everyone seems to sense the indicators. Worship numbers may have dropped in recent years; there is more white hair than noisy children in the hallways; church additions don't seem to keep up with losses; baptisms or confirmation classes have fallen off. The alarm bell grows louder. So the church turns to their denominational leaders or to outside consultants to try to fix the situation. It is a rare occurrence when the fix works. What is needed is not a new prescription—a new program of sorts, but rather different DNA.[3] The different DNA that I am referring to is a complete change, away from the corporate or institutional mind-set of the church and toward a direction of the church that reflects as closely as possible an orientation toward the kingdom of God. This book is about that different DNA, the kind of DNA that will serve to interface the church with a world that seems to be seeking answers.

On Mission in a Different World

The challenges for churches living in the pluralism of the twenty-first century cannot be adequately addressed by simply initiating a new program, no matter how popular the secular or religious media has made it. Congregations that are in decline cannot suddenly take on new meaning or identity within the community by simply tinkering with more effective marketing strategies that endeavor to pitch the church to an otherwise apathetic culture. The problems go deeper.

Church consultant Lyle Schaller wrote in the 1980s that we were living in a different world.[4] It is a world that is not just uniformly different, however. Churches today are faced with an entirely new world often divided by religious perspective and opinion.[5] It is a post 9/11 world, in which suspicion of religion is more widespread in the culture, and where caution and uneasiness rule the day.[6] It is a world in which global conflict is the norm. The problems that communities face are no longer simply local; they have global implications.

Yet, the reality is that people are still searching for answers to spiritual problems. Much of the research on religion seems to affirm that America is a nation of spiritually interested people. Many denominations and churches are in decline at a time when the largest religious demographic encompasses people who believe in God and affirm Jesus Christ as Savior, but never attend church. The potential for ministry to large numbers of people who affirm Christianity yet do not attend church is significant. Tapping that potential will require commitment to an identity that is markedly different from the present *status quo*. Both Christians and churches will have to reexamine who they are through the lenses of the cultures around them, and begin to take seriously the challenges and implications of living as witnesses who reflect the character of the kingdom of God. Churches, as much as possible, will have to make an effort to avoid the corporate or institutional mind-set, most often mirrored in American business, that characterizes so many.

There has been a renewed interest in the kingdom of God. Several new books have appeared on the shelves that speak of the ethics, the work, the hope, and the place of mission in the kingdom of God. It seems entirely appropriate to redefine the true essence of the kingdom-focused church so that Christians can understand the implications of the language. This will need to be language that is used inside the church. It will make little sense outside to people who do not know the language of Zion. However, the issue is critical to the church becoming what our Lord intended. If the church can recover a vision of mission the way it is viewed in Scripture, it can be renewed and become a powerful force in the world. Paul Hiebert writes, "If in Christian missions we recover that vision, we will be freed from the tyranny of activism and human-centeredness and recover the long-range perspective and coherence that we now lack. We will joyfully participate in God's mission because we have met a missionary God, and because he has sent us into the world to proclaim salvation, righteousness, justice, and peace."[7] When Christians fully understand the implications of the kingdom of God, the associated fears can be laid to rest and the true nature of the kingdom can be seen as an appropriate characteristic of churches. To do so will require a boldness to confront the critics who do not want to address the true nature of a church that focuses its life on the kingdom of God. Many of the critics may well be found among the loyal members of local churches who feel much safer in a controlled spiritual climate and less comfortable with the challenges Jesus set forth when he talked about the kingdom of God. Nevertheless, the shift has to occur.

Changing the Genetic Code

For most congregations, the first step in moving toward a kingdom orientation is the honest admission that they are often more institutional or businesslike in their orientation than they are spiritual. For example, when most churches choose to build a building, their first thoughts are often which bank to use, what the interest rates will be, and how to raise the money. I once met a pastor in New York whose congregation believed that if they would build a new building, God would be their banker. They literally prayed and believed the new facility into reality. "It was amazing," he said, "how the more we prayed about the building we needed, the more people stepped up and helped. People donated their time, money, and labor. We never borrowed a cent."

Of course, there are many who will doubt that such an approach is possible or efficient. The point is that many churches, large or small, often conduct themselves like any other business in town, adopting many of the same strategies to accomplish goals that are seen in the corporate world.

Moving toward a kingdom orientation where total trust in God is the norm will be difficult: many in the church will doubt it can work.

Another major hurdle to be overcome is that many Christians and churches hold an assumptive position about their place in the culture and the way they have been engaged in mission. For most believers who have grown up in the churches, the mission and evangelism foundations they learned have asserted that Christians are naturally equipped to conquer the world for Christ. The music and rhetoric we use in our churches builds confidence that suggests victory. But the assumptive position that has been taken has generally not allowed for serious questioning of methods or programs, theological foundations, or an exploration of the challenges presented by the emerging postmodern world. Christians cannot simply assume that we know how to be on mission today and how to effectively share the gospel. Assuming that what we need are newer programs that will reach postmoderns or newer methods that will reach the increased numbers of new immigrants, holds fast to the idea that we know what to do. In reality, we are repeating the same old patterns of behavior. This is a highly rationalistic, modern approach that often does not fit a world that is increasingly postmodern and relativistic.

One of the greatest challenges to becoming a kingdom-focused church is theological in nature. At the very heart of most churches is their understanding of salvation. But many Christian faith traditions have understandings of salvation that are quite narrow in scope. Many conservative traditions in particular must face the fact that, very often, their understanding of salvation is only in terms of the apocalyptic; in other words, saving people from eternal disaster. An understanding of the holistic nature of salvation in terms of not only the soul, but of the total experience of humankind, is vital to helping people today understand Christianity. There are hosts of people today who are not worried about heaven or hell. Those concepts are far off for them. Rather, they are more concerned about living a life that has some meaning or purpose. What many people today want to discover is whether there is any redemptive benefit to the life they are currently living.

Each Christian and each church has to discover, or perhaps rediscover, a holistic theology of the kingdom of God within the experience of human life. Instead of focusing on the abstractions of meaning for the Christian life, an honest examination of the concrete biblical intention for human life will need to be paramount in the believer's communication of God's purposes in the world. Connecting a holistic theology to human life means that every aspect of human life is a matter of God's concern. Social justice and ministry issues can be taken seriously and viewed soberly in a more holistic theology. Christians and congregations will realize that to approach salvation holistically will engage them to be as concerned for the issues of poverty, abuse, hunger, and addiction as they are about heaven or hell.

A more holistic theology will appreciate the fact that God is always redeeming, and that the Divine is always in the process of revealing to humanity the intentions of the Creator. Thus our attitude toward persons outside the Christian tradition can be more effective. Secularists and persons from the world's various religions can be related to more inclusively through the lens of divine revelation to all humankind. We understand that God is concerned with the redemption of every sector of the human condition. Christians who develop a more holistic view of salvation will be equipped to take seriously the reality of revelation expressed in world religions. They will be able to enter into authentic dialogue with those who are seeking to follow the revelation of their own religion. If as Christians we understand that God is seeking to be known in the entirety of the human condition, and proceed from that theological position, each Christian will be more fully able to express through dialogue a sense of the uniqueness of Christ within the context of the search for meaning found within the world's religions.

Approaching salvation as exclusively the end goal for persons ignores the present reality of the human experience and the dynamic process of faith development. Simply believing that Jesus will come again to receive the saved and to usher them into a perfect world ignores the words of Jeremiah 9:23–24. In this passage, God wishes to establish steadfast love, justice, and righteousness on the earth. These are the issues in which the Lord delights, according to Jeremiah. It is notable that God wishes to establish these on the earth and does not speak of them as needing to be established in heaven.[8] These attributes are already in the heavenly realm, but they need to be on the earth. Evangelistic concerns should take seriously the earth issues that affect all of humanity.

Another hurdle that will need to be crossed is the ecumenical barrier. To believe that any one denomination or church or faith group can relate to or evangelize the world with its own considered understanding of the biblical mandate simply ignores the reality of witness as a communal effort. More needs to be done across denominational lines, faith traditions, and in cooperation with other Christians to accomplish mission to the world. Interfaith dialogue and cooperation is essential to kingdom-oriented vision that will renew the mission of all churches.

It is simply time for us to become students of demographic change, postmodernism, and lifestyle orientation in the world around us. The regional nature of some faith traditions, for example that of Baptists in the South, has insulated them in the past from the problems of demographic change, worldview shifts, and the need to understand the dynamics of culture. It is no longer the case today. Baptists, Methodists, Presbyterians, Catholics, Lutherans—all denominations now find themselves in a different world. They must face the challenges that have been unmet and that threaten to place not only their particular denomination but Christians in general in a small subcultural position if they fail to take seriously what is happening in the world. Denominational leaders need to listen to the work of sociologists and missiologists. Church agencies need to embrace dialogue with scholars who are studying cultural trends. Churches need to move away from a programmatic approach designed exclusively for religiously oriented persons, and toward an incarnational model of mission that will place the church among persons who follow other faiths or philosophies.[9] Engaging the culture, instead of insulating away from it, is a must for the future of every church.

While there are other hurdles that need to be overcome in order to accomplish a major shift in the mission of Christians, the corporate or institutional hurdle seems to be the most formidable. Since the 1950s, the corporate model of denominational life and church life has dominated. The corporate or institutional model has caused churches to invest in cooperation as the primary model for mission, and to fund home and overseas missions by sending money to centralized mission agencies. The passion for mission has therefore been delegated, along with considerable funds, to the work of agencies who then send others on mission for the churches. As a result, the passion of local churches for mission has been generally diminished to local or community-based efforts, or has not been inclusive of the world, except through identification with the work of the mission-sending agencies they sponsor. The average church member is led to feel that giving money to missions is the sum total of mission involvement to the world. Mission has been institutionalized instead of being incarnational.

The corporate or institutional–and most often denominational–model can also limit the evangelistic passion of churches. The sharing of the good news of the kingdom has suffered reproach as it has been reduced to crass recruitment: a set of spiritual laws, a plan of salvation, or a host of other programs that resemble a "bait and switch" mind-set. Many of these programs are passed along to the churches by their agencies for the churches to implement in their context. Little to no consideration is given to the community in which the church finds itself. It is rather assumed, in an efficient and businesslike corporate sense, that what will work in one part of the country will work in the whole of the nation. Thus evangelism is limited, reduced to a program often participated in by the most passionate, and seldom practiced in ways that reflect the holistic nature of the kingdom. Such an approach does not usually carry the invitational characteristics of the messianic banquet, at which all are invited to taste and sample the good things of God. An evangelistic witness that touches the deepest needs of human life with all of its questions generally fails when it is reduced to a package to be opened and poured out on the culture.

Much is being written today about the missional church.[10] We need to be careful, however, that the emphasis on the kingdom-oriented church does not itself become reduced to just another new programmatic response.

If the focus on the *missio Dei,* or God's mission in the world, becomes the way denominations package what they think is needed in the twenty-first century, we will be no better off. The missional church requires DNA change, as Craig Van Gelder suggests.[11] We must move away from the mere business of church and religion, and toward participation within the incarnational nature of the kingdom of God.

Validating a Missional Model for Mission

In order to suggest what might be a paradigm shift for mission and evangelism, it will be necessary to examine some of the concepts of the kingdom of God. Many scholars have investigated the subject, and it is not necessary to review all of them here. However, foundational concepts need to be explored to properly apply them to a model for mission and evangelism that takes the subject seriously.[12]

Given the evidence that the good news is central to the mission of the church, the kingdom of God becomes "an important image for understanding the biblical vision of God's saving activity."[13] God's saving activity, however, must be enlarged within the vision of each individual church. God's mission in the world reminds us that, as Christians, we must focus on the entirety of the human situation and not be limited to only the spiritual. The missional or kingdom-focused model has the potential to turn the churches inside out rather than allowing them to focus exclusively inward, thereby overlooking the reality of the human situation. While most Christians indicate that they believe in mission to the world, "the outward thrust of Christians and Christian communities into the world for the conversion of every human situation in Jesus Christ remains problematic."[14] A shift to a model that takes seriously the kingdom of God will radically change the focus of most churches and challenge most Christians in ways that may make them uncomfortable. Our tendency is to avoid such discomfort. Jürgen Moltmann indicates that the ideal of Western progress suggests that Christians can lead a life free from pain or suffering; but such a vision is impossible because it inflicts suffering and pain on others.[15] The ideal, often found in the institutional or corporate church, is of a life without suffering and of easy "believism." However, the dividends that are paid with such a view can cause Christians to think of themselves as powerless in helping those who are in the midst of suffering throughout the world. The temptation, then, is most often to focus their vision inward on their own congregation's need. Many churches feel helpless to meet the world's need and thus limit their missiological vision to those nearest to the church community.

Moltmann warns Christians to remember, "Humanity only has a future if it looks to a common future."[16] Each church will thus have to be responsible for the totality of humanity and make every effort to meet human need and spiritual need as far as its resources will allow. Beyond local resources, churches will need to link up with other churches to reach out to humanity and to the world. This kind of mind-set will in itself be a challenge, since most of Christendom is so divided along faith traditions and denominational lines.

Many churches will not be able to depend on the corporate or institutional model to furnish them with answers to the need for world mission. They will find increasing challenges to become more creative and more visionary in order to accomplish the goals of mission to the world. The priority of vision will thus have to be a world perspective, beginning at home and moving dynamically outward. John Jonsson has summed up the need by saying:

> As long as there are growing numbers of people in the world who do not have the opportunity of hearing about Jesus Christ, the vocation of each witnessing church must be multiplied and intensified. The fact that the majority of the world's population is poor means that the promises of God must be shared in the gospel. The fact that people are struggling for personal justice, human freedom, and spiritual liberation means that the hope of the kingdom of God must be promised to them. The fact that there are dropouts in societies calls for the proclamation of the One who gives fullness of life. The fact that people are seeking meaning in life means that we must heed the call of Jesus Christ to discipleship, service, and risk. The fact that there is so much nominal Christianity means that we must return to our first love. The fact that there is so much threat to our future global existence means that we are being called to be peacemakers, announcing the One who "makes all things new."[17]

Jonsson's analysis sums up the challenge for individual Christians and indeed all churches to become focused on a kingdom of God orientation of the gospel.

The movement toward a more missional or kingdom-focused model should be an attractive one, since most churches speak so often of the early church as their model for mission and evangelistic outreach. However, the need to discover the larger implications of the kingdom of God is the real challenge. The kingdom of God must not be limited to a local church's worship, fellowship, ministry, or outreach. To do so means that we will only design worship that suits us, and relates to persons like us, and seeks to enlist persons close to our own tradition. We will, in effect, create our own version of the kingdom. To do so misunderstands the nature of God's kingdom and kingdom-focused people.

Jesus was always careful to listen to God and to understand what God was doing in the world. George Beasley-Murray shows that Jesus understood the kingdom of God to consist primarily in God's actions in salvation and judgment. Jesus was "...'borne along' by God's sovereign action in his ministry. It is axiomatic that Jesus does not lead God but rather that God sends, guides, empowers, and sustains him."[18]

This is the position that the church must adopt. The church is sent, guided, empowered, and sustained as partners with God in the *missio Dei*. We must always remind ourselves that the church is nothing less than the missionary people of the kingdom of God. Glasser has correctly said, "The church does not establish the Kingdom. It is rather the custodian of the good news of the Kingdom."[19] Taking seriously the task of custodian of the good news is central to a church that partners with God in what God is doing in the world. Local churches will need to actively visualize themselves as a part of the larger work of God's kingdom, yet vital within God's reign throughout the world, beginning where they are and moving outward to embrace the world.

John Fullenbach has pointed out the following:

> There are 114 occurrences of church in the New Testament referring to the Christian community, but the word church occurs only twice on the lips of Jesus. Can we conclude from here that the central teaching of Jesus was the Kingdom while the church occupied no significant place in Jesus' thought? Did the early church substitute the church for the Kingdom because the parousia did not come? It would be dangerous in theology to measure everything by the range of the names applied to it. The word church may not appear often in Jesus' teaching, but the very concept of the messianic community intrinsically bound up with the Kingdom implies what is meant by the concept church.[20]

Hence, churches should recognize the large scope of the work of the kingdom and be willing to participate in its work with all churches on mission to the world. As Peter Kuzmic points out, it is precisely because

> ...the Kingdom of God and the Church are two key New Testament concepts, both are crucial for the understanding of God's plan for humanity. They are central to the fulfillment of his redemptive purpose. While the Church cannot be identified with the Kingdom, for the latter is a large and more comprehensive term, the two are nevertheless in such close correlation that they cannot be separated either.[21]

According to Fullenbach, the kingdom of God is to be understood as all-embracing and a dynamic concept that signifies God's active rule over all reality.[22] The present prevailing image of the church among many Christians, however, is that of organized religion with by-laws, constitutions, and structures that narrowly define the church's mission. Many view the church as an institution in society that fulfills spiritual functions the way other institutions fulfill business, government, educational, or labor needs. All too often, the church becomes just another competitor for the attention of the culture and succeeds when it can successfully package its program in entertaining ways. It is therefore easy to understand how Christians have limited the scope of the church within the kingdom of God and how society in general has allotted religion a role in the culture that keeps it a comfortable distance away from the more inclusive aspects of human life.

The symbol of the kingdom of God offers the church "a horizon of transcendence that will save it from enclosing itself again and again in stifling structures."[23] Many churches have enclosed themselves within the stifling structures of an identity that has limited their missional or kingdom-focused vision. A recovery of understanding of the true nature of the kingdom of God has the potential to create new images and visions of mission and evangelization to the world.

For many churches in decline, a kingdom-oriented vision offers the only hope for renewal and growth. For churches in transitional areas, new visions of unreached peoples can become a reality. For churches content with their weekly worship routines, the vision of God's messianic banquet can create a healthy discontent that there is much more that needs to be accomplished. Hence, a missional model for churches will produce the promise of a praxis of mission and evangelism that has the potential to fulfill the call of God upon each messianic community.

The Praxis of a Missional Model for Mission

Churches that choose to follow a model for mission and evangelism that takes seriously the reality of the kingdom of God have the potential of developing a more holistic ministry to the world. Within the praxis of mission, kingdom-focused churches will be less concerned with many of the barriers that keep churches from a creative vision of mission to the world. Within the evangelistic mandate, churches can find themselves closer to a New Testament model of evangelization that moves away from evangelistic formulas and mini-theologies, and toward apostolic proclamation, while in keeping with Jesus' holistic method: teaching, preaching, and healing.[24]

The missional or kingdom-focused model offers three possibilities of praxis in mission for local churches, according to Fullenbach: the recovery of word and sacrament; the opportunity to offer the church's own life to the world; and a model for society as a whole to follow.[25]

The church in mission today should be about proclaiming in word and deed that the kingdom of God has come in the person of Jesus Christ. The culture has apparently only *overheard* the gospel.[26] Many seem to have never truly heard it. The kingdom-oriented church, therefore, should not be about the business of moralizing the gospel, but announcing it. It should be clear to anyone who observes the reaction of the culture around us that moralizing the gospel has not worked. Such an approach has turned people's ears off to the potential of the gospel's promises. Mortimer Arias quotes Gabriel Fackre in saying that in order to get the gospel out of the church and into the world, the story must first be told in all its fullness.[27] This is especially important because, as Fackre says, the world is aggressively telling its own tale. And if we are honest, that tale is more attractive, since so many have judged the gospel that is often presented as antiquated and not relevant to their lives.

When Christians truly perceive the kingdom of God as good news and the church as an instrument in the telling of the story, the potential for evangelism becomes clear. The power of the witness is in the story. It is not in manipulation of evangelistic formulas or strategies built around it. It is to be found in everyday lives that communicate the story they celebrate each Sunday.

A student's reaction to one of my lectures related to worship made an impact on me. I had made the statement in class that there are many instances in Scripture in which God makes it clear that the worship of the people was not pleasing because they had neglected God's mission to the world. All the smoke and songs of sacrifice had done little to please God. I encouraged my students to remember that our highest praise and worship of God occurs when we are doing what God is doing in the world.

This student, in order to fulfill the requirements of the course, had consistently participated in a missional setting that required him to work with people who were homeless and poor. His *verbata* and case studies shared in the class made it clear that the experience was changing his vision of ministry. He took me aside and related the story of counseling a homeless person and how he had shared his vision for what God was doing in human life. He told me that as he shared the good news of the gospel with the homeless man, he felt a sense of God that he had never experienced in formal worship. He said that it was during this time of ministry to the homeless person that, for the first time, he felt truly in the presence of God. This is the kind of experience that every Christian needs to fully understand the worship of God. Learning to tell the story of God's care for all is liberating to the Christian who may have lived his or her life of faith as abstract yearning to be on mission with God, and is fresh hope for another who may have never really heard of the potential of a life lived in response to God.

The importance of the story of the gospel was summed up in a World Council of Churches meeting in Melbourne in 1980:

> The proclamation of the word of God is one such witness, distinct and indispensable. The story of God in Christ is the heart of all evangelism, and this story has to be told, for the life of the present church never fully reveals the love and holiness and power of God

in Christ. The telling of the story is an inescapable mandate for
the whole church; word accompanies deed as the Kingdom throws
its light ahead of its arrival and men and women seek to live in
that light.[28]

Mortimer Arias has indicated that it was because the story was good
news that it was remembered, told and retold, written and passed on.[29] If
the gospel is to become alive in the culture, it must first become alive
through story within the churches.[30] A kingdom-oriented church has the
potential to open themselves up to the world and have greater opportunities
for telling the story. As Eduard Schillebeeckx explains:

> The Church is not the Kingdom of God, but it bears symbolic
> witness to the Kingdom through its word and sacrament, and its
> praxis effectively anticipates that Kingdom. It does so by doing
> for men and women here and now, in new situations (different
> from those in Jesus' time), what Jesus did in his time: raising them
> up for the coming Kingdom of God, opening up communication
> among them, caring for the poor and outcast, establishing com-
> munal ties within the household of faith and serving all men and
> women in solidarity.[31]

As the church recovers the power of the story of the kingdom of God
and of the gospel, its proclaimed Word has the potential of taking on new
life and its sacrament new meaning as the church reaches out to the world
to include them in the story. This becomes authentic worship that goes far
beyond the worship wars being fought in churches.

Another possibility for the kingdom-focused church is that it has the
opportunity to offer the possibilities of its own life to the world. The
kingdom-focused church model constantly holds images of justice, peace,
freedom, respect for all persons, and redemption. God's reign over the
world becomes not a judgment of human failure but a liberating reality full
of possibilities to become fully human.

The practical nature of the kingdom-focused model emphasizes that
the messianic community has embraced for itself such images and that
they are practiced within the community of faith. The issues of daily life
are brought into redemptive focus and are made concrete by a kingdom-
oriented community that chooses to practice peace, to call for justice, to
honor all people, and to seek salvation. This reality alone has the power to
change the culture's appraisal of what it means to be part of a community
of faith.

As Gerhard Lohfink affirms, "[T]he church should offer itself as a
'contrast society' to society at large."[32] Churches that delegate through
corporate or denominational agencies the issues of justice, ministry to needy,
human rights, and evangelistic outreach will be unable to offer themselves

in authentic ways to the communities around them. Postmodern persons in the larger society are not easily impressed with institutional or corporate attempts to meet human need. However, churches who are willing to give their lives for the sake of the issues at the heart of the kingdom of God are more likely to gain the attention of persons in the larger culture.

A most exciting possibility of the kingdom-focused or missional model for the church is that it has the potential to challenge society with its unique message in ways the corporate or institutional church often does not. Since the ultimate goal of the kingdom is the transformation of the whole of creation, the church must "understand its mission in the service of the imminent Kingdom."[33]

Each church that follows the kingdom-focused model will decide for itself appropriate ways to engage the culture around it, and thus will properly contextualize its message. The corporate or institutional church usually depends upon agencies far removed from the local context to furnish it with a vision, strategies, and materials for outreach. As has been stated, such an approach is not likely to be properly contextualized. No community is like another. Human needs vary. The way people-groups process information is often culturally unique, and demographic shifts make it impossible to assume that persons in monocultural churches are like those in the larger multicultural society. If the church's message is to properly engage society as a whole, it will require that each church fashion for itself the vision given to them by the Creator for their local context and for the world.

These possibilities function together for the sake of mission and evangelization. The kingdom-oriented or missional model for the church does not allow for the dichotomization between ministry, mission, and evangelism, as does the institutional or corporate model. Rather, the complex mission of the church is fully realized as the church understands itself participating with God in the world. Such an approach to mission finds its expression among Catholic authors in *Redemptoris Missio*:

> The Church is effectively and concretely at the service of the Kingdom. This is seen especially in her preaching, which is a call to conversion. Preaching constitutes the Church's first and fundamental way of serving the coming of the Kingdom in individuals and in human society.
>
> The Church, then, serves the Kingdom by establishing communities and founding new particular Churches and by guiding them to mature faith and charity in openness toward others, in service to individuals and society, and in understanding and esteem for human institutions.
>
> The Church serves the Kingdom by spreading throughout the world the "Gospel values" which are an expression of the Kingdom and which help people to accept God's plan. It is true that the

inchoate reality of the Kingdom can also be found beyond the confines of the Church among peoples everywhere to the extent that they live "Gospel values" and are open to the working of the Spirit, who breathes when and where he wills.[34]

The missional or kingdom-focused model is not a perfect one and must always view itself as a preliminary anticipation of the kingdom. Yet the church that is focused on God's mission to the world, the *missio Dei*, has the best opportunity to challenge itself to actually participate in the reality of the kingdom of God. Doing this allows the church to break away from a corporate or institutional identity that may not fully challenge its understanding of mission and that may dilute it or delegate mission away from the church.

Howard Snyder adequately sums up the practical nature of the kingdom model in five points:

1. Kingdom consciousness means living and working in the firm hope of the final triumph of God's reign. In the face of contrary evidence, Kingdom Christians hold on to the conviction that God will eventually swallow up all evil, hate, and injustice. It is the firm belief that the leaven of the Kingdom is already at work in the dough of creation, to use Jesus' own parable. This gives Christians an unworldly, audacious confidence that enables them to go right on doing what others say is impossible or futile.

2. Understanding God's Kingdom means that the line between sacred and secular does not exist in concrete reality. God's Kingdom means that all things are in the sphere of God's sovereignty, and therefore, of God's concern. All spheres of life are Kingdom topics.

3. Kingdom awareness means that ministry is much broader than church work. Christians who understand the meaning of God's Reign know they are in the Kingdom business, not the church business. They see all activity as ultimately having Kingdom significance.

4. In Kingdom perspective, concern for justice and concrete commitment to the word of God are necessarily held together. An awareness of God's Kingdom, biblically understood, resolves the tension between the two vital concerns. Those committed to the Kingdom want to win people to personal faith in Jesus Christ, for the Kingdom is ultimately the longing of every human heart. They are also committed to peace, justice, and righteousness at every level of society because the Kingdom includes "things in heaven and things on earth" (Eph. 1:10) and the welfare of every person and everything God has made.

5. The reality of the Kingdom of God can be experienced now through the Spirit who gives the believer the first fruits of the fullness of the Kingdom in the here and now. Particularly in their liturgy Kingdom people anticipate the joy of the Kingdom. The different charisms given

by the Holy Spirit witness concretely to the Kingdom present and are appreciated by all as clear manifestations of the powerful presence of the Kingdom in the midst of their daily life.[35]

Each of the five observations made by Snyder are critical in the understanding of the church that takes the kingdom of God seriously. As they merge together, they help to fashion a vision for the church that allows its mission to flourish and to fully participate in God's salvific intention for the whole of humanity.

Hope for Holism in Mission

The evangelistic focus of Christianity has historically fueled the mission advance of churches and agencies. Some have therefore concluded that evangelistic witness is the highest priority of the church. While it is certainly true that evangelistic witness is essential to the work of the people of God, the passion that it generates can sometimes limit the vision of churches with regard to the comprehensive task of the church in the world. Basing the mission of the church on a monolithic evangelistic thrust misses the holistic nature of mission.

David Bosch approximates more correctly what the task of the church is about and provides a corrective to an inadequate theology of mission and evangelism by saying:

> Mission refers to *Missio Dei* (God's mission), that is, God's self-revelation as the One who loves the world, God's involvement in and with the world, the nature and activity of God, which embraces both the church and the world, and in which the church is privileged to participate. *Missio Dei* enunciates the good news that God is a God-for-people.[36]

If Christians define mission exclusively as an outreach or evangelical activity of the church, they will miss Bosch's approximations of mission, which are holistic and emphasize the fullness of God's mission in which the church is privileged to participate. Denominations and faith traditions have divided over this issue with some believing that the church is only about gospel witness and salvation issues, and others negating salvation issues for an emphasis on social ministry without a verbal witness. This restricted view is unfavorable to a holistic encounter with a kingdom-oriented model called for in this book, but entirely favorable to a corporate or institutional approach in which mission can be easily separated into missions, evangelism, or ministry functions.

A further problem is that dichotomized evangelical approaches to mission do not adequately take into account a concern that evangelism be properly defined as the whole gospel for the whole person in the whole of society. Evangelicals who reject conciliatory approaches to the holism of mission miss the importance of bringing into the full context of human life the word of God that touches every aspect of human experience.[37]

Bosch can inform Christians and help them understand that the missionary ventures of the church, properly called "missions," refer to particular forms, and relates to specific times, places, or needs, of participation in God's mission, *missio Dei*. Focusing on missionary ventures with an exclusivistic evangelistic passion often leads in directions that ignore the larger realities of *missio Dei*.

If churches are to move to a model that promises a more holistic approach to mission, they will have to commit themselves to

> service to the *missio Dei*, representing God in and over against the world, pointing to God, holding up the God-child before the eyes of the world in a ceaseless celebration of the Feast of the Epiphany.[38]

Such a holistic approach will be critical to the shift needed to become the kind of church that takes seriously the kingdom of God. The kingdom-oriented church fully embraces the *missio Dei*. It recognizes that it is God's mission and that we are pleased to participate with God in it. The church and Christians of all stripes participate, fully representing God to the world in the fullest expression of Gods word.

A Practical View of the Kingdom-oriented Church

There are five critical components that churches should take into account in order to shift from the institutional ethos to that of a more kingdom-oriented sensitivity. Such a shift will require an honest appraisal of how a particular church currently functions with regard to its missional task. This appraisal should be undertaken from the outside in: each church should first attempt to understand what the culture around it is saying about the church's interface with its community. Internally, the church should attempt to discover where its priorities lie and what would be needed if the church undertook a major shift toward a more kingdom-centered approach. One note of caution needs to be sounded here: no two churches are likely to transition in the same manner. Neither should the church rely entirely upon others to discover the essential mission of the church. It is a matter of concentrated and earnest "prayer-hearing" from God, Scripture study, and sober commitment to the task ahead.

Component One: Immersed in Mission

The first component suggests that churches need to become fully immersed in mission. This is vital, as Paul Knitter has said, because "if the mission of Jesus was the Kingdom of God, it cannot be otherwise for the mission of the church."[39] In order to accomplish such immersion, churches will need to see missional opportunities from at least two perspectives: full-time—or vocational—mission and lifestyle mission.

There are those in the church who feel called to vocational mission, while others catch a vision for being on mission in their everyday careers. For persons who feel called to a vocation of mission, it will be essential for the church to distance itself from the traditional dependence on the corporate or institutional model of mission that has been so familiar. The local individual church will find itself more involved in the calling, blessing, and sending of career missionaries into the world. It will not be not dependent upon national agencies to accomplish the task for them.

National agencies must move beyond an entirely pragmatic and rational thinking mode toward a more catalytic approach. Mission-sending agencies should focus their energies not upon exclusive appointment of missionaries but upon advocacy, training, and research, joining hands with local churches to prepare persons called to vocational mission. They should help build a climate and vision for mission internationally and at home. Agencies should not be charged with setting standards for those who wish to go on mission—this is the job of the local church. They rather should be an additional resource to missionaries commissioned and sent by local churches.

As long as the mission-sending agencies are seen as placement organizations for career missionaries, local churches will continue to be limited in their missional vision. There are persons, though far too few in comparison to the total membership of all churches, who visualize themselves as being on mission with God as a career. These persons should be encouraged in their missional vision. The local church should embrace their vision, commission them, and bless their efforts as they respond to what they are hearing God say to them.

The concept of lifestyle mission should be emphasized for the church as a whole. People in the church should be challenged to see themselves on mission in their respective vocations. The church should also bless them, and send them in ways that make it apparent that they are responding to what they are hearing God say to them as they are involved in industry and commerce. Laypersons need to be encouraged to see their vocation as service to God, and their fellow workers as persons to whom they minister each day. Creating an atmosphere in the church that honors ordinary laypersons and their vocations will encourage them to find ways that God is working redemptively in their particular workplaces.

Component Two: Salt, Light, and Context

The second component concerns the evangelistic thrust of the local churches. Kingdom-oriented churches take seriously their role as witnesses within the culture, but are careful to understand the context of the culture and how to properly communicate the good news. Alfred Krass has suggested that the kind of evangelism that is needed is contextual evangelism, one that is "alert to the current historical and cultural moment in each place where the church is called to witness."[40] Evangelism programs should not be developed by national agencies and merely handed to the churches for implementation. Missional churches should instead focus on their witness according to the biblical metaphors of salt and light within the context of their own communities. They should be willing to add the flavor of the gospel to the daily dialogue of the culture, thereby enhancing the human experience of God. Missional churches should also be light expressing the hope of the gospel in ways that challenge the darkness of the culture's misunderstandings of God.

Church agencies concerned with evangelism should seek to help local church members express the story of their faith and to find entry points to the culture that they might otherwise overlook. Churches should be able to utilize consultants that could be provided by church agencies and evangelistic leadership within national boards or agencies. Churches who seem to have difficulty in understanding their cultural context, for example, should seek the help of specialists who can spend time in the local church field. National church leaders could work with the local church to properly contextualize evangelistic activities within the communities surrounding the church. Demographic research data could be provided to churches in the form of community studies conducted with the help of consultants. Local associations of churches could benefit as specialized consultants help analyze data with the churches.

Specialists should seek to help the church be holistic in its outreach by addressing every aspect of human need within the mandate of the gospel. Churches desiring to become more kingdom-oriented should be helped by specialists to properly contextualize their total ministry efforts within communities. Above all, the specialists should help lead the local church to discover God's vision for its ministry and suggest ways that the vision of the church can be implemented within the community.

Component Three: A Ministry-based Mind-set

A third characteristic of a church with a kingdom-centered vision is a ministry-based approach to the whole of its mission. The passion of Christians for the communication of the gospel can be best realized through a ministry-based approach.

One of the most difficult transitions is moving away from a propositional approach to evangelism, which Henry Knight says "misconstrues personal revelation and misunderstands the relation of language and truth."[41] Postmodern persons are reluctant to accept propositions historically used in a modern form of evangelistic presentation. The idea of presenting the gospel in five minutes using tracts or memorized presentations is not warmly received by most persons in the secular world. The message of the gospel has its best chance of being heard as it is ministered within the context of the human story.[42]

Each member of the church should be taught the importance of ministry and that they are called to ministry regardless of their vocation. Laypersons should work alongside ministers as the gospel is demonstrated in word and deed. Ministers should serve as mentors of laypersons and teach skills of ministry.

An ethos of ministry that takes seriously the character of the kingdom of God needs to permeate the church. Krass has said, "to be personally attached to Jesus is thus to understand oneself as called to the same servant ministry as he was."[43] Every opportunity to meet human need and to address the human situation should include the story of the kingdom of Christ and his gospel. Ministry should not be focused exclusively on those who are needy but should be practiced toward all persons. Every person with whom a church member comes into contact must be viewed as one whom God loves and toward whom the church wishes to demonstrate care.

Ministry should not be used as a license for the proclamation of the evangel, rather the gospel should be viewed as woven within the total fabric of the missional church's ministry. Ministry should expand its focus to every issue within the human experience. Because social justice concerns, ecological issues, health concerns, the need for reconciliation, and peace are all part of the *missio Dei*, they should also be part of the missional church's outreach.

A ministry-based mind-set will focus the kingdom-oriented church's attention on the world. Its reason for being will reflect the concern of Jesus that all persons might have life in abundance. The missional church will focus its energy, its resources, and its attention toward the demonstration of abundant life in Jesus Christ for all humankind.

Component Four: An Inclusive Spiritual House

A fourth characteristic is culturally inclusive worship opportunities. The household of God (Eph. 2:19), the family of faith (Gal. 6:10), the dwelling of the Holy Spirit (1 Cor. 3:16), and numerous other images are used throughout Scripture to invite persons to encounter God. The fundamentally social character of God's temple, according to John Driver, means that relationships are important.[44] The kingdom-focused church will invest in relationships that are open and invitational to all who wish to worship God.

The missional church will understand the reality of seekers who are interested in spirituality but who are not necessarily well-informed about Christianity. George Hunter III asserts that many pre-Christian persons "have little or no experience of church."[45] The missional church, therefore, will not establish prerequisites about worship or spiritual exploration for those in the general community. Instead, the image of the messianic banquet will dominate. All will be invited to explore the spiritual feast.

The church that wishes to reflect the kingdom of God will be sensitive to those who do not "know the rules" of worship. Educational opportunities will be available for persons who wish to know more or to "test the waters" before they commit to church participation or membership. The emphasis of the kingdom-oriented church will be upon invitation and not upon recruitment of persons. One of the most important concepts to remember is that people today do not readily join any organization. They want to test the waters, often for an extended period of time, before they commit themselves. We should be reminded that Jesus often invited people to "come and see." We should be willing to invite persons to come and see, touch, taste, and feel the character of the missional church. Pressure exerted on them to join will only reinforce their belief that our desire is to get them on the roll or perhaps to access their finances. Once they taste the character of the kingdom of God, the Creator will enlist them to service.

Missional churches do not feel a need to adhere to church or denominational labels in order to define themselves. They define themselves in terms of distinctives, such as believer's baptism, but offer persons opportunities to explore the distinctives for themselves. Emphasis is not upon numbers in the missional church, but upon the worship and knowledge of God.

Component Five: Commitment to the Family of God

The missional church model suggests a commitment to the concept of the family of God. Christians are not isolated by traditions but are embraced in the household of faith. The church is ecumenical in its vision, outreach to communities, ministry involvement, mission advance, and concern for the world. The church that takes seriously the challenge of the kingdom of God should be eager to work with all Christians for the sake of the gospel. The primary reason, according to Knitter, is that the focus of the church's mission is that of "building up the Kingdom of God and building up the Church to be at the service of the Kingdom."[46]

The isolation that has existed in Christendom, brought about by church differences, must be broken down if mission is to advance. If the world is to encounter the living Christ, it cannot witness divisions in Christ's body, the church. Every attempt should be made to foster openness and dialogue between faith groups.

The missional church should be an advocate of willing participation with any church community that feels called to mission. In doing so it recognizes that the kingdom of God is broader than any denomination, church, or Christian group. Sharing of resources, information, and expertise should be a natural expression of the church so that the kingdom of God can benefit from all sources. Knitter insists that the church is called to a twofold service: One is to witness to the kingdom and to promote the realization of the kingdom of God in the world. The second service is to proclaim Jesus Christ and to build up a community of faith as disciples.[47]

As Christians embrace the concept of the family of God in the ecumenical sense, they soon discover that the mystery of God is at work everywhere. The wholeness of the kingdom is strengthened, and fellowship is enhanced as churches work together for the sake of God's reign over all creation. According to Knitter, "In a Kingdom-centered mission theology, Christians are better able to keep their priorities straight."[48] This is perhaps one of the greatest needs of the church. It must keep its priorities in focus at all times. It is far too easy to be distracted by simply going through the motions of religion, its rules, its customs, and its isolation from the culture. Keeping the focus of the church on its mission to the world will center its theology appropriately.

Conclusion

The missional model implies participation with God as God's kingdom is made known on the earth. Every realm of human experience is touched by the kingdom concept. The reality of the kingdom of God opens the door to life in the kingdom and extends the kingdom through the participation and witness of all believers in God's mission.

Many Christians are not used to thinking along kingdom lines. They are more at home with church or denominational identity. Yet the challenge to shift to a kingdom-oriented model as the basis for mission is crucial to the survival of all churches, given the uncertain direction of most mission programs, aging membership, and the realities of post-denominationalism. The missional church model offers hope because of the fundamental character of kingdom people. As David Bosch so aptly explains in his quote of Snyder:

> Kingdom people seek first the Kingdom of God and its justice; church people often put the church work above concerns of justice, mercy, and truth. Church people think about how to get people into the church; Kingdom people think about how to get the church into the world.
>
> Church people worry that the world might change the church; Kingdom people work to see the church change the world.[49]

Kingdom people are eager to participate in the *missio Dei*. They realize that "the *missio Dei* purifies the church. It sets it under the cross—the only place where it is ever safe."[50]

Does Your Church Really Know Itself?

"Know thyself." Most of us have probably heard this famous quotation, often attributed to Socrates. He probably did say it, but if we are to believe Plutarch, the famous two words were originally inscribed in the vestibule of the sun god Apollo's Oracle of Delphi temple in Greece. Plutarch is believed to have served for a period of time as one of the two priests of the temple, so he should have some idea as to the origin of the phrase, "Know thyself." The challenge has continued through the centuries. People today spend untold millions of dollars in counseling, self-help books, and chasing spiritual gurus trying to figure out who they are. It doesn't seem as easy as Apollo would have us believe. I once bought a T-shirt in Greece that has a simple saying on it from Socrates, "One thing I know, I know nothing." That may sum it up for a lot of people.

When it comes to knowing who we really are, the jury is still out for most of us. But perhaps we should realize that congregations are like human beings that way: it is hard for them to really know who they are. For one thing, they are composed of human beings, so what else should we expect? The idea of a church personality may have never been explored by the ordinary Christian. Newcomers to a congregation often pick up on the surface personality of a church quickly and may make some initial judgments, but as Herb Miller points out, they are not yet acquainted with the congregation's invisible personality or the personality that actually drives the organization.[1] Therefore, it is accurate to say that congregations, like people, have personalities, moods, and attitudes. So do businesses, universities, and most other venues where people gather. Restaurants would have us believe they are family-friendly; banks are caring; even cars are given personality traits by Detroit.

It takes more than hype to sway the average consumer, however. People tend to believe what they experience. In spite of a slogan boasting about the bank being a caring bank, if the customer gets shortchanged by a teller, he or she will probably look elsewhere. And a bad steak at a family-friendly restaurant will be remembered long after the indigestion has subsided. That customer will not be seen again. Reality is more important than image. Likewise, to advertise that your church is family-friendly and yet to not minister effectively to the whole family will convince no one.

Your church congregation exudes personality to the community around it. A church may think of itself as a warm and friendly congregation, but might be surprised to find that the community, when surveyed, views the congregation as wealthy elites who do not experience the problems ordinary people face every day. Joseph Litterer has explained that many people who observe organizations become confused and disturbed when they observe an organization doing that which runs counter to what its objectives say it ought to be doing.[2] If the community around a church believes that churches in general ought to be advocates for the poor, for example, and yet observes richly adorned buildings or expensive vehicles in the parking lots, they are likely to be confused about a church's real mission. In order to be on mission in today's world, every congregation has to invest in discovery of the image they portray to the world and who they are in terms of the context around them. Industry today spends billions in research to discover how their products are perceived, yet most churches follow the assumptive pattern discussed in chapter 1. They just believe that somehow everyone knows who they are and what they are about. And most often they are dead wrong.

The Making of a Church Personality

Churches are not born with personalities. These develop over a period of time. Almost everyone knows of the church in the community that runs away every pastor, or the ones that fight among themselves, or the church that is known for standing in the gap for the poor and oppressed. These impressions are most often accurate: the characteristics did not develop overnight, but rather were reinforced through the years by patterns of behavior that were observed over and over again by the community.

A congregation has to recognize that religious and corporate organizations always fight the battle of presenting an accurate picture of who they really are in the community, and that picture can be helped or damaged by any one member or incident. Many of us remember the incident with a popular over-the-counter pain medication during the 1980s. In 1982, seven people collapsed and died in Chicago after taking capsules laced with cyanide. Americans were introduced to product tampering, which, by some accounts, has cost companies millions of dollars per year. In recent years and in light of several acts of terrorism, public sensitivity to product tampering has put pressure on companies to package products in ways that will make it obvious if tampering has occurred. What we have learned from such incidents is that the public is now much more suspicious and careful about who they trust. People are often suspicious about both individuals and organizations.

H. Wheeler Robinson has indicated that the idea of a corporate body comes from English law, which viewed a corporate body as being legally authorized to act as a single individual.[3] English law advanced the idea that a corporate body could legally exhibit a response much as an individual would. Interestingly, the ancient Hebrew concept of a corporate personality viewed large or small bodies as a unity. Robinson says, "The whole group, including its past, present, and future members, might function as a single individual through any one of those members conceived as representative of it." The group was not confined to the living, but included the dead and the unborn as a part of it forever.[4] There were sometimes positive results and sometimes very negative ones. One only has to read about the sin of Achan in Joshua 7 to view the impact of one individual's sin on the whole group. Achan broke the taboos on the spoils of war at Jericho, and, as a result, his whole family was destroyed.

A second truth is that a church's personality can be helped or hindered by its associations. With whom does the church cooperate to accomplish its mission to the world? If the church is viewed as linking with organizations that have similar goals to accomplish good in the community, the image of the church and its personality will most likely be positive. Churches that form linkages with social service agencies, health care institutions, job banks, and educational services will enhance the culture's view of the personality of the church as a caring place. Likewise, if the church associates itself with organizations that have a negative image in the community, the problems will be compounded as a church tries to present itself to the community around it. For example, one church in our community associated itself with a travel company promising tours to the Holy Land. The church cosponsored the travel and placed ads in the local paper and on radio. Many of the senior citizens in the church and in the community fell prey to the dishonesty of the travel company, who stole the money and left town. It took years before the church overcame the negative image in the community.

A church I once served linked its ministry of caring to a local food bank and opened its doors one Saturday each month to provide food for the poor of the community. It was quite an undertaking, since the church had to set up scores of tables, truck in large quantities of food, enlist volunteers from within the church and the local community, advertise its ministry, and assist those who came in for the services. It took a host of caring volunteers to provide food for the hundreds of persons who came. That partnership did much to portray the church as a group of persons who not only said they cared for people but demonstrated that care in the way they linked to outside agencies and organizations for the benefit of the community.

A third truth is that the personality of a church can be made clearer or distorted by the language the congregation uses as it relates to the community. Inclusive language that addresses race, gender, lifestyle, and religious orientation does much to clarify the receptivity of the church congregation for those outside. Harsh judgments that are voiced from the pulpit, on the church sign, in church newsletters, or from the conversations of church members as they interface with the general public can create the impression of coldness.

One of the greatest barriers to those who are not members of any church is religious language. The religious code words that are natural to church people are for the most part entirely unnatural to those outside. Many people have written and studied religious language and how it is used both inside the church and outside the church. Paul Mundey says, "Some speak the language of Pentecost—a vocabulary accenting the work of the Holy Spirit. Words such as 'spirit-filled,' 'baptism with the Spirit,' and 'anointed' flow freely. Others speak the language of Amos—a vocabulary lifting up the prophetic. Words such as 'justice,' 'peace,' and 'liberation' punctuate conversations. Still others speak the language of Calvary—a vocabulary dominated by images of the sacrifice of Christ. Words such as 'born again,' 'washed in the blood' and 'redeemed' prevail."[5] Many postmodern people today simply do not understand this language.

In communicating the mission of any church to its community, every effort has to be made to clarify what is meant. Garrison Keillor has done a very good job of explaining, during his weekly radio variety show, what it is like to be raised a Lutheran in Minnesota. While he pokes fun at Lutherans, he has also let non-Lutherans in on the language, customs, history, and habits of Lutherans in Minnesota through the lens of his experience. We have come to know Pastor Inkqvist and his family, as well as some of the sermons he has preached. Whether representative of most Lutherans in Minnesota or not, we have a feel for being a Lutheran.

Religious language has to be interpreted. That is best done through the use of story, illustrations, metaphor, and imagery. Whether we are talking about Lutherans or Baptists, about salvation or sanctification, most of it makes little sense to those who do not have a church background. It is always the task of Christians to translate the language of Zion into the ordinary conversation of the day. Church signs, in their attempt at humor, often betray the codified language of the church. Often they make little sense to the general public, may communicate judgment on those who do not attend church, or may be laughed at not because they are creatively humorous, but because the language may be offensive or confusing.

The issue of language is complicated as we attempt to communicate to persons whose native tongue is not English. A Spanish-speaking person has enough difficulty learning a new language, adapting to a new culture and to new customs, and can be entirely confused by the religious jargon used by different faith groups. I once had dinner with a pastor friend who felt it was important to speak an evangelistic word to every person he met. At the Mexican restaurant, we were served by a young man of Hispanic background. My friend immediately asked him, "Are you a saved young man?" The waiter, who apparently knew very little English, responded, "No, I was raised in an orphanage." From what I have observed in the general unchurched culture, one does not have to be from another country to be confused by a question so loaded with religious meaning. An unchurched person raised in this country might not have understood the church language either. Churches that do not pay attention to the way they chat with the world will make sense only to themselves.

A fourth truth is that the personality of a church is most often realized by the public or defined by the way it successfully or unsuccessfully interfaces with the community around it. Generally speaking, a church's personality is known in the community in several ways:[6]

■ *"Advocate" or "Against"*–The church that is known as an "Advocate" for the community is often perceived as a gathering place or focal point when issues arise. People often sense that the members of the church are empathetic with whatever situation arises in the community due to the past responses of the church in times of crisis or concern. Advocate churches tend to be verbal in their advocacy from a philosophical or theological point of view. During the 1960s it was easy to identify churches across the South that marched with those who advocated civil rights. It was also very easy to identify those churches that preached against and developed resistance toward integration of the society. In the 1980s, the sanctuary movement offered an ethical response and dissent toward U.S. immigration policy regarding refugees from Central America.[7] Advocate churches are willing to engage and dialogue about social issues for the benefit of the community or those who are on the margins, and they do not become concerned if they are perceived as being on the wrong side of the issue by some. They have a heightened sense of the ethics of the kingdom of God and are sometimes persecuted by their sister churches for their stance. Nevertheless, they stand firm in spite of being the lone voice on some issues.

Those churches who are perceived by the community as "Against" often have a negative image. They can be seen as narrow-minded and closed in matters that are usually being hotly debated in the culture. They often appear to take a righteous stand against certain hot-button issues and can be politically vocal. They are sometimes judged as having a very narrow view of right and wrong, preferring to pass judgment quickly. They ally themselves with other churches that react as they do if the issue is significant enough. Many of these churches are character-ized as fundamentalist theologically, but often prefer to characterize themselves as being faithful to biblical mandates. In recent years the issue of homosexuality has polarized many of the Advocate and Against type churches. Advocate churches tend to elevate the human condition, while Against churches hold up what they perceive as spiritual idealism as the test of Christian fidelity.

■ *"Responsive" or "Repressed"*–There are churches that have a strong image of their importance to the community. They are often the first ones to answer the call to disaster relief, to build homes for people, or to engage in other projects that benefit humanity. They are always aware of issues such as world hunger, HIV-AIDS prevention and management, or ecological disasters. "Responsive" churches move quickly and often mobilize volunteers at a moment's notice. They tend to be less philosophical or theological in their response, but, rather, action-oriented. They are capable of motivating ordinary church members and raising large sums of money or foodstuffs to benefit others. Responsive churches have an openness to social issues and to the headlines they read in the newspaper. Their language is very often peppered with current events and they exhibit a great deal of sensitivity to the plight of human beings caught up in the joys and sorrows of everyday life. They not only exhibit the character of the Advocate churches, but they put their beliefs into tangible and measurable action.

At the other end of the continuum are the "Repressed" churches. They hold back or are tentative in nearly every response to the community around them. They are often smaller churches with only a few resources that they feel they must conserve for themselves. They often suffer from a diminished image of their importance, though this is not always the case. Many Repressed churches have little national strength or support, have unclear historic recognition, or are independent churches who struggle to keep themselves viable, so the larger issues are always beyond them. Some Repressed churches have such a narrow theological definition that they feel consumed with the need to protect their view of life. Many of these churches seem to be responsive, then, only within the conversations of their own faith group. They are largely undereducated to larger theological issues or critical issues in the community. They may feel inadequately prepared to comment on public events, preferring their view of the spiritual world to the difficult issues of everyday life.

■ *"Neutral" or "Isolated"*–"Neutral" churches do not have an opinion on very much in the community. Some of them have been so quiet for so long about the issues that face the larger culture that no one ever seeks their advice or counsel on any matter. They are faithful to the flock of members but largely prefer not to offend anyone by addressing issues that may be hotly debated in the larger culture. They prefer to keep the peace both inside and outside the church. A few Neutral churches have been hurt in the past when they attempted to give an opinion regarding a community issue, becoming reluctant to venture subsequent opinions on other matters. A significant number of Baptist churches that suffered through the denominational wars in the 1990s, when Southern Baptists and Moderate Baptists were trading blows and drawing lines in the sand, found themselves becoming more Neutral. This was especially true in many small towns far removed from the larger and more vocal city churches. The issues were so hot in Baptist life that many of these churches feared losing membership and vitality if they took sides. A large number of them chose to seek a Neutral posture with regard to the Baptist denominational war, formulating policies that attempted to satisfy the church membership so they could all live in peace together and not split the church. Some pastors did not want to be a part of the controversy, so they publicly ignored it and led their church to ignore it. Many denominational churches have faced similar crises and have chosen to remain as Neutral as possible until all the shooting stopped.

Isolated churches are not of this world. They choose to not engage with their community on public issues. Some of them feel disconnected enough with the world that they perceive their task is to simply speak of the spiritual and to let the physical take care of itself. Often these churches feel overwhelmed by the needs of the world and so they retreat. Theirs is a spiritual family, they take care of their own, and they seldom focus on reaching others outside the fold. Their attitude is largely reminiscent of the old spiritual song: "This world is not my home, I'm just a passin' through." Isolated churches are often critical of the world around them. They have given up on those who do not love God as much as they do. Isolated churches are also those that are dying. Many churches that are shrinking in membership and aging or in a transitional community feel trapped and hence turn inward until the end comes. Theirs is a lonely existence. One of these churches was located in downtown Atlanta. It was a powerful church throughout most of its history, with many hundreds of members. But as the downtown changed in the 1970s and people moved away, the church found its membership base shrinking. It held on in spite of small numbers as long as it could. By the 1980s, the church had closed its doors and ended its hundred-year-old ministry. Researchers later discovered that the church circled the wagons and chose to isolate itself and die at a time when many hundreds of people were beginning to move back to the downtown in renovated communities near the church.

Churches that choose the more positive images of Advocacy and Response find themselves, at the very least, in conversation with the community. Those who choose to be Against, or display characteristics of the Repressed church, cut off the avenues of conversation and opportunity. Churches who are Neutral or Isolated are most often judged by the community as being irrelevant. A church's personality develops in relation to the way it reads the world in general. Each of the above responses is a way of describing how some of them have chosen to respond.

A fifth truth is that a church's personality develops as a result of its spiritual self-identification. No matter what size the church might be, the members have a sense of who they are, spiritually as well as corporately. I will never forget the first church I served as pastor. It was a small country church in Kentucky. On the morning of my first Sunday there, I was met at the front of the church by the chairman of the deacons. He had a simple message for me, but it spoke volumes about the church, and he probably did me a favor since I knew their mind-set immediately. He said, "Preacher, you ain't the first one we have ever had, and you sure ain't gonna be the last one." Two things stood out in his appraisal of my future there. One, I would not likely change that church overnight. Two, I would probably get so tired of trying that I, like all the others before me, would give up and leave. An older friend of mine once told me that churches are patient. They will sit and listen to new challenges and new ideas and in the end just wait it out until things get back to what they believe is normal.

The spiritual self-identification of churches also depends on the health of congregations. I once served a church in rural Georgia that perfectly exemplifies this. It was a church of about 300 members, with about 150 attending on a regular Sunday. The church looked like one you might see in a Norman Rockwell painting: beautiful to look at on the outside and obviously an historic fixture in the community. Inside the sanctuary, pews were on the right and on the left with a crimson isle in the center, terminating at the communion table and pulpit area.

I will never forget the faces I saw from the pulpit on my left and on my right. Many on both sides smiled and nodded their heads from time to time as I spoke to them. But I also noticed something very peculiar that very first Sunday. At the conclusion of the service, many of the people on the left exited by way of a door located at the front of the church; a good many people on the right exited through the back doors.

I observed this pattern as they came into the church and as they left on the next several Sundays, and it soon became apparent that some of the folks on the left side of the church did not speak to the ones on the right side! When I asked a trusted church leader, he told me the story. It seems that the church had experienced a sharp division during the last pastor's tenure and the church had split. What made it so strange was that no one left. They just split up into the right and left sides of the church!

Sunday after Sunday there was a feeling of coldness and deadness in the worship services. I believe I prayed harder for that church than for any other I have ever served. I spoke on love one Sunday and talked about love of neighbor and of each other as Christians. One old deacon in the right-hand camp who sat near the back of the church crossed his arms over his chest and shook his head from side to side all the way through my sermon. It was clear that he did not agree with me on anything I said.

After almost a year of pastoral care with many of the individuals of the church, and after many sermons about the mission of the church and the need to be faithful, loving witnesses, the break came one Sunday evening. Halfway through my sermon, a lady on the right rose to her feet. I stopped speaking and looked at her. She said, "Preacher, I just have to say something. Forgive me for interrupting you, but I cannot remain quiet any longer." She then confessed her anger and hostile attitude toward another lady on the left side of the church. She began crying and openly pleaded for forgiveness. The other lady rose to her feet and began to weep and made her way out of her seat toward the woman on the right. They both embraced each other in the middle of the church aisle. Slowly, others in the church began to stand and move into the center aisle. Men who had not spoken to each other for months shook hands. Women embraced their estranged friends. Even the youth and children responded as they embraced adults.

I had not seen any movement in the church for months and months, but that evening a spirit of revival broke out. Over the next few months, more than a dozen people were baptized into faith. The church began to grow. Two years after I left, I was invited back by their new pastor to speak one Sunday. I was astounded that the church was full. Chairs were brought in to provide additional seating. The climate of the church was contagious, warm, and friendly. The church had moved from an unhealthy congregation to one exuding health and vitality when reconciliation and love replaced bitterness and anger. And the old deacon? He was not at the service, and I dared not ask about him. I suspect he had left the church.

It was clear to me that this church had no chance of partnering with God in the world as long as it was divided, hurt, and angry. Membership had suffered, witness had dried up, and ministry to the community was nonexistent. But when the spiritual climate was restored, things changed. The church reached out to others in the community and grew. I interviewed one young man who was new to the church. He told me that he had lived a life of bitterness toward God and toward churches. He lived near the church and had observed the fighting and bickering there. It had reinforced his negative feelings about Christianity. But he began to notice when the church was made whole again. People from the church visited the young man, and confessed their sins to him and invited him to worship with the newly reconciled community. For several months he remained skeptical, but visited one Sunday to see if it was true. What he found changed his life. He was warmly ministered to over the course of several months and found love in that church that he had been missing. The young man became a

Christian as a result of the transformation of the church. It is clear that unhealthy churches cannot be fruitfully engaged in mission to their community. They have to be healed of their sins. Otherwise, they will develop a dysfunctional personality that will embed itself in the ethos of the church so deeply that all vision for the kingdom of God will be lost.

Many other factors contribute to the health of congregations. But as it is related to the mission of the church in the world, probably no other factor is as critical as a spirit of unity and love based on the character of God's kingdom. Love, peace, justice, righteousness, and reconciliation are but a few characteristics critical to the essential nature of the kingdom-oriented church. These characteristics are best demonstrated as churches work proactively to demonstrate inclusivity in every aspect of ministry to the community. Herb Miller has helped us to understand, "Like other voluntary community organizations, a church is a social system. Its attendees measure much of its effectiveness by how well members get along with each other and how well it lives out the 'be a good neighbor' maxim."[8] I would add to what Miller says in that it is not only the attendees who measure much of a church's effectiveness, especially in terms of unity, peace, and love, but those on the outside who are observing the church in its daily ministry and toward whom the church seeks to be neighbor.

A sixth truth is that a church's personality develops as a result of missional leadership models. My colleague, Karen Massey, who teaches Faith Development at the McAfee School of Theology, explains that the formation of missional leadership should be thought of in terms of how children learn. A child learns, among other ways, by doing. Children will often copy behavior—both positive and negative—and eventually learn to integrate the models they observe into their lives, both positive and negative. In order to develop missional leaders for the future, she suggests, children and youth should be involved in missional outreach and ministry. They should be exposed to people who have a missional heart and vision for the church's task in the world. They should have the opportunity to work alongside adults who are involved in missional activity and whose lives embody the characteristics of the kingdom. As a result, they can be exposed to characteristics of leadership that are flavored with missional vision.

Missional leaders have to be people of vision and of courage. They must have their eyes and ears tuned to what God is doing in the world. As such, they have to be people whose prayer life is consistent and probing into the very heart of God. Often they represent those on the fringe of the church's total life. As such, they suffer the potential of not being taken seriously, being thought of as dreamers, or even being considered antagonistic to the normalcy of the church's present ethos. But missional leaders cannot let themselves be discouraged. They have to be people of hope. They have to develop confidence that what they seem to hear and what others seem not to hear and see is consistent with God's activity in the world. Most church members are so used to corporate or institutional religion that the unique activities of God in their community fail to fit their expectations. For missional leaders to emerge in the church, they will need to become like novices.[9] They will have to learn to recover the essential vision of the people of God called to mission in the world. A helpful pattern, according to Darrell Guder, is to revisit Paul's account of leadership found in Ephesians chapter four. Paul's definition of the function of missional leaders is to "equip the saints for the work of ministry" (4:12a), which emphasizes the formation of God's people so that they can "lead a life worthy of the calling to which [they] have been called" (4:1b).[10]

Missional leadership depends on persons in the church who live between the times, as Wilbert Shenk has said. They are people who understand the nature of God's kingdom as "already" but "not yet."[11] These leaders take seriously the journey of faith toward expressing the values and character of God's kingdom in the community. This will require that the goals, expectations, and ethos of the church be reformed away from institutional patterns of church, and toward patterns characteristic of the covenant community of faith.

A seventh truth is that a church's personality develops as a response to denominational identity. For most churches, history is a shaping factor. Churches in the South have a long history of reflecting Southern values, while Northern churches no doubt reflect a history of their Northern values. People in the community often characterize the personality of a church according to what they know of the larger denomination. Hence, if the denomination has been in the news because it has engaged in advocacy for people in need, the local church can also benefit from positive media attention. Likewise, denominational controversies in the news can have a negative impact on the local church, lumping it into stereotypes. No matter the situation, good press or bad press, the church has to transcend its historic labels. This can only be done as church members move beyond dependence on denominational identity. Denominations do not, by and large, minister to people. Congregations do. People in need of pastoral care do not call the headquarters of a denomination, and people who are hungry do not visit national agencies. They show up on the campus of a local church. Therefore, a church's personality can transcend its denominational identity by elevating the importance of the covenant nature of the missional community and presenting that face to the world around it.

The values and theology of denominations impact local churches. Catholic churches, for example, cannot sidestep the fact that the Vatican condemns the use of birth control. Therefore a local Catholic church may have to work very hard to minister to people who have theological differences with that official position. Denominations that have restrictive policies or theological positions against ordaining homosexuals or against women in ministry communicate those positions through local churches.

A local church wishing to minister to persons with an alternate lifestyle will constantly battle the culture's assumptions about the church. Those who wish to be inclusive of women, for example, will always be pointing to their local church as the exception to their denomination's restrictive official position. For many denominations, the ordination of women for ministry is not an issue. As a result, they will have fewer obstacles to overcome with the community. But others who do have restrictive policies will always be on the defensive with the community.

A church's personality is the sum total of these factors and others as well. In order to become more kingdom-focused, every church has to seriously engage the issues that present the church to the world and seek ways to communicate what the church senses is God's agenda. If a church is serious about asking the question, "Why can't our community hear what we are saying?" it will examine its personality carefully in light of the ethos of the kingdom of God and it will take the necessary steps to modify, enhance, or change its personality in order to be the kind of witness to the world that the gospel demands.

Are We Ready to Listen to Our Community?

Now that we have addressed the fact that every church exudes a certain personality to the community around it, the logical question is, "How do we assess our church's personality?" Chapter 4 discusses the mechanics of such a process, but before getting into the actual evaluation tool, we must consider two additional issues. One relates to the assumptions we often make about culture as a whole. This will be discussed in the next chapter. The other is simply whether your church is really willing to listen to the culture around it and willing to learn from what it discovers.

It has been my observation that churches seldom assess what the community around them thinks of them or their ministry. This is not only the case with churches; it is often the case with other social organizations, and even business and industry. In order to assess the personality of the church as seen from the community's vantage point, a deliberate process needs to take place.

First, the church has to decide that it really does want to assess its true reputation in the community. The subject will need to be explored among church leaders, the pastor, and other ministry personnel. Spiritual preparation time is vital. Sermons, Bible studies, and spiritual formation groups will need to examine the implications of becoming a kingdom-focused church. Laypersons should be challenged to study the Scriptures to discover the essence of Jesus' words about the kingdom. The church's spiritual leaders should suggest key passages and write brief commentaries to encourage church members who want to conduct their own biblical discovery.

Each church will need to decide how best to adopt the planning process according to its church polity. This cannot be the vision of any one person, but will require commitment from as many as possible. If the church as a whole is not interested, any effort to change will be slow, might create resistance, and be futile. Therefore, a period of discovery and visionary leadership can benefit the process.

Second, church persons have to be enlisted who are interested in knowing why their community can't hear them. These persons must also be willing to do the work necessary to discover the answers. Once those people are found and enlisted, a period of training is necessary, using the principles listed below under "Training the Troops," and the creative vision of the church.

Third, the church has to pledge itself to take seriously the information they find and be willing to put into place a response to the findings. People will not be interested in contributing if they believe that nothing will come from the investigation. They have to know that there is a serious commitment to shaping the church in terms of the kingdom of God and to refocusing the ministry of the church missionally. Educational opportunities need to be provided to the larger congregation through special teaching sessions, sermons, and printed materials that explain the goals and needs of the discovery project. It should be widely known that the emphasis on the project is to reformat the ministry of the church based on missional goals. This will change the church's main focus and basic personality.

Fourth, adequate funding, time on the church calendar, and prayer support are needed. Enlist as many people as possible to pray for the process and for what the church discovers. Allow plenty of preparation time and encourage excitement to build from week to week in anticipation of "Discovery Sunday." Above all, remind the church family over and over again that this is not just another program of the church, but a life-changing period of discovery that will affect the future ministry of the church and its goals.

Fifth, begin equipping the people who will engage in the discovery process. Make sure the church understands each stage of the process. You will need one set of volunteers to go out into the community and another set who will assess everything the church does for its own membership. Religious educational materials will need to be examined, worship services evaluated, church budgets will need to be looked at, and church programs carefully scrutinized. A single criterion must be used to do this in-house survey: everything will be examined in light of how it prepares the church to be more kingdom-of-God–oriented. Are budgets mostly weighted in terms of service to the members, or are budgets focused toward the character of the kingdom? Do church programs benefit only those who are members, or do they touch the world with the love of Christ? Are people in the church educated in terms of God's mission in the world, or are they educated to be religious? Be very deliberate and focused, otherwise the in-house discovery process will turn inward or potentially critical, and it will then fail to be accountable to the larger goals of the discovery. The point is to not criticize the church or its leadership. It is to refocus the energies of the church toward a kingdom orientation, and away from a corporate or institutional religion.

Training the Troops, Implementing the Process of Discovery

After choosing the group of people who will seek to discover how the church is perceived in the larger community, provide them training in how to conduct interviews. Interview materials, complete with suggested questions to ask, will need to be carefully developed from an assessment of the church's goals for the discovery. Develop teams that will conduct focus interviews, draft persons who will produce mailings with questions about the church, and explore the possibility of telephone interviews if it is appropriate in the context of the church community. Develop as many channels of input as you possibly can, but do not give every team member the same questions to ask. You may, for example, have a pool of fifty questions or more. These need to be spread out among many team members so that all the questions are asked; so each individual asks only a few questions.

Most laypersons have limited knowledge or skills in interviewing others, especially in regard to church work or the mission of the church. Help them to prepare through role play and other activities that will let them practice before they "hit the streets."

One of the most critical aspects of interviewing others is the ability to listen. In a previous book, *How Will They Hear If We Don't Listen?*,[12] I provided methodology for how to listen to others in evangelistic dialogue in a caring manner. This book can be used as additional preparation for training the team during the interviews. Below are some key components that the interviewer will need to understand as she talks with people about how her church is received in the community.

First, pay attention to the personality of the community around the church. Who lives there? What is their lifestyle? What occupies their time? What other voices clamor for the attention of the community? How has tragedy or celebration affected the community? These are but a few questions you need to keep in mind as you interview persons from the community. Consider also the history of the community. How many people are young? How many seniors live there? Check other surveys that have been done in the community that assess the lifestyle of the community, its income, education, crime statistics, number of singles, and so on. This information is readily available through local or state Web sites that report demographic trends. Information is also available from collected census data. Check also with denominational agencies that will have profiles of communities in your area. In short, try to learn as much as possible about the factors that compete for the attention of the community around your church. Keep good records of the information you discover.

Second, invest in dialogue. Each interviewer must understand the difference between dialogue and monologue. You are not there to enlist the other person for membership in the church or to "bait and switch" them so they are confronted with someone who they believe only wants to make another convert. You are there to honestly gather the opinion of the other person about how he or she perceives your church, whether it seems correct to you or not.

Be clear about your purpose with the other person, whether the person is a stranger to you or a coworker or neighbor who lives in the community. When you ask them a question, make sure you have understood what they have said. Repeat their response to them, and ask them if what you heard is what they meant. You may find that the process will develop into a dialogue about your church or churches in general that will provide insight. Do not be defensive. Just listen, take notes, clarify what they are saying, and thank them for helping you to understand better how they perceive your church. Remember this: The process of communication is complex. Douglas Steere once described how difficult it is to really listen to another person. He said, "In every conversation between two people there are always at least six persons present. What each person said are two; what each person meant to say are two more; and what each person understood the other to say are two more."[13] Remember as you are chatting on the back porch with the neighbor who does not attend your church–there are six people involved in the conversation.

Third, listen to what people *don't* say. People are often reluctant to being open, especially to strangers. You will need to set the other person at ease as much as possible. But listen carefully to what they do not say in response to your question. Rather than confronting the person about whether they attend church or not, listen for the absence of religious language or knowledge of the work of churches. Such data is important to report back to the church because it provides a measure of how many persons in the community may not be religiously oriented in their worldview.

Often what people do not say is a reflection of the emotional baggage they are carrying regarding a subject. Some people become strangely quiet when certain subjects are raised in conversations. Maybe it is just too painful for them to relive the events that are brought to mind by the subject at hand. Carefully watch the body language of the person with whom you are talking about your church. You may be led to the understanding that he or she has been hurt by a faith community. Even if people do not say so, they may allude to the pain with what they do not say. Such an observation may suggest to you that pastoral care is an important need in your community among those who have been wounded by institutional religion, religious persons, or personal tragedies that raised questions about religious faith.

Fourth, ask questions that will get responses. Employ questions that are specific to learn the community impressions about the character of your church, its ministries, its facilities, and its programs. You may find many people who just do not have a clue what your church is about. If you hit a wall, ask the person to elaborate on any impression he or she may have about the church. If the person says something general, probe a bit further and ask, "I'm fascinated by what you are saying. Could you tell me more?" In other words, compliment the answers given and encourage the person to go further. Do not give the impression that you do not like the response or that you are frustrated because he or she seems to know little about your church. Be prepared to dialogue as completely as possible regarding what few impressions the person may have about your church.

Fifth, as an interviewer you will need to overcome the blindness of your own personal point of view. As a Christian you are likely to encounter persons who are not Christians. They will most likely not share the same level of interest in your church that you do. The longer we are Christians, the more we tend to view the world through our religious orientation. We have to try as best we can to see the Christian faith and our congregations from the viewpoint of those who live on the outside, or who express no strong religious orientation toward life. The attitudes and responses from persons in this category can help us understand how our church can better communicate the gospel to the secular culture and unchurched persons.

Sixth, take careful notes. You may choose to use a tape recorder for the interviews. If you do so, make sure you have permission from the other person to do so. Otherwise, take notes that can later be rewritten and made more complete. Let the person know that his or her name will never be used. You are collecting input from people to discover the perceptions of your church in the community, not to hold individuals accountable for their contributions. Pay attention to the fatigue factor. If the other person grows weary, stop the process and thank that person for his or her time; don't overstay your welcome. Respect the fact that people are busy and they have endured lots of interviews during their lives. If you only get two or three good answers, consider that you have succeeded in your task.

Seventh, after the interviews are complete and you have compiled the responses, be ready to compare your interview material with other team members'. This will provide an extra level of learning from the responses. Record the insights of the group as you discuss the responses from interviewees. These insights will suggest approaches and changes that will improve your interviewing in the future.

Eighth, summarize all input from the interviews. All the data will need to be collected and grouped according to function. Compile telephone interviews, focus group interviews, mailings' responses, and any other data you have collected into a single report. This report will be foundational to the analysis of your church's receptivity in the community.

Ninth, test your findings with other church members and leaders. Invite a fellow pastor and a group of laypersons from a sister congregation to read the reports and to meet with the team to discuss the implications. If you are uncomfortable with this process, invite an outside consultant from your denomination or a professional to help you sort out the implications of your discovery. Once again, record the responses.

Tenth, test the findings with the larger church membership. Make the results of the surveys available to church members so they can see what others are saying about your faith community. Ask church members to respond in writing to what they have seen in the data. All of the input from the interviews, church members, and outside readers should be used as information that will direct discussions and planning that needs to be done as the church refocuses its direction.

Risks and Benefits

Discovering the personality of the church from the outside is not an easy task. It is filled with time-consuming effort. Furthermore, there are risks. Some church members will question why this is necessary and will see it as a threat to what they have always valued about the church. They may fear that the church will change from what they have always known. And it will. No church I have worked with has remained the same after taking this journey. Each one has discovered something about themselves that shocked them.

I was in Tennessee to do a consultation with a church a couple of years ago. My purpose, as they defined it, was to help them discover how the community viewed their ministry and outreach. I drove from my home in Georgia to Tennessee, but realized on the way there that I had left the directions to the church at home. Furthermore, I did not know the church phone number. But I did not panic. I knew the city and I felt I could find the church.

When I arrived in town, I decided to look for the tallest steeple in town. I knew that would probably be the Methodist church, and I figured that the church that had commissioned me would be either on the corner across from it or nearby. That is the way county-seat towns are often arranged in the South. Most of the churches are all gathered close to each other. In larger cities they are spread out, and in very large cities many of the churches have long ago scattered into the suburbs. But in a small town, one can usually find where "First Church" is located.

Sure enough, I got to the center of the town and I found the Methodist church. It had the tall steeple. But I drove around the town for a while and could not spot the Baptist church. It was getting close to time for me to be there for the evening, so I began to panic. Then I spotted a local police cruiser. I ducked in behind him and decided to follow him until he stopped or until I could flag him down. Sure enough, he stopped at a local diner. I pulled up behind him and asked, "Excuse me, sir, I am looking for the First Baptist Church. Can you give me directions?" He looked puzzled, reached inside his car and radioed to his headquarters. I heard him ask for the directions. While we were waiting for a response I asked him how long he had been a policeman there. He said for about ten years. Then the radio crackled with the directions. I thanked him and left.

When I drove into the parking lot of the church, I could see why I could not find it—no steeple. There was no church sign where I expected it to be. I gathered my materials from the back seat of my car, turned to walk toward the church and noticed that across the street in plain view of the church…was the police station. The policeman who came every day to his police station could not tell me where to find the church, when for the last ten years he had worked across from it.

When I related the story to the congregation, it proved my point. At least to this policeman, they were invisible. Needless to say, I had to convince the people of the church that I was serious and that what I had just told them was indeed true.

A similar event occurred in Huntsville, Alabama, when I worked with a very large church there. I had stayed the night before in a hotel near the church. To test my assumptions, I asked the clerk the next morning for directions to the church. It is the largest one downtown. It was just across the street. She could not tell me where it was. Truth is stranger than fiction. Many people pass by churches every day in their normal work routines, yet take little notice of them. This is true even in the South, where most people believe everyone goes to church.

There will be people in every church who will find it difficult to believe there is a problem to be overcome. Some may use the discovery journey as an excuse to leave the church and go somewhere else. But if the process is done in the right spirit, casualties need not occur. If done in the right spirit, everyone can contribute—maybe for the first time—toward the church transforming itself in the image of Christ.

The benefits are so tremendously significant. The church has the potential to discover who it is in light of the community. It will have the capability to create opportunities for ministry that will touch human need in creative ways. It will find itself more sensitive to what God is doing in the world and more ready to join God in the process. Church growth can be a real outcome as more people are introduced to faith by a faithful congregation. Each church, however, must examine the risks and the benefits for themselves and measure them against the reality of the kingdom-focused church they can attain. If done in the right spirit, transformation can occur.

What Makes You Think the Community Cares about Your Message?

For many Christians who value their church tradition, the idea that there are those within the culture who do not care to participate in weekly religious services seems a bit odd. It is all the more confusing when a few pollsters seem to indicate that Americans, by and large, are Christians. Yet for many years my personal observations of the culture have hinted to me that the value of regular church life is declining within the general population. I have not seen evidence that large numbers of the American population are regular churchgoers.

I have tested this observation in churches across the country by asking a simple question in church outreach conferences. I realize that it is not a scientific poll, but the observations have been interesting to me. I have often quoted the popular figures on church attendance that some pollsters use. Then I ask this question: "What percentage of people in your neighborhood tend to leave for church services along with you when you back out of your driveway on Sunday morning?" I have *never* had more than a 10 to 20 percent figure cited. In a lot of cases, some people will respond by saying, "So far as I can tell, I am about the only one in my neighborhood who leaves the house on Sunday mornings."

The Gallup Poll has been fairly consistent over the years in reporting that Americans attend church in fairly large numbers. Beginning in the late 1930s, the Gallup Poll Organization has consistently asked Americans if they had attended church or synagogue within the last seven days. About 40 percent of Americans have consistently responded to the poll by saying that they did attend church recently.

To complicate matters, religious Americans have relied on these polls to confirm their belief that Americans go to church, are willing to be enlisted for church attendance, and are comfortable talking to religious people about their spiritual life. One only has to tune into religious broadcasters to pick up on their confidence and opinion that America is a religious country. They approach the nation with an assumption that Americans have perhaps been lazy about their church attendance and need to be reminded of its value and its place in what they believe to be the history of the nation. They use language that urges people to return to faith in God, read their Bibles, and proclaim their faith in a public manner, but they do not, by and large, seem to understand that a vast majority of Americans neither understand their language nor value it. Religious programs on television Sunday mornings are generally produced by large churches with large budgets and may give the casual viewer the idea that everyone is in church but her. She need not worry, however, because that is just not the case.

There is much controversy over the polling data. Some pollsters are refuting the idea that Americans who value church attendance are enough to represent 40 percent of the population. It may be that Americans want pollsters to believe that they are more faithful in their church attendance than they really are. Some critics have gone right to the heart of the issue by saying that Americans lie about their church attendance and exaggerate its importance in their lives.[1] Pollsters that rely on self-reporting are implicitly relying on the honesty of people. That supposition has served to skew the numbers away from reality. What they fail to take into account is that people often exaggerate as a matter of course when they speak. They will exaggerate their financial worth, an event in their personal life that may have been out of the ordinary, their giving to charities, how much they pay in taxes, the brilliance of their children, and so on. Why is it then that many Christians believe that the general public is so honest about its spiritual life? People will often report to pollsters what they believe pollsters are looking for; they want to portray themselves in a positive light to those who are checking up on them.

Andrew Walsh, managing editor of *Religion in the News,* reports that several contending pollsters have moved away from self-reporting and have actually counted the number of people who have attended services in sample communities.[2] Sociologists Penny Marler, Kirk Hadaway, and Mark Chaves, in an article entitled, "Overreporting Church Attendance in America: Evidence that Demands the Same Verdict," which appeared in the *American Sociological Review,* placed the numbers of average weekly attendance at around 20 percent of the American population.[3] Their ongoing research created a firestorm of controversy from people who did not believe the numbers. George Barna, a pollster from California, has placed the number at around 30 percent.[4] The controversy over the actual numbers of Americans who attend church on a weekly basis is likely to continue. But the reader can see that the evidence is strong that most churches are less than full on typical Sundays; likewise, activities such as organized recreation for youth, theme parks, shopping malls, and theaters seem to be well-attended on Sundays. It may be time for Christians to take another look at their assumptions about faith in America. It may be time for us to honestly ask the question, "What makes us believe that the communities around our churches care at all about what we are saying about faith?" They may indeed care, since many Americans tell the pollsters that they are spiritually minded people. But do they care enough to be part of the churches? If not, why not?

A Constantly Changing Culture

If we are going to assess whether the culture is interested in what our churches are saying, we need to view our churches as one of the many options available to people. Churches are often assessed in the same way everything is assessed by people in a community—that is, in terms of value. Thus, we need to have knowledge of the factors that influence, shape, and contribute to human assessment of the world around us.

According to Stanley Hauerwas and William Willimon, "Sometime between 1960 and 1980, an old, inadequately conceived world ended, and a fresh, new world began."[5] Hauerwas and Willimon began their book *Resident Aliens* by challenging Christians to face the changing world and by assessing the culture that has dramatically changed since World War II. This book, although now somewhat dated, was an important one for many people because it set in focus the way the culture had shifted in its religious orientation. Almost without our realizing it, faith communities themselves were quietly being eroded by many of the changes that Hauerwas and Willimon described. These changes may give us a glimpse into why people view organized religion differently today, and why they may not be interested in what we are saying to them.

The changes the authors cited need to be encountered in an honest manner in order to grasp the implications related to America's outlook on religion. Because the complexities of modern life that have escalated since Hauerwas and Willimon wrote, additional pressures on the church will need to be taken into account. These pressures can be found in the headlines of most newspapers. For example, the events of September 11, 2001, have made Americans both more cautious and more confused about evil in the world. People today are increasingly worried about violence and crime—from world terrorism to the personal invasion of identity theft. Each church therefore will need to assess carefully the levels of crime concern in their surrounding communities. What are the changes that are taking place in the world around *your* parish, and how have people responded within the community? How has the religious orientation of your community changed in the last 10 years? How is it that some people seem to be oriented in a particular manner to faith, while some do not appear to be concerned?

Religious orientation is often a reflection of a particular lifestyle that a person chooses. Demographic shifts can impact lifestyles. Culture as a whole often shifts as a result of the combination of these and other factors. While not exhaustive, the elements of cultural change, lifestyle patterns, general religious orientation preferences, and demographic realities contribute to the challenge ahead for Christians as they live out their witness in the twenty-first century. An honest assessment of these elements will give faith communities a creative opportunity to retool for the future without the temptation to merely repeat a dependency on past patterns. If the mission of Christians is to reach the world for Christ, they will need to critically evaluate their response to each element that contributes to the changes within the patterns of human life.

The Impact of Culture

People learn culture. It is not genetically encoded. Culture can be defined in a general way as a collection of learned behaviors that are common to a human society. Culture shapes behavior, identification, outlook on the world, and the expectations people have about their place in the world. Cultural identification is passed along from generation to generation, and is modified to some extent by each succeeding generation. Although definitions of culture are complex, three characteristics emerge that help to focus the meaning.

First, culture is a dynamic force. Like human beings, culture grows by adapting certain structures and discarding others. Contemporary culture is being shaken, for example, by technical modernity, and is constantly adapting to technological trends. While adapting to technology, certain manifestations of old technology are being discarded by the culture. Very few people, for example, insist on manual typewriters in today's culture, but will insist instead on the latest word processors to facilitate their work. Additionally, while technology impacts the culture, "its essential components will certainly always be related to art, ethics, and religion."[6] These disciplines, like technology, do not escape the dynamic forces that call for adaptation of the new and the discarding of the old. Often, it is a painful process as some people feel left behind while others seem to advance.

Second, culture is inevitably connected to human history. This history is rooted in certain traditions of the past that inform both consciously and unconsciously. History is important to a culture because it provides a heritage that is transmitted and that further defines the culture as a whole. Culture is an invisible but very tight link that binds human beings to their predecessors, contemporaries, and successors.[7] The narratives of this history shape the norms of the culture and further define it. The subsets of a larger culture that remember the stories of the past are likely to remain more consistent into the future compared to those who forget their past. Therefore, the importance of the function of narrative and storytelling can be seen in the definition of a culture.[8]

A third characteristic formulating a definition of culture relates to ethics as a process that has the ability to humanize people. In many ways, culture is what makes human beings human.[9] Any culture carries with it an ethical imperative. However, the struggle to define humanistic causes tends also to carry with it ethical dimensions that have the potential to unite or divide people, especially among groups who hold to ethical categories emerging out of their different definitions of humanity. The lesson of World War II is informative. For the Nazis of Germany, the definition of humanity centered around their ideal of the "super race" and carried an ethical framework that could exterminate with impunity those deemed as inferior. For the Jews, whose definition of humanity was formed in part within the crucible of oppression throughout their history, an entirely different ethical framework existed that may have contributed, in part, to millions being led to their deaths without struggle, much as their forefathers were led to slavery in the brickponds of the Egyptians. While at times problematic, ethics communicates the values that shape the culture throughout the generations. Cultures, regardless of how self-serving they might be, tend to view their ethical frameworks as having a value that contributes toward a greater human potential and social good. While these three characteristics contribute toward a definition of culture, it is also necessary to view the impact of religion upon cultural development. Self-identification is often linked to how a group views its culture. It is evident that American culture, although multicultural, tends to think of itself as largely Christian and with Christian value sets, while, for example, India views its culture as largely Hindu, and various Middle Eastern countries define their culture as Muslim. The truth, however, is that religious categories are not monolithic. Each nation on earth is a patchwork of many cultures and varied religious traditions.

Claude Geffre says, "Culture tends to be of greater importance in modern societies. Culture signifies a certain system of values and elements that induce modes of life."[10] These modes of life are communicated in schools to the larger populace and within the churches to the Christian community. What results are commonly held worldviews on national, regional, and local levels. One example is the notion of America as a free and democratic nation. Regional worldviews would include the notion that the West is populated by rugged individualists. Local worldviews vary in towns, villages, and communities where founding families, regional themes, historical landscapes, or traditions determine uniqueness. The culture of a nation, therefore, is a patchwork giving color and character to the whole.

The shifts in American culture during the last fifty years are not unlike those that have occurred in cultures worldwide. However, since World War II American culture has witnessed dramatic economic, technological, demographic, and lifestyle changes. Christians must become sensitive to cultural change. They cannot be the last to recognize that the world around them is changing daily. They must recognize the coming together of peoples from all parts of the world and the cultural pluralism that results. Wilbert Shenk warns, "To take culture seriously for the sake of the Gospel will demand a depth of cultural sensitivity not required in Christendom."[11]

If Christians in local churches are to be effective in the culture, changes in attitude have to occur. First, every church must embrace the dynamics of culture with a willingness to receive new forms and to discard outdated forms if necessary. There are still many churches, for example, that insist on worship forms that have changed little while the music, stories, and interests of the culture have shifted dramatically.

Worship wars have centered around the tension between those who prefer the old hymns and those who prefer contemporary choruses, or those who prefer to write their own songs of worship.[12] The culture has moved away from pipe organs and pianos to synthesizers, drums, and stringed instruments. Some Christian youth are adopting hip-hop as a way to express their spiritual journey through music. Many seminaries now find it difficult to offer traditional organ curriculum because of lack of demand by the students and by churches that call music ministers.

The church that finds beauty in the great hymns of the faith does not need to feel intimidated, however, in the face of so many changes. Music is a dynamic and ever-changing force in the culture. There are many young people who can find those hymns a delightful contrast to their current diet. They just need an opportunity to taste for themselves. In any case, each church will need to decide how best to respond to changing tastes and preferences found within its community, and to be prepared to honor those changes and yet to introduce with creativity some classic expressions of worship that the community may have never heard.

Churches that still insist on outdated outreach methods such as revivals as a means of evangelism will continue to decline in their ability to attract persons to the services. Instead of being effective outreach to the unchurched, revivals have become little more than ordinary worship services. Even on a larger scale, crusades no longer attract those from within the secular culture. Stephen Neill, while expressing appreciation for Billy Graham's ministry, notes that the vast majority of those who attended his crusades and responded already had some connection with the church and the gospel.[13]

Clearly then, a refusal to accept the dynamics of change in the culture affecting worship patterns, musical expression, and evangelistic outreach of the church is problematic. To continue to insist on forms that have been largely discarded as outdated by the unchurched culture will simply ensure that congregations will find it increasingly difficult to fulfill what they believe to be their missiological mandate. They will continue to feel frustrated as the community around them seems to care little for what they are offering.

Changes within the culture need not be feared. Emilio Castro has suggested that because cultures are not neutral, even today's subcultures that might not claim a particular religious tradition tend to idolize specific values.[14] These values present opportunities to congregations that learn to encounter the culture through dialogical and constructive ways. Dialogue within cultures has enormous potential. Dialogue can help us learn what the culture is interested in pursuing. Paul Russ Satari encourages the potential for dialogue in his observations. He writes:

> Since no culture is essentially foreign to God, it becomes imperative for Christian mission through the translatability of Christianity to realize the bridge of mutual interaction between the gospel and culture. It is this enduring dialogue between the gospel and culture that has the capacity to link the relationship of the source of life and truth with all human cultures, thus leading to a contextual understanding and experience of faith in God.[15]

But dialogue must be done honestly; it must be done with a response to the culture, not as targets of zeal, but with a desire to understand and to learn. It is necessary to approach persons in the larger culture, as Castro says, with an attitude of respect:

> We cannot approach people inside different cultures with a "hunting attitude," as it were, of looking for people to get them out of their realities or subcultures, and to incorporate them into our own sub-cultures, that we sometimes call the church. Rather, in evangelism, we are going to the encounter of a spiritual construction, where we will expect the signs of the Spirit of God to be at work, and fruits that will enrich the common heritage of humanity. Without a sense of respect and admiration for what we could find in the situation of the others, it would be very difficult to avow it a judgmental attitude that would falsify our evangelistic encounter.[16]

Old patterns of witness, especially in the South, may have been effective in a culture that did not mind the "hunters." But today's culture, increasingly bombarded by sales campaigns, has rejected them. This shift in culture is simply one example that should be noted and allowed to contribute to a church's outreach philosophy and practice. Congregations should routinely reevaluate their outreach programs in light of the changing culture, with respect for those who live within each cultural setting.

Churches must respond to the second characteristic of culture as well: its connection to history. Rather than treating unchurched people as all the same, every congregation needs to be a student of the history of peoples and their cultures. Most churches have spent very little time or effort in trying to understand the historical context of the communities around them. Christians must put forth the effort to actively embrace the history of communities and the various cultural groups within localities. David Bosch reminds us that, "History is not only the 'context' of mission, but its 'text.'"[17] The reading of the historical "text" enables the Christian witness to rightly communicate the gospel within the context of the culture, and dialogue in a way that the gospel can be understood.

Craig Van Gelder proposes that the reason why so many fail to understand history as vital to the construct of cultures is because radicalized modernity has distorted time. Time and history seem to have collapsed, in his view; the new reality forces people to experience time and history in a new way based upon the constant process of change.[18] Thus, the historical context is rarely considered. Because of this, it is necessary to be deliberate in constructing communities of faith with a historical consciousness. To become more kingdom-oriented in the outreach and work of the church, it will be necessary to build into the church's very character an understanding of persons as being "part of an ongoing history being shaped by the God who was, who is, and who will be forever."[19]

Most congregations will continue to be at a loss in understanding the shifts of culture until they make the effort to understand their own history as a cultural subset and to invest in the cultural subsets of others to whom they seek to minister. Having done so, they will be better able to contextualize the gospel within the culture and will not be accused of merely trying to indoctrinate those they seek to reach with the gospel. They will be far more sensitive to integrate the history of the people of faith with the history of the community around it.

There is a third aspect to consider, related to the characteristics of culture. It is the ethical dimension. Churches that have not settled the ethical dilemmas within their own congregations have little hope of reaching a world for Christ. President Jimmy Carter said to a group of seminary students that he had a difficult time going into countries embroiled in civil war to talk about reconciliation and peace when his own religious denomination had failed to reconcile its divisions. Carter spoke to the pain he felt over the racism, theological conflict, and division evident to even casual observers of his denomination.

Carter's dilemma in trying to explain the ethical inconsistencies within his denomination merely points to the surface of the problem. The deeper problem is directly related to an improper ethical response to the culture. Rather than functioning in arenas of peacemaking, reconciliation, social justice, or racial equality, some church members are more concerned about aligning the culture to their way of thinking and to their behavior.

George G. Hunter III has identified the outreach goals of people in traditional churches. He says that we want to make the culture religious, believe like us, behave like us, have an experience like us, become like us, be good citizens like us, share our politics, support the church like us, worship like us, and prepare for heaven.[20] Such expecta ions point to an inadequate understanding of the purpose of the church in the world. Oftentimes congregations are evaluated by the larger culture as being interested enough in the world to get people to come and join the church, yet not interested enough to care about the issues that impact ordinary people in their everyday lives when they fail to join.

The dualism between this age and the age to come is often viewed as an absolute by Christians. This is precisely why so much attention has been given to evangelistic programs that many churches view as central to their mission. But the problem among those who hold to such dualism is the working belief that "believers are not called to engage in working for peace, justice, and reconciliation among people."[21] For example, it was not until 1995 that the Southern Baptist Convention adopted a resolution apologizing to the African American community for the convention's historical involvement in support of slavery. While an appropriate response, it took 150 years to address the problem and to debate the issue among the convention's dissenters. When the resolution finally passed, it did nothing to demonstrate a proactive approach to "tear down the walls" within the infrastructure of racism in the churches or in the larger culture. A proper ethical response to the culture will ensure that all Christians resist racism, and work for the equality of all people. Churches are often afraid of confronting the culture around them. Yet, "authentic apocalyptic hope compels ethical seriousness. It is impossible to believe in God's coming triumph without being agitators for God's Kingdom here and now."[22]

Likewise, any church that has an oppressive policy with regard to women discounts an ethical approach to the culture around it. Every congregation would do well to honestly study the apostle Paul's theology of inclusiveness and apply lessons learned to the issue of inclusivity, whether racially, in terms of gender, or in other areas. As Bosch explains:

> Paul's vehement reaction signifies that since Christ has accepted everybody unconditionally, it is preposterous even to contemplate the possibility of Jews and Gentiles acting differently on the "horizontal" plane, that is, not accepting one another unconditionally. There is, indeed, no longer Jew or Greek, slave or free, male or female.[23]

What Christians sometime communicate to the larger culture can present an ethical dilemma. Not speaking on issues of vital concern is as problematic as speaking in a narrow and legalistic manner. Thus, the voice of the church can become negated in every other matter as well. If the church's voice is to be taken seriously, it must learn when and how to be prophetic and to communicate its prophetic words in ways that do not ignore the emotions, questions, and investments of the community to the issues at hand. Failure to do so may be part of the reason why the community can't hear what we are saying.

Demographic and Lifestyle Changes

Lifestyles change as cultures change. Since World War II, the changes in American lifestyle have been profound. Demographic changes occurred as people moved from the countryside to the cities, as they became more affluent, more diverse, and as they moved from community webs to isolation from neighbors. The erosion of regionalism in many parts of the nation presents challenges to every congregation regarding their cultural identity and to their mission. They must decide if they are going to continue to be regional, or if they are going to become more inclusive of persons who are not the least interested in a particular regional way of life or in a denomination that is heavily weighted to the value sets of regionalism.

The demographic shifts in the population of the country away from the industrial North have been dramatic. The fastest growing areas are in the Mountain West, the Upper Great Lakes, the Ozarks, and the South.[24] Migrants to a new region of the country often have no idea of the folkways of the region and may have a difficult time understanding variances in culture and language. This is especially true in churches heavily flavored with programs and worship styles unique to the region.

The movement of people from rural lifestyles to urban lifestyles has been dramatic since the 1900s. Now, rural areas are once again witnessing widespread population gains as urban persons spread into the countrside. Studies published on American demographics indicate, "Three in four nonmetropolitan counties gained population between 1990 and 1994, a stunning reversal following a decade of rural decline."[25] The state of Florida is an example. Statistics indicate that in 1900, 79.7 percent of the state's residents lived (made their living) on family farms in the rural countryside. Cities were smaller in terms of population. The statistics reversed throughout the last century: 84.8 percent now live (make their living) in cities or in metropolitan areas, whereas 15.2 percent live (make their living) in rural areas.[26] What this implies is that the cities have grown much larger and the countryside no longer represents the economic strength as it once did. However, people are moving into the countryside, driving back into the city to make a living, and maintaining their residence in the countryside. As cities continue to grow, growth is impacting rural areas, which are being assimilated into the urban context. The rural rebound of the past decade and beyond has not been fueled by births, but by more rural residents remaining in rural areas and by metropolitan residents moving to the small towns, and to rural homes. Falling interest rates in this time have made it possible for homeowners to own not only larger homes but larger tracts of land on which to place the home. The study continues: "Specifically, 56 percent of nonmetro growth between 1990 and 1994 came from net gains in migration."[27]

The new rural migrants are not moving from the city to work on farms, or to simply get away from civilization. Rather, they reflect a new pattern of urban development. "Edge cities," major metropolitan areas developing outside the central city, are pushing the suburbs further into the countryside: "As a result, 84 percent of nonmetropolitan counties that are adjacent to a metropolitan area gained population between 1990 and 1994, and 73 percent had net in-migration."[28] These migrants bring money and urban attitudes with them into the countryside.

Most people now relate to the cities by way of employment, rather than depending on the small villages and farms for their economic lifestyle. Even those living in rural areas commute long distances to the city for employment. For example, the average commuting distance to the city of Atlanta, Georgia, is now 34 miles: Many people draw their economic resources from the city while living far removed from it.

These lifestyle changes have forced many persons who live in small towns and rural areas to think and live more like urban dwellers. Many rural dwellers, like their urban counterparts, now do not know their neighbors, a shift from fifty years ago. Their friendship webs are more often related to the city than the small town in which they live. Even in a rural home, it is difficult for urban dwellers to escape the pace of the city. Hence, the city pace is brought into the rural town. Lifestyles are more complex, more diverse in interest, and more influenced by the urban ethos than the rural.

For churches, the impact is dramatic. Long commuting distances, the opportunities for multivaried activities offered by nearby cities, and economic change has given people the disposition to also commute to the churches they like, the opportunity to be involved in activities on Sunday other than church, and the economic resources to travel on weekends or be involved in leisure activities that were not available when America was a rural complex.

Many churches are working hard to compete with the lifestyles of people in the larger culture. However, most are finding they simply cannot do it. They cannot compete with the opportunities that are afforded to people today.

It is interesting to pick up a church bulletin and note the weekly activities. Many of these are built around the expectations that people have little else to occupy their time and will attend the church's functions, that they are willing to spend their money for church involvement rather than on the lifestyle the city offers, and that the familial interpersonal webs within the church will be desired by persons who are unchurched. However, Ron Dempsey cautions that unchurched people have lifestyles that are incompatible with those they find in churches.[29] Their lifestyles are simply not aligned with the lifestyle patterns of churched people.

Those churches caught in the growth patterns of urban-to-rural population change fostered by edge cities often find themselves surrounded by new industry, new housing complexes, and increasing traffic. These all contribute to radical changes in the lifestyles of the people who populate the area. If these churches are unable to cope they will wither and die.

This fact became apparent to me when I interviewed church members in a once-small rural community now surrounded by the urban sprawl of a nearby edge city. When members of the church were confronted with questions of change in their church and of reaching the new people living in the suburbs that were once open fields, their consensus response was, "They are not like us. They are city folks. They won't be happy here." It is no surprise that this church has continued to decline even while the area around it explodes in growth as the city expands.

Affluence has also contributed to lifestyle change. Americans now have more money to spend on themselves than before. David Wells lends insight to the affluence of Americans and to the problems affluence has caused:

> Between 1945 and 1973, the average family income in America increased by two-thirds in constant dollars, unemployment dropped from a high in the Depression of one in three to less than one in ten by 1993, and the American Way of Life rapidly became a byword in many parts of the world. But study after study conducted during this period suggested that although newly prosperous Americans had the money and the leisure time to own and do a multitude of things that had been mere dreams for many of their parents, they were increasingly less satisfied with their lives.[30]

Affluence, as Wells has noted, has given Americans more time and resources to fulfill their dreams. The pursuit of these dreams has more often than not been the primary activity of Americans, while percentages of religious involvement have suffered. Although the churches *have* benefited by the affluence of religious Americans, most have not used the money they have received to minister to persons in the culture for whom money has not been the answer to happiness. While Americans and their churches bask in relative plenty, those whose lifestyles are spiritually bankrupt have largely been overlooked. Instead of furthering the *missio Dei,* Christians have used affluence to make themselves more comfortable in their lavish sanctuaries. Church buildings in America tend to reflect the aesthetic concerns of the members rather than their concern for the mission of God in the world. They tend to also be homogenous with regard to symbol and structure and suggest little acceptance of diversity within the culture.

Diversity is the watchword of today's lifestyle changes. The racial composition of America's heartland is an indicator. In October of 1995, *The Wall Street Journal* ran a front-page article on the changing demographics of small towns in America. Its focused example was one small town in Minnesota. The article pointed out that the town was "virtually all white a decade ago," but in just five years had become "20 percent immigrants, mostly Mexicans, Laotians, Vietnamese, Sudanese, and Ethiopians."[31]

Today's immigrants are from "vastly different racial, cultural, and religious backgrounds," according to the article, than the "white, European, and Christian" immigrants who came to America in the nineteenth century. The article links this town's experience to many others like it. "The number of Asian immigrants living in small towns has jumped 42 percent to more than six hundred thousand, and the number of Hispanics has increased 23 percent to more than three million."[32] These changes, according to Calvin Beale, a senior demographer at the U.S. Department of Agriculture, are leading to a "permanent change in the ethnic composition of many small communities."[33]

Small rural communities, where lifestyles were built around family farms, neighbors, family businesses, and local churches, have grown smaller in number and have shifted to larger multicultural realities. The small towns of America now reflect the cities' ethnic diversity as never before. As America continues to grow, it will increasingly become less European and less white, according to Phillip Jenkins: "By 2000, the United States was home to 30 million immigrants, about 11 percent of the population. Over 13 million migrants arrived in the 1990s alone. Almost 5 percent of Americans have been in the country for a decade or less."[34]

Other demographic changes are reflected in the nation. The senior adult population continues to increase each year. From 1990 to 1994, for example, the increase was nearly eight percent. The Baby Boom cohort (79,352,000 persons) now represents 30 percent of the population, and the oldest of the cohort will reach retirement age in about six years, adding to the increase in senior adults. Compounding this shift, however, birth rates are slowing. Since 1994 the decline has been over two percent every year. The estimated median age at first marriage is higher than ever before: 26.7 years for men and 24.5 years for women. In 1970, first marriages occurred at 23.2 years for men and 20.8 years for women. Shifts in the age distribution of women of childbearing age, decreases in age-specific fertility rates, and declines in the total number of women having children add to the slowing birth rates.[35] As a result, America is aging. Churches will find themselves growing older unless they deliberately emphasize a ministry to the young.

The number of traditional nuclear households has also changed dramatically. One in nine adults now lives alone. This represents about 23.6 million persons. The increase has been most dramatic among men: "Between 1970 and 1994, the number of women living alone increased 94 percent (from 7.3 to 14.2 million). During the same period, there was a 167 percent increase in the number of men living alone (from 3.5 to 9.4 million)."[36]

There has been a sevenfold increase in unmarried-couple households since 1970. Of all the children who live with one parent, the proportion who live with a parent who has never married has grown by one-half in the past decade to 36 percent: "In 1983, a child in a one-parent situation was almost twice as likely to be living with a divorced parent as with a never-married parent; whereas today, the child is just as likely to be living with a divorced parent as with a never-married parent (37 percent compared with 36 percent, respectively)."[37]

Congregations that have traditionally relied on nuclear families to populate their churches are facing the challenge of a twenty-first–century world that has redefined family. Most divorced persons who have found themselves stigmatized in their home church have either transferred to another church or denomination or dropped out of church attendance altogether.

Demographic and lifestyle shifts challenge congregations more than any other factor largely because these shifts hit the core of their traditional value expectations. With a missiology heavily tied to the traditional values they espouse, a radical reevaluation of attitudes, theology, and methodology will be needed. However, the trend is away from all three.

Religious Orientation

Today's societal differentiation has stripped religion of many of its former responsibilities and roles. The religious orientation of the culture today is different than in the early days of America. The dominant conception of religion within that culture was its emphasis on influencing cultural values. Religion was thought to be a primary force in shaping the politics of culture. Oscar Blackwelder said the main role of the church was "to declare moral and spiritual principles" and "to inspire and instruct individual Christians to apply Christian principles in all their relationships."[38] The implication carried in Blackwelder's statement placed religion at the forefront of shaping public opinion, utilizing the influence of Christians. Religious leaders, according to Robert Wuthnow, widely assumed that influencing society through religious individuals was more effective than passing legislation.[39]

Public officials also reinforced the belief that religion should influence society. Wuthnow quotes a speech by President Harry Truman in 1946 in which he addressed the matter of the religious orientation of the nation and its hopes for the future, saying, "Without a religious revival we are lost."[40] Dwight Eisenhower, in a postwar 1946 address, averred that religion nurtures men of faith who are "needed in the building of a new world reflecting the glory of God."[41]

The religious orientation of Americans connected faith to America and to its prosperity. Indeed, some believed there could be no American way of life without Christianity. For many people, being a good American was to be a Christian. To be a good Christian was to uphold the American ideal. Wuthnow says, "It was the conviction that public life could be influenced chiefly by the religiously informed consciences of individuals that in part accounts for the churches' tremendous interest in these years in membership drives."[42]

Today, the place of religion in public life has largely been diminished through court decisions ruling on prayer in public schools and the placing of the Ten Commandments in public or government buildings, through lawsuits brought against religious organizations such as the PTL Club, and as a result of increasing secularism. Religion, more than ever, has been relegated to a private affair for millions. Robert Bellah writes, "Religion is displaced from its role as guardian of the public worldview that gives human life its coherence. Religion is now relegated to the purely private sphere."[43]

George G. Hunter III highlights the shift away from a general religious orientation in which people in the culture honor the church and Christianity, to a general populace that knows little of the "stories" of the faith. Hunter says, "Consequently, we observe an increasing number of secular people– who have navigated their whole lives beyond the serious influence of Christian churches. They have little or no Christian memory, background, or vocabulary. Many of them do not even know what we are talking about, and have little or no experience of "church."[44] In Hunter's estimation, about 120 million Americans have little to no religious orientation in the sense of church involvement. Ron Dempsey finds, "The result is an unchurched religiosity based on the Christian faith but supplemented by the inclusion of values and meaning from other sources plus the emergence of the idea that faith is a private matter and has no need for institutional grounding."[45]

The importance of the church in public life has been displaced by other institutions. Most churches no longer offer general children's education, health care, social services, or recreation and leisure outlet for the community as they did in days past. The responsibility for community leisure outlets have been passed to county recreation departments, malls, movies, and TV.[46] Although many churches provide divorce counseling, child care, grief support groups, senior adult ministries, and other offerings, the general populace does not tend to participate in them. The ministries of most local churches are focused toward the members of the church. Community services sponsored by government agencies and social service groups have largely replaced the church in the larger culture. Dempsey sums up the situation by saying, "The church that once played a very distinct role in the community no longer has such a role. The church has become one choice among many."[47]

The shifting in the religious orientation of the culture is a serious matter for every congregation. They have generally drawn most of their members from persons who have been patriotic, conservative, denominationally oriented, involved in community, and centered in close-knit family relation-ships.[48] But today most congregations find themselves amid opposing influences that will make it harder to draw members from the general culture. An effective missiology for churches will demand a serious appraisal of the religious orientation of the general unchurched culture. New entry points to the culture must be found. Many of these entry points will be found in everyday experiences. As persons look for meaning in life, opportunities will arise to which the community of faith can speak. Christians cannot be reactive to the unchurched religiosity that surrounds the churches. Instead, they need to be proactive and focus energies on shaping the unchurched religiosity in ways that will be attractive enough to cause the unchurched to give the church "a second look."

Implications

I once met the late missiologist Lesslie Newbigin at a gathering in Birmingham, Alabama. He challenged me, as he did others, to think of the West as the new mission field for the twenty-first century. Newbigin's comments echoed those made to me by historian J. Edwin Orr in Amsterdam, in 1986, when he indicated that there were evidences of the movement of God in almost every nation of the world. "America," he said, "seems to be the exception." If the West is the new mission field, as Newbigin has said, and if, as Orr has said, America is in the midst of an religious drought, the need for an effective missiology is critical.

Given the changes that have occurred within the culture, lifestyle patterns, demographics, and religious orientation, the implication is that a shift toward a kingdom-focused orientation of the church seems to be overdue. No longer can any church fulfill its mission of reaching the world for Christ using the structures of corporate or institutional religion. Each one must begin to understand the changing realities of today's world and study carefully the effect of those changes upon the unchurched culture around them.

Such study will force a critical appraisal of the mission of every congregation. It will critically focus on strategies for effective outreach that take into consideration the shifts of culture. Critical appraisal that is willing to disregard idealistic rhetoric for sometimes harsh reality offers hope for any congregation wishing to embody the nature of the kingdom.

Every congregation needs to recognize the potential of reaching persons who are nonchurched. According to Dempsey, "Most nonchurchgoers have been involved in a local church at some time in their lives, normally during their childhood and adolescent years."[49] As such, they have some Christian memory. Yet they must be approached with the gospel in a way that recognizes the barriers that have been erected in their understanding and appreciation for religion. This category of persons has historically been the focus of evangelical churches. But there is another group that offers a significant challenge for a critical appraisal of outreach efforts directed toward them.

Large numbers of persons have never attended church and come from families that have never been exposed to church at all.[50] They have little to no Christian memory. These people cannot be reached with the gospel without pre-Christian cultivation efforts. Reaching both groups of people with the gospel will necessitate critical shifts in the way Christians view the culture around them. Reaching both those with Christian memory and those without a functioning Christian memory will require of the approaches a critical realism with regard to a church's outreach.

Paul Hiebert says, "Christian theologies, like other systems of human thought, emerge in different historical and cultural contexts."[51] Most Christians have sought to root their theology in what they believe to be the revelation of God in history, particularly as it is recorded in the Bible and applied to the culture. Strong biblical conservatism among a number of congregations has led them simply to overlay biblical revelation as they understand it onto the culture. With a dominant religious ethos formerly functioning in the society, especially out of the "Great Awakening," the receptivity of biblical revelation applied to the culture contributed to the prominence of religion within the society.

Today the situation has shifted. People are deeply influenced by both the positive and negative attributes of the culture in which they live and that fact must now inform churches as they are on mission in the twenty-first century. Such a shift will not be without dissent, especially from those who refuse to recognize the problem that mission faces in today's world.

Many forward thinkers who are evangelical are aware of the shifts that are occurring within the culture and are moving from old positions of naive realism to that of critical realism. Critics have interpreted the writings of these thinkers as a march toward liberalism, and have asserted the certainty of theology as a complete system of thought with little need for revision. They have become increasingly resistant to a critical realism for fear that the trustworthiness of Scripture as historical revelation will be violated. But in doing so, they have brought the majority of the churches into what Paul Hiebert calls "an idealist epistemology that absolutizes ideas over historical realities."[52] Critical of realism with regard to cultural, lifestyle, demographic, and religious orientation shifts, the antagonists of a proactive view of missions for the twenty-first century have become ahistorical and acultural. Hiebert says, "Realism looks at the events in the real historical world within which we live and focuses on the nature of truth in specific situations."[53]

If, in their theology, congregations become more aware of the paradigm shifts throughout history with regard to mission, they will be more likely to embrace the possibilities for the future, for example, ministry-based evangelism approaches that are sensitive to the culture. As Hiebert has suggested, those who aver a theology of mission devoid of cultural and historical realities become the liberals they loathe. They do so by placing the dynamic of the gospel into a narrow functionalism that is culturally specific, self-serving, and historically inert. Therefore, they tend to deny the realities of mission advance both biblically and historically. Realist theologians, however, emphasize biblical theologies that look at God's acts and self-revelation in specific historical and cultural situations.[54]

Effectively confronting the cultural shifts that are occurring in the larger society against the backdrop of critical realism will necessitate that every congregation first confronts the problem of their missiological idealism. Seen most clearly in missionaries who once considered most local customs to be evil and in the suggestion that mission fields were "foreign," little attention was paid to local customs and to the felt needs of people. Although sensitivity to mission fields has increased over the years, the underlying motif is still exercised within the evangelistic paradigm practiced by some. The world is still viewed as "evil" and "foreign" to many Christians. A critical realism will shift the view of the world as evil to the world as a place of potential within the kingdom of God, thus placing the mission of the church in a proactive role of fostering such potential.

Critical realism will examine demographics, lifestyle, and religious orientation as aspects of culture and will lend itself to a more missional orientation. Alister McGrath has defined "mission orientation" as including greater awareness of the social context in which evangelism and mission takes place.[55] Given the massive changes that have occurred within the culture of the United States in the last fifty years, the shift to mission orientation will call for the best critical thinking that Christians can incorporate into their missional strategies. Perhaps then the gospel will be proclaimed as holistically as Scripture challenges, and will make positive movement to the accomplishment of God's mission in the world.

The Postmodern Opportunity

Although much has been written in recent years about the emergence of postmodernism, there are still many faithful church members who do not understand the change that is taking place with regard to the modern world. They are confused about what they see, and very often I hear them confess that they just do not understand what is happening, especially among young people. It is therefore necessary to remind ourselves how we are witnessing a major shift in worldview that is as dramatic as the shift from the ancient worldview to a modern one. This fact also contributes to the frustration that many churches have as they watch the community around them turn a deaf ear to what they are saying.

Caleb Rosado has said that a great chasm exists between the church and contemporary society.[56] The chasm is growing wider: The two poles of modernity and postmodernity are moving apart and in different directions. The challenge to the church is to bridge the chasm and to find ways to communicate the gospel effectively through theological reflection and sociological research. Many churches are vulnerable to the widening gap between modernity and postmodernity, due in part to their lack of response to cultural shifts. For many, the issue of a postmodern worldview may prove to be the most troublesome of these shifts, as they seek to contextualize their message within the emerging postmodern culture. The culture of the postmodern is increasingly free of the assumptions of the Enlightenment view that has dominated modernity. As Diogenes Allen suggests, "[A] culture free of these assumptions is also free of assumptions that prevent one from coming to an appreciation of the intellectual validity of Christianity."[57] Historically, most churches have depended upon the structures of modernity to enhance their cultural assumptions, evangelistic strategies, theological position, and missiological approaches. The systematic view of religion, morality, and scientific method has aided them as they have categorized their worldview. Postmodernism, however, with its movement away from the assumptions formed by religion, morality, and science, challenges churches to respond in entirely new categories for which they are largely unprepared. Craig Van Gelder's concern is that most churches are failing to face the postmodern paradigm shift.[58]

A survey of programs and analysis of literature produced by denominational presses related to evangelism, mission, and ministry reveals a lack of attention to the emerging postmodern paradigm as it impacts the culture. Attention will need to be paid to the shifts that are occurring if Christians are to be effective in their missional objectives in the decades ahead.

Definitions of Postmodernism

The postmodern worldview represents an aspect of the contemporary period in which Enlightenment thought is beginning to lose its dominance. The emerging postmodern worldview represents a transition away from the philosophical thought patterns of modernity and associated lifestyles to an emerging pattern that is quite different.

Jean-Francois Lyotard describes *postmodern* as the "state of our culture following the transformations which, since the end of the nineteenth century, have altered the game rules for science, literature, and the arts."[59] Hans Kung says that in the transition from the modern to the postmodern paradigm a change occurs in the "entire constellation of beliefs, values, techniques, and so on, shared by the members of a given community."[60] In this book, the word *postmodern* will reflect Kung's analysis, though other writers such as Jacques Derrida, Michael Foucault, Diogenes Allen, Craig Van Gelder, Stanley Grenz, Thomas Oden, and David Bosch expand the analysis as they have sought to clarify their own definitions of the emerging period.

Allen, for example, suggests that the postmodern worldview began with the development of modern science—science that began with Max Planck's discovery that energy is emitted in discrete units or quanta.[61] Van Gelder says that after 1890, dramatic transitions occurred both on the technical level in the arts and sciences, and on the popular level within the broader culture. All these fields shared in common the gradual shift from objective reason to subjective experience as the basis for knowing and sharing human meaning.[62]

The late Stanley Grenz believed that modernity had been under attack since Friedrich Nietzsche fired volleys against it in the late nineteenth century, but that the "full-scale frontal assault did not begin until the 1970s."[63] Thomas Oden defines the period after modernity in terms of attitude, conceptualism, and ideological tone.[64] David Bosch contends that, in postmodern times, the "edifice of the preeminence of reason is being challenged."[65] All such definitions seek to clarify the issue, and are themselves reflective of postmodernism in their struggle to understand, formulate, and conceptualize the structure of the emerging worldview.

Kung believes postmodernism adequately describes an epoch that only began in the twentieth century.[66] Stanley Grenz and Thomas Oden concur, as they describe the closing of the modern era. Derrida uses metaphor to describe the shift from modernity to postmodernity as "the end of the book and the beginning of writing."[67] For Derrida, "everything that for at least some twenty centuries tended toward and finally succeeded in being gathered under the name of language is beginning to let itself be transferred to, or at least summarized under, the name of writing."[68] It is a work in progress, creative, and yet to be concluded. If the modern period can be described as a book and the postmodern period as writing, a study of the contrasts suggested by the metaphors will be helpful.

The Modern Worldview

The modern era is generally thought to have come into being with the Renaissance and the Protestant Reformation.[69] Thomas Oden offers the image of two "falls" to describe the modern and postmodern era. Oden says that the fall of the Bastille in 1789 ushered in the modern era, and that the fall of the Berlin Wall marked the postmodern era's rise to prominence.[70] David Bosch clarifies the evolution into the modern era by pointing to a series of events that helped to solidify an emerging worldview. He says:

> Through a series of events–the Renaissance, the Protestant Reformation (which destroyed the centuries-old unity and therefore power of the Western church), and the like–the church was gradually eliminated as a factor for validating the structure of society. Validation now passed directly from God to the king, and from there to the people. During the Age of Revolution (primarily in the eighteenth century) the real power of kings and nobles was also destroyed. The ordinary people now saw themselves as being, in some measure, related to God directly, no longer by way of king or nobility and church. We find here the early stirrings of democracy.[71]

The full birth of the modern spirit, therefore, came to form in the Enlightenment period.[72] It was through the Enlightenment that the age of reason became the most adequate epistemology and thus the intellectual foundation for the modern world. David Bosch writes, "[T]he Enlightenment brought about the elimination of God from society's validation structure."[73] Truth, which once had its locus in God, now could be determined through scientific research and reason. As such, "[T]he role of God was dethroned as a valid claim to authority."[74] The desire to know and to understand the physical and objective world drove the scientific method to its place of prominence during the modern period. George Hunter summarizes in detail six thinkers who greatly influence the thought patterns associated with the modern era:

> Copernicus and Galileo, by discovering the structure of the solar system, challenged the church's traditional understanding of the cosmos. Ptolemy had placed the earth at the center of the universe, with the sun revolving around it. But Copernicus and Galileo demonstrated that the earth revolves around the sun, and the earth's rotation on an axis gives us our days and nights; the cosmology assumed from the New Testament through the Middle Ages was now ludicrous.
>
> Newton's theory of gravity challenged the doctrine of Providence, as traditionally understood. Prior to Newton, people assumed that God's providential hand kept the moon, planets, and stars in place. Newton's *Principia* demonstrated, mathematically, that the universe's cohesion could be explained by his theory of gravity, and for many people God was edged out of the providence business. The long-term effect of the Newtonian revolution was even greater, as people came to see the universe as a self-enclosed system, or a "machine" that did not require "God" to explain or manage it.
>
> Darwin's theory of evolution challenged the doctrine of the creation and nature of humankind–as traditionally understood. Darwin's *Origin of Species,* with theories of natural selection, survival of the fittest, and progressive evolution, made it possible for people to understand their species in a very different way–as rational animals, without the dignity and purpose assumed in the biblical doctrine of creation.
>
> Marx's writings provided an alternative to the traditional Christian understanding of the goal of history. Marx seems to have retained the Judeo-Christian structure of history, but he substituted for Christianity's promised Kingdom of God a promised economic utopia.
>
> Freud wrote a question mark over religious belief and religious experience, charging that belief in God and experiences of God

could be explained psychologically, and thereby explained away as "illusion."[75]

As a result of the perspectives mentioned above, science became the new reality. It became the source of ultimate and objective truth. The modern era came to be conceived of as "the society in which the Enlightenment project is realized, in which the scientific understanding of the human and physical worlds regulates social interaction."[76]

The Enlightenment's emphasis on reason was the glue that held together the scientific method upon which modernity rests. This emphasis suggested that the human mind was viewed as "the indubitable point of departure for all knowing."[77] One scientific approach that characterized the Enlightenment period was the rationalism of René Descartes. His approach operated on the premise that human reason had a certain degree of autonomy. Rick Gosnell says, "Descartes postulated that the human approach to knowledge must be governed by doubt. According to Descartes, humans reject everything which, when tested by pure reason, appears uncertain."[78] The legacy of Descartes assumes that it is the individual's task to justify all knowledge by the use of other disciplines that contribute to indisputable facts upon which they stand.

The modern era also brought with it a naturalistic emphasis. According to Huston Smith, human reason is "capable of discerning the order of reality as it manifests itself in the laws of nature."[79] Lesslie Newbigin explains reason as

> essentially those analytical and mathematical powers by which human beings could attain to a complete understanding of, and thus a full mastery of nature—or reality in all its forms.[80]

Thus, human reason becomes the chief means of attaining belief. Naturalism becomes a sustaining belief when nature is viewed as all there is, and any existing reality is only a natural part of the universe. Richard Cunningham explains, "All things come to be and pass away solely from natural causes."[81] Naturalism, therefore, views humanity as deriving its existence and validity "from 'below' and no longer from 'above.'"[82] Transcendence is lost to the naturalists when religious explanations for the universe are no longer persuasive.

Modernity also holds to a humanistic view of life. Pauline Marie Rosenau avers, "Humanists are optimistic about the nature of humankind, the potential for improvement in the human condition, and the scope of human accomplishments."[83] Humanists taught that by nature people were good and not bad. Their primary concern is with life in this world and not with life in the hereafter.

A leading proponent of humanism was John Locke, who held three optimistic principles regarding human beings. First, Locke believed the chief end of persons is happiness in this world and probably the next.

Second, he believed persons' rational powers, if rightly disciplined and employed, provide a means for solving the problems of life and attaining happiness. Humans, he believed, had the potential for influencing the future toward a better life for the human race. Third, Locke thought the essential truths of the preceding views are so self-evident, and humans are so responsive to such evidence, that progress in human happiness is inevitable.[84]

The emphasis upon progress is most visible in the modern ethos. The modern era placed a high premium on progress, on expansion, advance, and modernization. Western colonization, industrial development, economic prosperity, and growing understandings of an expanding universe suggested unlimited progress. Modernity suggested that human beings, working together, could free humanity from want and enrich daily life. David Harvey says, "The scientific domination of nature promised freedom from scarcity, want, and the arbitrariness of natural calamity."[85] Progress became in the modern era the end to justify exploitation of nature, people, nations, and economies for progressive thinkers.

Many of the above characteristics of modernity contributed to an increasing secularism, largely due to a movement away from the Divine as the source of truth and prosperity to science, rationalism, and human confidence as primary ingredients. Arnold E. Leon defines the process of secularization as "the historical process by which the world is de-divinized… as far as human consciousness is concerned."[86] Autonomous science and technology became the religion of the public realm, while individualistic pietism became the religion of the private realm. Gosnell says, "Religion was, in the course of time, relegated to the realm of the private world of opinion and divorced from the public world of facts."[87] Religion, thus, became increasingly polarized from the rest of society. The gap between the sacred and the secular widened as modernity increased its grip on the world.

Although the picture of modernity seems to contrast sharply with the outlines of religion, many denominations found elements within modernity to be friendly. Modernity's emphasis on progress, for example, provided an uncritical preoccupation with growth and prosperity within denominations. The scientific method provided a context in which programs could be developed using rationalistic structures and deductive reasoning. Humanistic optimism was in sharp contrast to much preaching about humankind's "lostness" and sin, but it also yielded confidence that Christians could achieve any goals they set for themselves with regard to the accomplishment of their mission. Churches embraced the structures of modernity that facilitated their growth. But as the secularism of the world became more evident in modernity, many religious traditions withdrew into the confines of their own subcultural worldview. The problem has grown more complex, however, with the decline of the modern era and the emergence of a new, more complex one.

The Decline of the Modern Period

While much more can be written about the historical rise and subsequent development of modernity, the decline of the modern era can be most sharply examined within the twentieth century. Many scholars have now declared that the modern period is at an end. There are several factors that lead to such a declaration.

The foundations that gave preeminence to the scientific method and to reason are being challenged in the contemporary world. Absolutes are being challenged. A researcher in physics commented that what passed as fact in his doctoral dissertation twenty years ago has been disproved in recent analysis.

James Miller asserts:

> In a Newtonian world, it was possible to conceive of absolute contexts of space and time within which an object could be isolated. But with Einstein's development of relativity physics, common-sense notions of the absoluteness of space and time have been abandoned. It can no longer be taken for granted that measurements of either distance or duration in one frame of reference will be identical to those taken in another.[88]

Today's scientists work with uncertainty as perhaps never before. The field of technology is changing so rapidly that old observations are constantly being exchanged for new ones. Absolute confidence in hitherto established scientific realities now runs counter to the new presupposition of the world as open and ever-changing. David Bosch undergirds this observation, quoting Werner Heisenberg in that the very foundations of science have started to move and there is almost a need to start all over again.[89] Van Gelder asserts that the world has come to be understood as operating with law and chance, both order and chaos.[90] Scientists are being surprised as new findings point to an ever-expanding uncertainty about the universe.

Additionally, the general population is losing confidence in science and technology. Many are frustrated as they try to keep up with changing technological trends, such as in the computer industry. Scientific achievements that have led to increasing efficiency in communications have isolated people from one another as they communicate by computer and cell phones, then retreat to their homes immersed in the latest technology of digital television. People are constantly faced with automated customer service systems that isolate the human touch from services once rendered freely. For many, scientific advance is more of a nuisance and a warning than a necessity. The explosions of Challenger and Columbia awakened many to the dangers that scientific advance poses. And while science has offered cures to many diseases, increasing resistances of some viruses to established vaccines now offer a new threat. Science is being viewed in the latter days of the modern era as not only helpful, but problematic.

The belief in inevitable progress has also contributed to the close of the modern era. Whereas the modern era promised that science and technology coupled with a humanistic positivism would inevitably advance humanity toward inevitable progress, the casual observer can point to the twentieth century as one filled with World Wars, the Holocaust, apartheid, structural racism, crime, and poverty. America is today embroiled in Iraq and numerous other places of conflict around the world. Regional wars and the fight against terrorism work together to keep the world embroiled in an ongoing global war.

The two World Wars shattered the belief in inevitable progress toward peace and prosperity. Much of the earth's surface had been soaked in human blood. And regional conflicts have continued warfare to such an extent that never before has so much of humankind been engaged simultaneously in war, "war which might be called internecine because it was really a civil war within the totality of the human race."[91] The technology of war has served to illustrate the negative aspects of scientific advance and its horror has depicted the failures of humanism. The bombings of Hiroshima and Nagasaki are evidence of the destructive side of the modern era.[92] Since World War II—or perhaps Vietnam—no other event has so greatly affected America's confidence in the modern world as the acts of terrorism on September 11.

The failure of inevitable human progress was seen most vividly in the Holocaust. Human knowledge did not lead to human advancement. Instead, the technology and scientific advances in warfare became an instrument of horrific destruction. The concept that knowledge leads to a beneficial use was totally undermined in the Holocaust. Kung reflects:

> Auschwitz is a place where modern science collapsed under the lies of propaganda, democracy was defeated by the control of the masses through seduction and terror of one man and his party, technology resulted in the murder of millions, and industry in the extermination of an entire people.[93]

Rick Gosnell has said that the "plausibility structure of modernity came to an end in the Holocaust."[94] Irving Greenberg's observations are that the assumption of moral progress and the sense of tolerance, love, and brotherhood—images of openness—came to an end in the experience of the Jews and other marginalized groups in the Holocaust.[95]

Secularization in the modern era led to the idea that religion was to be placed entirely in the private realm. Transcendence seemed to have no place within the secular. However, one manifestation of the demise of modernity has been the reemergence of interest in the transcendent. Large numbers of people now describe themselves as spiritual seekers. Hans Kung has commented, "[T]he death of religion expected in late modernity has not taken place."[96] Robert Wuthnow adds the following:

There is little indication in recent decades that American Religion has undergone what might be termed "secularization" in any absolute sense...religious commitment is as strong as it was 35 to 40 years ago.[97]

Lesslie Newbigin offers an explanation to the seeming paradox of religious interest in the modern era by explaining that increased religious vigor seems to travel farthest in any society that has proceeded along the road of rationalization, industrialization, and urbanization.[98]

The belief that the process of modernization would lead to the decline of religion cannot be established with credibility. Indeed, the reemergence of religious vigor seems to point to the decline in the modern paradigm. Newbigin believes that modernity did not "provide enough nourishment for the human spirit."[99] The narrowed Enlightenment perception of rationality proved to be an inadequate foundation upon which to build one's life.[100]

While it is true that increased religious vigor seems to be a rejection of modernity, the churches themselves are not witnessing a sharp increase in membership or attendance during the latter days of modernity. Most mainline denominations are witnessing declines. Although new religions have emerged, many people have sought to invest in less structured forms, preferring to gather in small groups and to pursue religious inquiry on an individual basis rather than to attend established churches. The return to religion in the latter days of modernity does not guarantee growth for the churches or denominations that grew during the era of modernity.

There are many other factors that point to the decline of modernity, and no doubt many more will surface. But it is becoming clear to many that an alternative worldview has emerged in the latter days of the twentieth century and into the new millennium. Philosophical thought patterns, worldview orientations, and lifestyle preferences are combining to contribute to the postmodern era and to the challenges Christians will face as they live in it.

The Emerging Postmodern Paradigm

The beginning of the postmodern era is disputed by many. Efforts to place a beginning date range broadly and depend on the individual writer's perspective on shifts away from modernism. Pauline Marie Rousenau, for example, views postmodernism as having evolved during the last 150 years, whereas Diogenes Allen places its beginning with the development of modern science.[101]

Several other writers look to the turbulent 1960s and early 1970s as the genesis of postmodernism and point to certain indicators. The civil rights movement, the Vietnam War, the peace movement, the women's movement, the sexual freedom movement, the hippie movement, rock music, and the emergence of new religions out of the 1960s and 1970s are indicators to them of the kinds of shifts that have occurred within the larger culture, signaling a new era.

Thomas Kuhn notes within the scientific method the presence of paradigm shifts or changes, which alter the view, implications, and processes of science that are regarded by those who wish to recognize them, but which are largely ignored by those who choose to remain in their accepted paradigm.[102] Such radical shifts serve as signposts to new beginnings. Brent Waters has stated:

> Postmodern is an adequate term if it is viewed as an interim phrase—a catchall word to identify a growing reaction to a historical epoch characterized by Western intellectual, political and technological dominance.[103]

Postmodernism is now a reality that is impacting the culture. The transition is continuing, much as modern science continued to influence the culture of modernity as it evolved. There is, however, sufficient evidence that the shift toward postmodernism has happened and that it is happening. Kuhn writes that when paradigms shift or change, the world changes with them. Joel Barker, a futurist, states that when a paradigm shifts everything goes back to the beginning.[104] Major paradigm shifts birth new thought patterns and possibilities yielding a new worldview.[105] Hence, postmodernism is not an apologetic for modernity, nor is it a condemnation of modernity. It is a new beginning with new thought patterns. Hal Poe has said, "Postmodernity as yet lies unfinished. People talk about it and try to describe it, but the most we can say now is that it will be different from modernity."[106]

Evidence for the paradigm shift to postmodernism can be seen within several categories. One of the most dramatic is in the shift to a relativistic and pluralistic attitude. The postmodern worldview is relativistic. Truth is relative to the postmodern. Jonathan Culler has said that postmodern persons view truth as either meaningless or arbitrary.[107] The postmodern person takes the position that different peoples have different concepts of what the world is like. There is no constant reality, since each people-group interprets the truth of reality within its own context, thus yielding a pluralistic attitude. Situations determine how the world is viewed. Gosnell writes, "Postmodernists argue that each situation is different and each situation calls for a special understanding."[108] This fact is especially resonant in the argument for religious truth.

Religious truth among postmoderns is perceived as a "special kind of truth and not an eternal and perfect representation of cosmic reality."[109] Whereas the ancient and modern worldviews were willing to embrace religious truth (in a variety of interpretations and traditions) as cosmic reality, the postmodern person tends to focus more on individualistic belief and experience to interpret what is true. Walter Anderson cautions, however, that "once we let go of absolutes, nobody gets to have a position that is anything more than a position. Nobody gets to speak for God, nobody gets to speak for American values, nobody gets to speak for nature."[110]

The assumptions made in the modern era about religious truth revolved around seeking wholeness and unity, although conflict and fragmentation was often reality. For the postmodern, relativism does not depend upon wholeness or unity, but assumes there *is* no center. As Van Gelder has observed, "life is lived in the local context as the only reality that matters for the moment."[111]

Given that postmoderns live in the local context, they object to all-encompassing worldviews. Being relativistic and pluralistic, postmoderns contend that questions of fact, truth, correctness, validity, and clarity can neither be posed nor answered.[112] Postmoderns live their lives without the need for explanations and are content with uncertainty. They are anti-foundationalists. They choose to believe that there is no one correct way to accomplish anything, but instead many ways.

Postmoderns have rejected the subject-object dichotomy found in modernity. They refuse to make distinctions between body and soul, the physical and the mental, reason and the irrational, the intellectual and the sensual, the self and the other, nature and culture, or reality and utopia.[113] Postmodernists do not wish to separate body and soul, for example, but rather wish to see a renewed connection between the two. They are comfortable with connections between the person and the cosmos. They are often described as holistic in their view of life. Postmodernists attempt to intermingle the aesthetic, the epistemic, and the sociocultural senses.[114] Thus, they are very interested in ecology, peace, and liberation issues.

Tex Sample, in his characterization of U.S. lifestyles, identifies the "Cultural Left" as a lifestyle group that seems to be reflective in many ways of postmoderns. These persons seek deeper and more lasting relationships and have committed themselves to issues that contribute to a more just and peaceful society. They have a strong inner direction and are committed to personal freedom issues. Conservation, consumer issues, environmental integrity, social justice, and peace issues are high on the agenda for the Cultural Left. They prefer to color outside the lines and to experiment with life rather than to abide by rules established by others.[115] Postmoderns may be like those that Sample suggests live in the Cultural Left. They do not believe in inevitable progress nor do they believe they will necessarily be a part of such progress.

Postmodern persons see themselves as possessors of beliefs and not necessarily believers.[116] They are often seekers who will experiment with a variety of beliefs they hold. As Gosnell has pointed out, "Postmodernists are concerned with their own lives, their personal satisfaction, and self-promotion and are less concerned with old loyalties and modern affiliations such as marriage, family, church, and nation."[117] Tex Sample avers that those in the Cultural Left use a kind of internal gyroscope that lends a more subjective and autonomous guide for personal life. They refuse to abide by the traditional "oughts" and "shoulds."[118]

For postmoderns, one's personal insights and views are more important than those of organized religion. Sample contends that members of the Cultural Left, as possible representatives of postmoderns, believe in God, but they are believers without belonging.[119] They believe that one does not have to go to church to be a good Christian. They are suspicious of organized religion as a reflection of modernity and feel it is vastly out of step with their lives.

The spirituality of postmodern people rejects secularism. They perceive the Eternal as revealing God's self at every turn within the culture and in the world. They are not institutionally minded with regard to church and they desire plurality in religious community. For the postmodern person, religion has meaning, but that meaning transcends the individual and the local congregation.[120] Religion becomes a private affair for the postmodern person, rather than a public one. Churches will continue to be challenged by postmodern persons who have a spiritual outlook on life, but many of them have little concern to express that outlook within the structures of traditional organized religion.

There are many other indicators of the shift from modernity to postmodernity. However, the characteristics mentioned above suggest a challenge in the years ahead. It is a challenge that will strike at the heart of church identity, church structure, and theology.

Implications for Missional Churches

The shift in worldview from the modern paradigm to the postmodern paradigm challenges congregations to evaluate their overall mission to the world. The methods developed by most church groups in the era of modernity seemed efficient. They were built upon a common cultural and religious ethos and presented an appealing contrast theologically to the world around them. However, churches today find themselves being limited in their ability to tell their story because of their failure to recognize the shift that postmodernism is causing in religious awareness among the larger culture. Churches may be still speaking, but much of the postmodern culture isn't listening. If Christians do not investigate the realities of the paradigm shift that has occurred, they will find themselves appealing only to those persons in the culture who cling to modernity, and will lose the majority of persons who are moving to a new worldview. Postmodernism challenges the modern mission of the church, but it also promises new possibilities for conversation with the world.

First, it can offer a needed expansion with regard to evangelistic witness and the definition of evangelism that some churches embrace. Although writers such as Delos Miles, Ben Campbell Johnson, George Hunter, Richard Stoll Armstrong, Michael Green, David Bosch, and William

Abraham have attempted fine definitions of biblical evangelism, some churches tend to have their own functional definitions.

Hunter, for example, offers a three-fold definition of evangelism: first, what we do to help make the Christian faith, life, and mission a live option to undiscipled people, both outside and inside the congregation. Second, it is what Jesus Christ does through the church's *kerygma* (message), *koinonia* (fellowship), and *diakonia* (service) to set people free. Third, evangelism happens when the receiver turns to Christ, to the Christian message and ethic, to a Christian congregation, and to the world in love and mission.[121]

Ben Campbell Johnson defines evangelism as

> that particular task of the church to communicate the good news of God's love to persons so that they may understand the message, place their trust in Christ, become loyal members of his church, and fulfill his will as obedient disciples.[122]

Richard Stoll Armstrong makes a strong case for evangelism in terms of service to others. He says that to be a Christian is to be involved in and concerned about every single issue of society. We speak to the world, relate to it, and work to make it better. "Service evangelism is motivated by a genuine interest in others, not by self-interest."[123]

William Abraham defines evangelism simply as "primary initiation into the Kingdom of God."[124] David Bosch offers a more complex suggestion that evangelism is

> that dimension and activity of the church's mission which, by word and deed and in the light of particular conditions and a particular context, offers every person and community, everywhere, a valid opportunity to be directly challenged to a radical reorientation of their lives, a reorientation which includes such things as deliverance from slavery to the world and its powers, embracing Christ as Savior and Lord, becoming a living member of his community, the church; being enlisted into his service of reconciliation, peace, and justice on earth; and being committed to God's purpose of placing all things under the rule of Christ.[125]

Michael Green accepts the 1918 Anglican definition of evangelism. He agrees that:

> To evangelize is so to present Christ Jesus in the power of the Holy Spirit, that men [*sic*] shall come to put their trust in God through Him, accept Him as their Saviour, and serve Him as their King in the fellowship of His church.[126]

Each of these selected definitions seeks to bring clarity to the task of the church for gospel witness. However, a propositional approach to the witness of the gospel is most problematic to the postmodern worldview.

Carl F.H. Henry, a leading proponent of a propositional view of salvation, provides a glimpse into traditional understandings of salvation. For Henry, revelation comes entirely at God's initiative. Revelation provides certain information about God so that salvation is a consequence of understanding or knowing God's plan.[127] Henry Knight has interpreted Henry's view by saying, "revelation directly addresses our ignorance, not our sin, and it is only if we accept the truth of that revelation that we can then respond in faith and receive salvation."[128]

God's divine revelation of salvation is seen as rational and propositional. Because the revelation is divine, it is reliable and trustworthy, logically consistent and without contradiction. Since a proposition is a "verbal statement that is either true or false; it is a rational declaration capable of being either believed, doubted, or denied."[129] Therefore, since God has revealed salvation's plan to humankind, and since God is true, the propositions offered within salvation are true. James I. Packer agrees that the Bible embodies the word of God, and conveys to us "real information about God."[130]

Knight concludes that propositional revelation implies verbal inspiration. Since propositions consist of words, divine authorship must extend not only to concepts but to the words used by the writers of Scripture.[131] The logical conclusion is that verbal inspiration implies the inerrancy of Scripture, a position that is embraced by many conservatives. Many conservative denominations join with others who extend their understanding of inerrancy to also imply that truth is to be expected in "scientific and historical matters insofar as they are part of the express message of the inspired writings."[132] Such a position means that "truth inheres in the very words of scripture, that is, in the propositions and sentences of the Bible, and not merely in the concepts and thoughts of the writers."[133] It is therefore easy to gather certain Scriptures together and to construct them along the lines of a propositional view of salvation that must be adhered to in a deductive fashion and to conclude that such a process is in keeping with the revelation of God concerning salvation. This process has been reflected in the designs of many outreach efforts of churches.

The problem that arises for postmodern persons is that a propositional view of Scripture with regard to salvation, while seeking to be faithful to Scripture, has embraced the methodology of the Enlightenment. Knight indicates that the transition to postmodernism is "increasingly exposing this as an accommodation to modern Western culture."[134] Propositionalists often see themselves as defenders of historic Christian principles. Postmodernity threatens inerrancy as an open door to uncertainty of truth as propositionalists view it.

In order to correct rational propositionalism, certain critics such as Alister McGrath, William J. Abraham, and Stanley J. Grenz have sought to warn against the problems of rationalism. Knight says they do not oppose propositional truth, but rather propositionalism.[135] The problem with rationalism is that the propositional approach assumes a human rational capacity that is untouched by either sin or cultural context, Knight says. Henry argues for a universal reason that, through testing for logical consistency or contradiction, can uphold the authority of Scripture.[136] Knight argues that there is no transcultural reason. There are only "fallible human thinkers whose categories and assumptions are supplied by their own cultures."[137] Knight would not argue that there is no transcultural *truth*, but would recognize the reality of cultural embeddedness of those who seek to know the truth.

Alister McGrath warns against the problems of rationalism when he examines human sinfulness. He says that rationalism makes "the truth of divine revelation dependent on the judgment of fallen human reason."[138] Rationalistic designs on a plan of salvation presupposed from God simply do not allow for the possibility of human sinful intervention. The essence of the *Imago Dei* within rationalism becomes a reflection of human categories of understanding based on cognitive and logical thought processes. For propositionalists, therefore, to formulate knowledge about God is to know God conceptually. Thomas Torrance criticizes a fundamentalism based on rationalism that identifies "biblical statements about the truth with the truth itself to which they refer."[139] The revelation of God is ultimately personal, and therefore must be "continually given and received in a living relationship with God."[140] For Knight, "knowing God involves not only the mind but the whole person."[141]

For the postmodern person, there is a need for a broader understanding of truth. Salvation must transform lives and correspond to reality. Postmoderns need wholeness and community. Christian witness must inspire persons to seek after God for that wholeness and community. Through revelation, persons come to know God and are brought into a living relationship with God. A more dynamic approach to the inspiration of Scripture and its revelation is therefore called for, especially when matters of salvation are discussed.

Congregations must not be distracted by a rationalistic and propositional approach to salvation. They must take seriously the Scripture, which is a medium through which the Spirit of God brings the truth of revelation. Clark Pinnock seeks to recover a more dynamic understanding of God's revelation, in which the Spirit of God uses Scripture to speak to persons in fresh ways and within the context of their experience.[142] Stanley Grenz calls for a reorientation of the doctrine of Scripture under the doctrine of the Holy Spirit, and a recovery of the role of the community in interpreting the Scripture.[143] This approach has the most promise for creative witness to postmodern persons. Christians must invest in a more dynamic interaction of the revelation of God through Scripture, in which the word is fresh, alive, and powerful because of the Holy Spirit's ministry. That interprets itself within communities of postmodern faith seekers who are increasingly reluctant to embrace the constructs of modernity.

Delos Miles seems to offer a credible approach to witness to post-moderns. While not exhaustive, Miles begins the conversation. His focus on being, doing, and telling the gospel offers the opportunity for the witnesses to dialogue with postmodern persons and invites them into a more dynamic understanding of God's revelation.[144] The issue of being can be discussed with postmoderns because of their belief in the unity of body and soul and the issue of connectionalism with the universe. To be a Christian offers the postmodern an opportunity to see Christianity as not allegiance to a specific group or set of propositions, but in terms of God's desire for the redemption of all creation, including persons.

The issue involves making appeals to the social and community concerns of postmoderns and of the community. Christianity can be seen against the backdrop of social justice issues, environmental concerns, and liberation movements. The issue of telling can suggest a narrative and open-ended approach rather than one of indoctrination or proposition. Miles' emphasis on the conversion of not only persons but structures appeals to the postmodern.

The missional church must recognize that Christian witness will have to be much more holistic and ministry-based in order to appeal to postmoderns. Postmoderns are not easily impressed by persons who try to indoctrinate them. Neither are they interested in recruitment to a particular church. They are more open to larger issues with which they may dialogue as they attempt to define their spirituality.

If mission concerns itself with the larger purpose of God in the world, the missional church must turn its focus upon the kingdom of God rather than the kingdom of the church. If John R.W. Stott is correct in his assumption that "mission concerns his [God's] redeemed people, and what he [God] sends them into the world to do,"[145] then every church will need to focus on larger issues that contribute to the building of the kingdom of God.

Christians may, for example, find themselves more immersed in social justice issues, more caring for the environment, more vocal about insti-tutional racism, more involved in advocacy for the poor, and more proactively ecumenical in joining hands with other Christians for the sake of the gospel. To focus on the kingdom of God can be most appealing to postmodern persons, since they care little for denominational labels or institutions, but rather want to invest in community. As postmodernity progresses, Christian witness as a function of mission will move away from indoctrination and recruitment toward a more holistic, ministry-based encounter that seeks to redeem not only people but corporate and social structures as well.

Mortimer Arias insists that Christian witness must be allied to the kingdom of God. He says, "the gospel in the Gospels is the good news of the Kingdom."[146] Arias promotes kingdom evangelization and is critical of the traditional evangelistic message that "has been centered in personal salvation, individual conversion, and incorporation into the church."[147] For Arias, the kingdom of God is multidimensional and relates to individuals *and* the society as a whole. He agrees with Bosch that the focus of Christian witness should not be on the church but on the irrupting reign of God.[148]

For most corporate or institutional churches, a radical shift in mission orientation will be called for. Postmodernism will challenge churches to seek to understand their role within the kingdom of God. They will need to examine carefully what they are being called to do in the world. As long as Christians are preoccupied with salvation only involving gaining heaven and avoiding hell, they will devalue the postmodern's quest for spiritual issues, since they do not fall within the categories of evangelical modernism. To reach postmoderns, an activist mission orientation will be needed. Because the postmodern person is interested in ethics, ecology, peace, and liberation issues, congregations that show spiritual sensitivity to such issues are those most likely to attract postmodern seekers. Congregations active in social concern issues will be most visible within the larger community and will be noticed as the postmodern person searches for meaning.

Postmodern people are intolerant of dogma. They do not embrace narrowed views of what they believe to be larger scriptural principles. George Hunter has said that they are offended by books in the Bible that they associate with dogma, yet they are open to the teachings of Jesus because they do not associate Jesus' teachings with dogma.[149] Many postmoderns are interested to know how Jesus' lifestyle can help them with their own.

Instead of dogma, the kingdom-oriented church needs to communicate with postmoderns in terms of spiritual formation. Christians must learn to begin with people wherever they are in terms of their spiritual journeys, and to walk with them in spiritual formation. Careful dialogue and guidance in the midst of their journey can inform their search for God.

Postmodern persons approve of the idea of spiritual journey. They see life as a journey, therefore the concept is not foreign to them. Tex Sample has suggested the journey metaphor produces a profound sense of the interspace and interconnectedness of all things.[150] Their daily lives reflect their belief in coherent wholeness, therefore spiritual formation built on the idea of journey can offer glimpses of the Christian life that have the potential to be embraced by the seeker. The Christian witness can communicate the idea that God is interested in their journey as much as the Divine is interested in every aspect of the world around them.

Further, it will be laypersons who will be most effective in reaching postmoderns. Michael Green suggests that laypersons "know far more about life, about celebration and friendship, about natural contacts with their friends than the clergy do."[151] Many postmoderns are suspicious of clergy and view them as narrow dogmatists.

Postmodernists can be attracted to the Christian message by churches that seek to build the community that postmoderns desire, by ministry that is holistic, by emphasis on spiritual formation and journey, by the use of laypersons as communicators of the good news, and by theological foundations that lend themselves to creativity of interpretation of the appropriateness of the Christian message for the daily lives of postmodern persons.

Concepts to Consider

The issues discussed in this chapter are key to understanding the factors that keep the community from hearing what the church is saying. In summary, the following concepts need to be kept in mind.

First, we have moved from a churched society to an unchurched society. Encourage the members of the church to take the matter seriously, look around at their communities, and notice just how many people do not make church attendance a priority in their lives. This understanding is foundational to any approach to Christian witness. We need not become discouraged—to do so would place the church in a negative position with regard to its self-image. Rather, the fact that we are living in a new mission field should be seen as one of the greatest opportunities for the church in the twenty-first century.

Take seriously the fact that we live in an emerging postmodern world. In the West, modernity is passing away and a new world is dawning. With it will come opportunities beyond our imagining to use technology and every available means to communicate the gospel. We will need to become much more entrepreneurial and creative than we have ever been before.

Make sure the congregation understands that Christianity is not the only game in town. Secularism, various world religions, increasing affluence, and leisure time all compete for the heart and soul of people. Instead of churches decrying secularism as evil, world religions as false, or the pursuit of affluence and leisure as condemned, the church must strive to make the gospel interesting to the world around it. It must offer to take people on a journey of discovery that can add to the quality of their lives. The church's voice has to be attractive and clear enough to the culture around it to signal the unique and compelling message of the kingdom, with its purpose of helping human beings become more thoroughly human.

Second, congregational life is different today. It used to be the case that people of faith automatically participated in all that the church had to offer. That is no longer the case. Today, many people believe they can exercise their faith without ever stepping foot inside a church building. Faith has become separated from congregational participation. As a result, a kind of designer religion has taken hold. People are free in their minds to design a faith response that makes sense to them—one that is holistic with regard to spirituality, the environment, ecology, justice and peace issues, eternal questions, life hereafter, and so on. They may mix Christianity with elements from other faith traditions if it helps them to make sense of faith. Many millions of people have never been a part of church life and have been raised to adulthood with no Christian memory. Today's postmoderns haven't rejected faith. As Hal Poe has said, "The postmodern generation does not have a theological position so much as it lacks a theological position. It has not rejected Christianity, because it is generally unaware of the Christian faith."[152]

The unchurched are now the majority of the culture; we can no longer assume anything with regard to church participation.

Third, denominationalism is no longer important. People in the communities around our churches do not care what flavor our church might be. To many people there is little difference between one church and another. A church is more likely to be thought of in a positive light when someone describes it to an unchurched person as having met a particular spiritual need that was important to a certain individual. As such, churches must be distinct and they must be able to make very clear to the community around them who they are, otherwise the community will make assumptions regarding the church that may lump them into categories they have long since rejected. Remember that church programs, worship experiences, and ministries are designed by church people who often do not think about the world in the same way that unchurched people think about the world. Every program and ministry has to be designed with the unchurched public in mind. To do otherwise is to ignore their needs and their agenda. Urge your church to think in terms of ministry to the world—to the bent and broken people.

Fourth, learn to think about mission as participation with God in what God is doing in the world, beginning in your community. When mission is limited to overseas, the implication is that America is not in need of God, when, as Newbigin has said, the West is the new mission field. For more than a hundred years, missionaries have departed American shores to take the gospel overseas. In the meantime, North America has grown neo-pagan. Mission must be seen in a broader concept as care for the whole world. Every church must have a passion for the world and for its local community with equal measure. As such, the message of the church has to be properly contextualized to its intended hearers, whether the church sends members to another country or whether it moves out into the community for ministry. Each church member should be retrained according to an understanding of the *missio Dei* so that they will function in everyday life as if they were indeed missionaries; as Christians participating with God in God's mission to the world, we are indeed a missionary people. Each church, then, must measure its ministry by the number of people who are engaged in the missionary enterprise, following an agenda that is kingdom-focused.

Fifth, encourage your church to focus on the nature of the kingdom of God in such a way that it learns to network with others in the community who are doing the work of the kingdom. These may be people who are not especially religious or who do not represent a religious organization. They may be a civic organization that is concerned for abused people, or that works to rid the community of violence. No church or denomination alone can effectively touch the world with the holistic claims of the gospel and of the nature of God's kingdom. Instead, work to be a transformational church, one that seeks to transform not only people but structures that oppress people. Networking in matters of justice, peace, and ecological concerns is vital.

Steps toward Being Transformational in a Transitional World

1. Ask your church to commit itself toward more concern for people in the community who may be caught in patterns of dysfunction. This will begin to sensitize church members to minister to those who are often overlooked in the community. One of the best ways to do this is by linking with service agencies that meet the needs of those who are ill from drug abuse, for instance, or are victims of domestic violence. When church members actively work among the homeless, or those whose need is very apparent, a new vision of the kingdom of God begins to emerge. This is but a beginning. It can, however, lead the church to much more inclusivity and begin to reflect the multivaried nature of communities around a church.

2. Learn to challenge traditions that hold the church apart from the world. What are those traditions that your church may be holding on to so tightly that it cannot see how the world around it has changed? This may move beyond just tinkering with the music program. It may have everything to do with the assumptions made by the church as to its place in the community. It may have to do with attitudes toward the community itself. Programs that have been largely directed at church people may need revision. Often churches hold so fast to their denominational traditions that they isolate themselves from other churches and people who do not care about church labels. Your church may have to consider what it is saying to the community when it boasts of being Presbyterian, Catholic, Baptist, Orthodox, Methodist, AME, or Disciples, to name only a few.

3. Work to advocate the removal of any barriers that hinder people from identity with your church. Is your church friendly to those who are physically challenged, those who have varied work hours, those who are poor, seniors who cannot drive any longer, youth who are away at

college, or families who have loved ones in prison? The kingdom-focused church cares for the widows, the orphans, those in jail, those in need.

4. Practice ministry-based evangelism. Every action done by the church should be prompted by ministry to persons. Gospel witness should proceed from natural care to the whole of the person, the whole of his family, the wholeness of her vocation. Never use physical ministry as a bait and switch method for evangelism. Be authentic in care for people and make it very obvious to the person with whom you are ministering that you are as concerned for their physical needs as you are for their spiritual needs. Minister to the whole person.

5. Use technology effectively. Communicate with the culture around you. Use whatever methods you find are most helpful to make it easier for a person to visit your church community. People often visit your church by way of the Internet before they ever step foot in the building. Give much attention to the way you speak of the mission of the church and its goals for touching human life. Train those who answer the phones to be sensitive to ministry needs. Follow up all who call asking for help. It is amazing how many times churches do not follow up on calls that are made by people asking for ministry. Let me illustrate:

Not long ago, a pastor friend of mine told me that someone called the church office just as the Wednesday evening service was about to get underway. The person on the other end of the line wanted a member to come by his house and minister to a need. The pastor told the person that as soon as the service was over, he would come.

That evening, after the service, the pastor showed up at the door of the person who had made the phone call. When the door opened, the man in the home replied, "I didn't think you were serious. You are the sixth church we have called this week, and so far you are the first to actually come by and visit us." Simple follow-up–faithfulness to what you commit to do–will go a long way toward changing the image of the church in the community and how it responds to people.

The Paradigm Question

Essential to any change toward being transformational is the response to one central question: "What is it that this church must do that once seemed impossible, but if it is done, will dramatically change this church so that it will become more effective for Christ and the kingdom of God?"[153]

With the above information in mind, churches can move outward toward their communities and begin to stimulate changes in the way the church is viewed in the community. Each church has to formulate methods and tactics to use in order to manage the changes that are necessary. Over the years, in many churches I have used a simple tool built off an ancient model. The "Enneagram" has been used for hundreds of years and adapted for multiple uses, but I have found that it works well as a tool to help a church discover its personality. An introduction to the Enneagram begins in the next chapter.

Using the Enneagram to Discover Who You Really Are

The purpose of this chapter is to explain the use of the Enneagram as a tool to help churches discover who they are and why the community may not be hearing what they are saying. The Enneagram should not be seen, however, as just another tool that might promise growth. A church grows by participating with God in God's mission and by taking on itself the character of the kingdom of God. It will not grow as a result of another program or gimmick. What is called for here is a sober engagement with some of the factors that may keep a community at arms length from the church. I have used this model with large churches and with small churches, but it is always up to the church to follow up and to use what they discover to transform themselves into a kingdom-focused congregation. Those that have taken the model seriously and have used it have seen the beginnings of transformation. Likewise, those who have not followed up and worked the model have continued to struggle. For hundreds of years, the Enneagram has helped people understand their personality. Churches have personalities as well, and if they are to change in order to become more effective, it will take a concerted effort by the whole congregation.

The Enneagram—A Short History

Hippocrates, who was born in 460 B.C.E. on the island of Cos, Greece, and is known as the father of medicine, wrote about the various moods of people he encountered. He described behaviors and moods as choleric (or easily angered), phlegmatic (or sluggish and unemotional), melancholic (or depressed). He based his observations on the study of human beings from a rational point of view and rejected the superstitions that often surrounded the illnesses of his day. Since Hippocrates, many more persons have attempted to understand human behavior and to classify people and their personalities based upon observation. Most of the classifications have tried to solve the associated problems found within human personalities, moods, and behaviors. The Enneagram has been used as a tool for that purpose.

There is a great deal of speculation regarding the ancient origins of the Enneagram as one of the tools used in trying to understand human personalities and behavior. The beginnings of the Enneagram are a bit unclear, but the word probably comes from the Greek. *Ennea* means "nine," and *gramma* can mean "letters" or "that which is written or drawn." None of the theories as to the Enneagram's origin are conclusive. We may say that the Enneagram evolved over time and that no one person or group of people is responsible for the way it is used today. Part of the continual evolution of the Enneagram has been its adaptation in form to apply to various disciplines. It has been used in education, business, the arts, and psychology, to name a few.

The Enneagram styles and its image seem to be very old. It is possible that the symbol originated long before any numbers were associated with it, and certainly long before any associated labels were ascribed to the numbers that eventually surrounded the symbol. According to Michael J. Goldberg, "The epic poet Homer (circa 750 B.C.E.) knew the nine basic styles essentially as they are today."[1] It appears that Homer must have known something about the design since he understood the sequence of the numbers. "In Homer's *Iliad,* the nine Enneagram types appear in their numerical order (one through nine.)"[2] It is not likely that Homer knew his model as an early Enneagram, but the styles and symbol seem to be present.

Others attribute the discovery of primary personality structures to the Cathars, a small gnostic Christian group that arose in about the eleventh century in the south of France. They believed in a pure lifestyle and recognized the factors that threatened serenity. They sought to balance negative attributes with positive ones and thus create harmony. They may have used the symbol in some fashion.

Regardless of its origins, the early use of the structure of the model is attributed to the ancient Sufis, whose teaching tried to explain the nine points of personality and their relationships with each other.[3] Around one hundred years after Muhammad's death, many pious Muslims wanted to lead much more simple lives. Some who were influenced by Christian monasticism renounced all possessions and wore wool garments, called *sufs* in Arabic, as a sign of their asceticism. Some became traveling sages or joined communal life in spiritual brotherhood.[4] Throughout the years of their existence these teachers helped people pursue their goal of discovering

God. The Sufi masters created nine models to explain why certain people could never find God; these models showed that the inner selves were barriers to God. Thus, the model helped the teachers explain how people could remove the barriers and know God.

The ancient Sufis called the nine points diagram the "Face of God," and likened it to light refracted out of a crystal. The nine points of energy of the Enneagram, as it is known today, were seen as refractions of the love of God.[5] It is not at all clear to what extent the Sufis used the symbol, but it has been largely thought that they both utilized the symbol within their spirituality and refined its usage from about the seventh century onward.

Regardless of its origin, many Enneagram spiritual leaders and researchers attribute the Westernization and further development of the Enneagram system to the Russian free thinker, George Ilych Gurdjieff (1877–1949).[6] He was the first major figure in the Enneagram's modern development and brought the symbol to the awareness of modern people. Gurdjieff was half Armenian and half Greek, and he enrolled in seminary at an early age. He left the seminary at the age of 13 and became heavily involved in the pursuit of spirituality. His travels brought him to Egypt, India, and Tibet, where he met a group of Sufis who lived in Central Asia.[7] Although his writings do not indicate the exact date he learned about the numbers that would eventually comprise the Enneagram system, they do indicate that he started learning about it during the early twentieth century.[8]

When Gurdjieff returned to Europe, he began teaching spirituality and psychology in Moscow and St. Petersburg, but he left before the revolution in 1919. He moved to Paris, where he opened up the Institute for the Harmonious Development of Man.[9] Many of the philosophical ideas that comprise the modern Enneagram derive from Gurdjieff's teachings.

A second main Enneagram system developer was philosopher Oscar Ichazo. He can be rightly called the father of the modern Enneagram. His ideas are central to the development of the system that most modern interpreters utilize. He was the first to relate the nine divine qualities to the Enneagram symbol. He created separate Enneagrams for passions, fixations, virtues, and holy ideas. He also contributed to the theory of how the arrows function as well as the theories behind the wings of the Enneagram. "In one way or another, all modern Enneagram authors have built their work on Ichazo's seminal insights."[10]

Another important contributor to the modern use of the Enneagram is Claudio Naranjo, who learned the Enneagram from Oscar Ichazo during a program that Ichazo offered in Chile in 1970. Naranjo began teaching the system and his approach to it to a small group of his students in California. He used his training in psychiatry to elaborate on the nine types and developed some additional ideas about the use of the arrows on the symbol.

Subsequent researchers such as Robert Ochs, who transmitted some of Naranjo's teachings to Jesuit priests and seminarians around North

America, and Helen Palmer, a noted Enneagram researcher, have further applied and interpreted the use of the Enneagram to the public.

The Enneagram and Faith

An example of how the Enneagram has been used in Christian faith can be seen in the work of Richard Rohr and Andreas Ebert. In their book, Rohr and Ebert discuss Jesus and the Enneagram, and conclude that many people refer to the Enneagram as an icon of the "Face of God" because they see Jesus' characteristics at every point.[11] It is interesting to see how Rohr and Ebert use each of the nine points to describe an aspect of Jesus' personality and ministry.

Rohr and Ebert point type ones' characteristics of teaching, tolerance, and patience to Jesus and use Matthew 5:17, 5:48, and 19:21 to support this claim.[12] The authors relate Jesus to Enneagram type two by focusing on Jesus' care, compassion, and solidarity. Matthew 20:28, Luke 17:11–18, John 13:1–20, and John 12:1–8 are key scriptures to this assertion. Rohr says, "the invitation to the Two is the call to freedom. Twos find in Jesus the model of a person who loves without losing freedom and without abusing the freedom of others."[13]

Jesus connects to Enneagram type three because of his ambition, energy, and vision. Evidence is found in Christ's pursuit of the kingdom of God, and Luke 4:16–21, 19:41–42, Matthew 5–7, and Matthew 23:37 also detail Jesus' type three personality. Rohr says that the hope of the kingdom of God prevents threes from settling and clinging to the security that money seems to provide.[14]

Enneagram type fours can connect to Jesus' personality. Fours appreciate that Jesus was never ashamed to show creativity, sensitivity, and simplicity, and that Jesus also demonstrated great joy, great sorrow, and great labor.[15] The authors compare the similarities between Enneagram fives and Jesus' characteristics of distance, sobriety, and wisdom. The Lucan story of Jesus withdrawing from his family to worship God in solitude, the Matthew story that recounts Jesus' mother and brothers who came to him, Jesus' reply that "whoever does God's will" are his brothers and sisters, and Jesus' urging of his disciples to be wise during the Sermon on the Mount are all characteristics of how Jesus exhibited the characteristics of a five.[16]

Jesus also displayed Enneagram type six because he displayed fidelity, obedience, and trust; examples of these are found in Luke 4:16, 13:32, 23:2, and Mark 12:17 as well as in 14:36. Each of these Scriptures describes Jesus' inner authority, which freed him from outer authorities and allowed him to have a trusting relationship with God. The authors recognize that Jesus had the freedom to obey the laws of his day (the outer authorities), as long as they were not meant to substitute for God (his inner authority). These boundaries gave Jesus the freedom to attend religious services in the synagogue, to listen to religious authorities, yet to be more accountable to the authority of his Father.[17] This is why Jesus would often respect and quote the Law, but then modify it with his insights into the kingdom of God.

Type sevens can relate to Jesus because they, like the Christ, are emotional and live in festivity, light-heartedness, and pain. See how Jesus uses the imagery of a wedding celebration to describe the kingdom of God. Other stories such as Jesus supplying the wedding with wine, accepting dinner invitations to tax collectors' homes, and warning against superficial joy in the beatitudes are characteristics of sevens.[18]

Eights also identify with Jesus. Their ability to confront, and to explain with clarity and authority are present in Jesus. Matthew 5:6, 21–23, 37, and 39–41 support what Rohr and Ebert say, "Jesus knew what he wanted. He defended his position without compromise and steadfastly bore the consequences of his words and actions. He never beat around the bush."[19]

Finally, Jesus is similar to Enneagram type nines because of composure, peace, and love. Despite his power, Jesus embodied peace. Mark 4:35–41 is one example of this, when Jesus urges the disciples to remain calm in the midst of the storm. Rohr and Ebert say that Jesus' love did not judge and did not exclude anyone. "He was a good nine. His life work was the reconciliation of people with God and the reconciliation of people with each other."[20]

The above examples compare Jesus to each of the characteristics found in the Enneagram model, but the model is not limited to Christian use. Jewish mystics that follow Kabbalah have also used it. The Hebrew word *Kabbalah* means "to receive" or "to accept." Kabbalah includes meditative, devotional, and mystical practices, which were taught only to a select few. Many Jews regard it as an obscure development in Judaism.[21]

In his book *The Enneagram and the Kabbalah* Rabbi Howard Addison writes that during the first chapter of Genesis, God says to Adam, "Ayeka?" ("Where are you?"). He says this is the question that God calls all human beings to ponder. God calls people individually because God understands each person's strengths and weaknesses. Addison believes, "If we seek God's personal message that is meant only for us, we might begin by learning about ourselves and our own traits."[22]

Addison believes that the human soul is rooted in a distinct aspect of the divine personality. The "Tree of Life" is the design of that divine personality, and the quest for the essential self beyond personality might lie at the individual's soul root. The Enneagram can aid people in discovering this root. Addison believes that the Enneagram depicts both the core aspects of personality and the structure of ultimate reality. Both the Enneagram and the Tree of Life imagery "draw upon many common historical sources and share several points of correspondence. Perhaps their most profound joint assertion is that our highest virtues and most troubling vices are actually rooted in the same source."[23] Jewish tradition says that God created human beings with two inclinations: the *Ha Tov* (selfless inclination) and the *Yester Ha Ra* (self-serving inclination). By recognizing and confronting both of these, human beings can begin the journey toward redemption.[24]

The Enneagram and Prayer

Richard Rohr and Andreas Ebert compare the universal three kinds of prayer to the Enneagram. They note that the first type is from the inside out, when a person lets whatever is on the inside rise to the surface. Inner moods and images develop and then the person expresses them verbally, through writing, or in art. The second kind of prayer is from the outside in, when something on the outside, generally a picture, symbol, or text, reaches a person and something happens inside the person due to this. The third type of prayer is emptiness. Zen Buddhism is a good example of understanding emptiness, since it strives to let go of the outer and inner impulses in order to gain stillness.[25]

These three types of prayer can be related to the three centers of the Enneagram. Those whose personality reflects the heart often express themselves from the inside outward. The contemplative personality seeks input from the outside. Those who are more emotional seek emptiness.[26] The Enneagram helps explain how certain personalities prefer certain patterns of prayer life. This can become an important observation for churches as well. Prayer in services should be expressed in different ways so that all personalities along the Enneagram spectrum can be ministered to within the congregation.

Positive and Negative Uses of the Enneagram

One of the most positive aspects of the Enneagram is that it provides insight into different personality types. This insight can guide people in relating to others both personally and professionally. Congregations that understand the dynamics of personality are better equipped to develop successful relationships with persons inside and outside the church. The Enneagram can provide an objective framework regarding relationships with others. It can help assess value differences in people, identify strengths and weaknesses in persons, establish boundaries in relationships, and gauge "the compatibilities and tensions between people, and build a framework for discussing emotional issues."[27]

Enneagram theory is emerging within institutions and in the business world. Stanford Business School offers a course on leadership concentrating on Enneagrams.[28] In 1994 Stanford University hosted the first International Enneagram Conference. Many corporate Enneagram researchers believe that it is a powerful tool for empowering organizations, executives, managers, and consultants. It is often used in motivational seminars and training sessions. Corporate leaders recognize that professional style flows from personality, and, similarly, actions reflect characteristics of the self, which help explain the essence of behavior.[29]

Enneagrams are helpful in relationships because relationship styles flow from personality type. With a better understanding of personality types and the characteristics of each Enneagram type, people can see relationships in terms of how personality affects communication, conflict management, rapport, irritants, and avenues for growth. Patrick Aspell and Dee Dee Aspell sum up the use of the Enneagram: "With knowledge of different relationship styles, you can develop successful relationships. Follow the Golden Rule: Treat others as they like to be treated."[30]

The Enneagram has potential within human relationships. However, Arthur Hastings, professor at Palo Alto's Institute of Transpersonal Psychology, warns that using the Enneagram to judge others is just like using race and gender to judge others: it inherently poses the risk of "typism."[31] Helen Palmer warns that people should not simply use "Enneatypes" to classify people and base job-hiring on their type. For example, even though a person may be classified as a "four," which is artistic, that person should not be hired in an art gallery if they do not have an eye for art. She also says that the Enneagram offers one of a variety of ways of classifying personalities, and should not just be used for categorizing people. Palmer says, "The reason for discovering your own type is so you can build a working relationship with yourself."[32]

Likewise, congregations should be careful as they use the Enneagram to assess the personality of their churches. The key to its effectiveness is in self-understanding, not as a source of concrete identity. Every church will manifest a certain tendency in its personality. However, that personality can be informed and modified in ways that help the congregation interface more effectively with the culture around it. It will be an exciting discovery for many churches. They will find clues that reveal how they process change, conflict, routine, growth, and decline. As they use the Enneagram, congregations have the potential to discover what may be at the root of why the community around them can't hear what they are saying.

Exploring Your Church's Personality

My introduction to the Enneagram was in a spiritual retreat some years ago. It occurred to me that the dynamics of the model could also be applied to churches that had little or no idea how they were perceived by others. An adaptation of the Enneagram followed as I introduced the concepts to churches where I ministered. Once the model is understood, it has the potential to unlock many insights for the church and make it more effective as it tries to communicate to the communities that surround the church.

As detailed in the last chapter, the Enneagram has been used to identify an individual's personality pattern and can explain some of the characteristics behind personality motivation.[1] The nine points on the circumference of the Enneagram's structure are split into a triangle and a six-pointed figure. A person's Enneatype is found at a distinctive point on the symbol. Each point on the Enneagram connects to two other points, which are marked by arrows. The arrows indicate how people deal with stressful and nonstressful moments in their lives. The arrows give a sense of direction since they explain the route of both development and decline for each specific Enneatype. It is a dynamic process. Basic personality types often change under certain conditions. When people are under stress, they often revert to the direction of decline, which involves following the arrows that point away from their basic Enneagram style.[2] Likewise, when people are healthy and growing there is positive movement in the direction of the arrows toward the person's Enneatype.

The Enneatypes located on either side of a point may influence personalities. For example, nines may have some characteristics of a 1 or an 8.[3] Neighboring Enneatypes are called "wings": they can act as a second kind of Enneatype moderating the primary type.[4] "Wings" are auxiliary types that characterize development and provide individuals with distinctive personality types. One wing tends to concentrate on dominant personality types, while the other functions at least as a possibility. Therefore, there are nine basic types, with eighteen subtypes.[5]

Likewise, in assessing the personality of the church there are nine basic types and associated subtypes. These types are general in nature and cannot, of course, be representative of every church in every locale. Just like human personality, there is surprise, shading, fuzziness, blending, and distinction in every type. Your church congregation may quite quickly recognize a dominant personality trait, but more than likely there will be lively discussion as the congregation sees traits or manifestations of several other personality patterns. It is not necessary for the church to completely agree on one type or another. What is beneficial is for the congregation to recognize the dominant traits that can keep its message locked behind the doors of the church.

Church Personality Types

The Enneagram's nine points are divided into three groups of three. These are called *triads*. The triads are composed of a dominant personality type and the associated "wings," or those types that immediately surround the dominant one. Usually, one of the wings is stronger than the other. For example, a church that is a 2 is part of the triad of 1s and 3s. In assessing personality types for human beings, Enneagram researchers have grouped the triads into categories according to the way people relate to the world. For example, the instinctual types are generally grouped around points 8, 9, and 1. People in this grouping respond intuitively, or with so-called "gut feelings." They tend to place a lot of emphasis on how things feel (bodily) to them. A second grouping includes those who relate to the world according to the heart or emotional feelings. These usually gather along points 2, 3, and 4. These people often respond emotionally to new situations and worry about how others feel about them. The last grouping includes the thinking or contemplative ones, who are usually grouped along points 5, 6, and 7. These people are likely to analyze, evaluate, and assess the world around them, usually due to the fact that they are suspicious of the world.[6] As we will see, these categories can also be applied to how churches respond to the world around them. These models are broad characterizations that I have noticed over the years as I have worked with each of the churches that are represented in the models. As you think about them, I would invite you to have a little fun with them and add your own insights.

Church Type 1: The Superhero Church

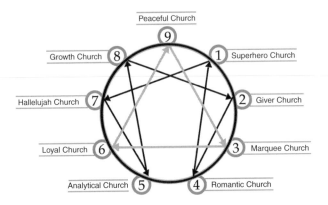

■ A PARABLE: The city council of Olympia voted almost unanimously last month to authorize the taking down of the Ten Commandments plaque in the city hall. This was the first time the city had faced the sticky problem of separation of church and state issues. They felt they needed to respond to what had happened in other communities and avoid the possibility of litigation in the future. They also passed a resolution that they no longer would open city council meetings with prayer. Further, they decided to ask every church in the community to refrain from placing direction signs on public streets on weekends. The council passed the last action in an effort to remove the clutter of what they called, "Sunday morning signs" that churches would often place on the street on Saturday evening and then remove on Monday morning.

Olympia's large downtown church responded. On the Wednesday evening following the city council's action, the church met in business session to discuss what they called the "continuing decline of moral values" in their town as evidenced by the removal of the Ten Commandments. They were outraged to learn that the business of the city would be conducted without the guidance of God. The pastor of Olympia noted that this country was built on Christian faith and that many of the problems they faced in their city could be laid at the feet of people who cared little for the church or God. They decided the sign issue was not a problem since they had already planned to erect a large billboard in the heart of downtown. The new billboard would be more effective, they felt, than putting signs along the main street. The church passed a resolution calling for the city council to repent of its actions and to take a stand against secularism. They appointed five people to attend the next council, took out ads on the local radio station, and placed an editorial in the local newspaper. If no one else would stand against the erosion of faith in their town, Olympia Church would. ■

Olympia Church, a "type 1," is a Superhero Church. It can simultaneously reflect positive images of church, emerging tension as conflict builds, and very negative images of church life.[7]

Superhero Church Characteristics		
POSITIVE IMAGES	EMERGING TENSIONS	NEGATIVE IMAGES
High moral values.	Narrow definition of morality.	Intolerant of those who do not share their value system.
Very active church life, hardworking members.	Conflicts with program leaders.	Pressure on church members to make church life their top priority.
Biblical foundation and strong Christian rhetoric.	Restrictive theology. Literalism.	Dogmatic in their theology. Resentful of so-called "liberals."
Commitment to the history of their tradition.	Resentful of those who do not appreciate or who misrepresent their history.	Rigid. Stuck in the good old days.

Olympia Church, like many other type 1 churches, has a good self-image. Its high moral values are locked tightly to its Christian commitment. Church members are loyal, hardworking, active in the community, and represent the church well. Church members are always trying to live better lives and to stay faithful to the "high calling" of Christian faith. The Bible is their guide and everything they do is tested by Scripture. They are concerned for the world and they wish that the world could be as committed to Christ as they are. They are a highly visible church in the community because their members are confident in their ability to improve the world through witness. The church members are dependable and give large sums of money to the outreach of the church and to its programs. They have a strong commitment to their tradition and wish to represent the best in the history of their faith tradition. Members feel blessed to be a part of the church and actively recruit others.

But when they are pressed by the world around them, the veneer sometimes cracks a bit. They value the standards they feel are biblical, like marriage between a man and woman. They refrain from alcohol, drugs, and legalized gambling such as lotteries. They can be very vocal about those who are caught in what they believe are "vices." They tend, when pressed, to rid communities of their problems. If the problems grow too severe, some of the type 1 churches will move to another location. They are so busy with ministries that sometimes conflict arises over budgets, personnel, and time slots. Some of the leaders of the ministries can become possessive of their turf. When denominational controversies occur, they react loudly and work to get their tradition back on course.

When the Superhero Church is at its worst, the strain is felt both within the community and within the church. They are often seen as bigoted people who are not tolerant in the least of persons who do not hold to their standards of morality, especially in the area of sexual ethics. Even within its own membership, the church can turn up the heat when there is a controversy to "be more faithful," or to give more money to a specific cause. Members can become resentful and frustrated as they preach against the sins of the world, only to see those sins increasing around them. When they are at their worst, they long for how the church used to be. They grow more and more unsure that anyone cares about God or their tradition as much as they do.

Wings—Neighbors

The Superhero Church has some adjacent neighbors. The wings of type 1 are types 9 and 2. Type 9 is the Peaceful Church. Type 2 is the Giver Church. Either type 9 or type 2 can exert the greater influence on type 1, but one will emerge as being more significant in its influence than the other. Type 9, with its even-tempered programs and modest goals, can positively influence type 1, which is always functioning at a fever pitch. Type 2, a church that avoids conflicts and works to develop intimacy with newcomers, can soften type 1's image of responding to perceived threat as a closed fellowship of people who think alike. Type 1 will lean a bit in either of the two directions.

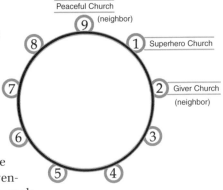

Directional Arrows

In response to various moods, churches will move from their type toward another type or receive input from the characteristics of another type. Howard Addison explains it by saying that personalities (in this case, churches) relate to their

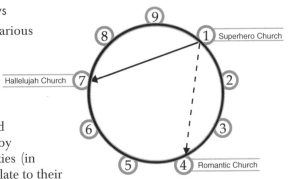

security points when things are doing well, and to their stress points when things are not going so well.[8] Type 1, the Superhero Church, can relate in two directions. When everything seems to be moving in directions that type 1 approves of, it gathers to itself some of the characteristics of type 7, The Hallelujah Church: optimistic, upbeat, positive, and always praising. But when tension arises, a type 1 church tends to move toward the characteristics of type 4, The Romantic Church: very sensitive, preoccupied with life, holding on to ideals, and closely monitoring itself for any hint of "letting down."

Broadening Type 1's Personality

Type 1 can broaden its personality by drawing from the strengths of types 4 and 7. Type 1 should become more spontaneous, upbeat, positive, and celebrative. Rather than always carrying the heavy burden of solving all of the ills in the world, the church can affirm its faith and its commitment to God's kingdom and be less critical of itself and the world around it. The church should seriously engage the question of where God is working in the community and seek to join God there. It may be among the poor, the uneducated, or the lonely.

The church should seek to offer to its members more help with issues of personal spirituality and sensitivity. It should engage members to focus on lifestyle witness and service to others as an extension of their Christian calling. Instead of fighting against all the evils in the culture, the Superhero Church should focus on helping those who are victims of evil. It is not likely that the church will make the community into the image it has of itself, rather it can become more dialogical with the community and seek to understand the pressing needs of the community and begin addressing those needs, one by one, in a nonjudgmental way.

Is Your Church a Superhero?

The following statements may help you determine whether your congregation is a type 1 Superhero Church.

❏ Yes ❏ No Our church communicates, in deliberate ways to the community around us, a value system that we believe the community should follow. We are vocal in the community when we believe biblical values have been violated.

❏ Yes ❏ No While being critical of the world's behavior around us, we are most critical of our own behavior as Christians.

❏ Yes ❏ No We have lots of energy and commitment that is focused on our programs and activities, and dedication to those programs is very important in our church.

❏ Yes ❏ No We feel Christians in our church should work hard and be faithful to church life.

❏ Yes ❏ No We tend to see things as either right or wrong.

❏ Yes ❏ No We tend to want people in the community to adopt our
faith tradition.

REFLECTION: Based on what you know of your church, what other
characteristics might point to Superhero tendencies?

Church Type 2: The Giver Church

■ A PARABLE: Mount Pleasant Church has a congregation that seems
never to meet a stranger. Even visitors have commented that as soon as
they entered the church, someone met them and told them how much they
looked forward to knowing them and being their friend. There is a lot of
laughter in the aisles of Mount Pleasant before each service, and the
congregation betrays the fact that people seem very much at ease in the
church. There are people who seem very poor sitting with people who
seem very rich. The church is a cross-section of the community around it:
black, white, Latin, Hispanic, Asian—it seems like the world has taken up
residency. This Sunday morning was given to an emphasis on homelessness.
New programs were announced from the pulpit that would give church
members an opportunity to serve the homeless. A special offering was
taken. The sermon was entitled, "Unto the Least of These…" The sermon
was politically correct in every way, and no criticism was leveled at any
failure in society to care for the less fortunate. Everyone agreed that if
other churches were like Mount Pleasant, the world would be a better place.
The only problem that seems to surface now and again is that the same
people seem to be doing the majority of the work in the community…and
they look tired. ■

Giver Church Characteristics		
POSITIVE IMAGES	EMERGING TENSIONS	NEGATIVE IMAGES
They avoid conflict.	Conflict makes them anxious.	They tend to run away from or ignore conflicts.
They exude compassion.	Some complain about the workload of ministry to the needy.	Compassion leads to self-service. Can manipulate the needy.
Intimacy with newcomers.	Newcomers do not always share the vision of the older members.	They can instill guilt when every member is not involved in some ministry to others.
Positive image in the community because of their programs for the needy.	They can feel that other churches just do not care as much as they do.	A sense of being used or ignored no matter how hard church members work.

Mount Pleasant Church is a Giver Church. They give to others time, money, and ministry because it makes them feel needed in the community. They tend to define who they are by what they do for others.

As a Giver Church, Mount Pleasant can be a real blessing to the community, especially in terms of taking care of the less fortunate. The members are empathetic to the stories they hear and supportive to the extent that the church is often a refuge for people with various needs. They tend to be socially conscious, but the stands they often take on moral issues appear to some on the outside as liberal. They often appear to be a church who cares for the homeless one month and a church that is defined by advocacy for women the next month; they will then shift the next month to advocacy for people with AIDS, or refugees. They seem to always be changing who they are in terms of the most pressing social issues at the time.

Mount Pleasant tends to be independent of sister churches within its own tradition. The members give help to anyone who comes through their doors, but they receive little to no help from sister churches, nor do they seek help. They pride themselves on being able to give without measure.

Mount Pleasant is generally in the denominational news, but not always in a positive light. It functions at the edge of its tradition, especially in terms of advocacy for alternate lifestyles. The members can grow resentful when challenged by the fact that they seldom appear to speak to the moral beliefs that others hold on certain issues, especially when it comes to homosexuality, illegal immigration, or crime and punishment. The church can manipulate others without realizing that it does so. It does not place much emphasis on helping people emerge out of poverty or illegal activity, rather it tends just to meet the poor's immediate needs. The church has little evangelistic outreach or emphasis. It depends on ministry to need as a way to attract others.

Wings–Neighbors

Type 2, the Giver Church, also lives in a neighborhood. The wings of type 2 are type 1 and type 3. Type 1, as we have seen, is the Superhero Church, while type 3 is the Marquee Church. Type 1 can influence type 2 by its confidence and its commitment to core principles of Scripture. Type 3, the Marquee Church, is very efficient. It has great organizational skills and is very energetic. Type 2 can learn from the Superhero Church. Confidence in and commitment to core principles in Scripture will not necessarily turn people away. Under type 1's influence, the Giver Church can start to emphasize personal accountability for actions and challenge persons to break cycles of dependency or manipulation. A type 3 leaning can help type 2 to set its ministry goals to be more effective and comprehensive. Rather than simply ministering to every need that arises, type 2 churches can learn from type 3 to construct their ministries along lines of accountability for money, personnel, and time spent.

Directional Arrows

Type 2, the Giver Church, is connected with type 8, the Growth Church, and type 4, the Romantic Church. When activities are going well in type 2 churches, they receive inspiration from the character-istics of the Romantic Church. That is, they have a sense in the way they define themselves, that all is well and

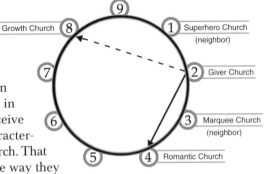

they pride themselves in sensitivity to others. By constantly monitoring themselves, type 2 churches bathe in the glow of a job well done, especially when they see the smiles on the faces of those they help.

But when they are challenged or pressed by the weight of controversy over their ministry approaches, their theological position regarding social issues, or denominational isolation, they move toward the characteristics of the Growth Church. They become preoccupied with their own identity and programs, or become resentful that other churches see problems with their approach. They can become boastful about what they do, especially when challenged.

Broadening Type 2's Personality

Type 2 can broaden its personality by paying attention to type 8 and type 4. Always being focused on others can ignore the need to strengthen the church from within. The church should become self-reflective and understand more deeply the "why" behind its ministries to others. Type 2 should get in touch with the reality of the cost of ministry and actively work to change the structures that oppress people rather than always trying to rescue those who are caught up in those structures. It should look for creative ways to attract others to its caring nature and not be afraid to engage in outreach. Its ministry to others should have a committed evangelistic thrust. The church should work to connect its sense of ministry to what God is doing in the world and view it redemptively.

Is Your Church a Giver Church?

The following statements may help your church determine if it is a type 2 Giver Church.

❑ Yes ❑ No Our church is very sensitive to the plight of others and is compassionate and nurturing to the less fortunate.

❑ Yes ❑ No We develop instant intimacy with others.

❏ Yes ❏ No We think we know what others need even without asking them.

❏ Yes ❏ No We work hard to project a good image of our church in the community.

❏ Yes ❏ No Our church is good at giving help to others, but we are less comfortable when we are in need of help.

❏ Yes ❏ No Sometimes we can be self-serving; at times we contribute to dependency in our ministries.

REFLECTION: Based on what you know of your church, what other characteristics might point to Giver Church tendencies?

Church Type 3: The Marquee Church

■ A PARABLE: Broadway Church is located in the heart of the downtown. All roads seem to lead to this church. Out front there is a large sign with a pithy quote intended to bring a smile to the face but a challenge to the soul. Every day on the local radio station the pastor provides an inspirational moment, "brought to you by your friends at Broadway Church." It is a modern complex with plenty of parking and rows of visitor's parking signs near the front door of the church.

On this bright Sunday morning, you have decided to visit Broadway. The sanctuary is very large, and as soon as you enter you are met by a greeter who provides you a colorful handful of materials about the church, its programs, and today's service, then ushers you to a seat. As you are seated, you notice people greeting each other in the aisles and soon you are greeted again, by a church member who wants to know everything about you. You feel very welcomed, but a bit uncomfortable with all the questions about your family, your work, where you live, and when you first heard about the church. Things quiet down as the choir files in and the music starts, but before very long you are on your feet again as the congregation formally greets each other. The service is a production. The energy is high and things are fast paced. At the end of the service, a church member greets you again and wants to know what you thought of the service and when you will be back again. You are anxious to leave but can't get away from the church member. Finally you make your way to your car, only to notice that the driver's window has been broken and your cell phone and camera are missing. Shaken, you go back inside the building and find the pastor down front talking to two other people. At first they do not acknowledge that you are there, but finally you get an opportunity to relate the problem. You are shocked to hear the pastor say, "I'm sorry for your loss, but this sort of thing happens around here all the time. It is one of perils of being a church in the downtown." He then turns back to his conversation, leaving you speechless. On the way home with the wind rushing through the broken window, you can't quite place how you feel. You wonder if you really mattered to them or if perhaps you were just another prospect. Somehow, you are not sure. ■

This example illustrates both the very best and very worst potentials of the type 3 Marquee Church. If human standards are any measure, then this church is a successful one: Large membership, varied programs, financial resources, and reputation place Broadway a cut above any in the area, at least in the minds of those who are members there.

Broadway Church, a representative of type 3, is a high-energy church that functions like a well-oiled machine. The church is self-assured and secure in its role in the community. It is very image-conscious, especially with regard to the buildings, the campus, and the programs. The members promote the church constantly and there is a budget item for publicity. Broadway Church prides itself on representing its tradition well and counts itself as important within its denominational life. It gives large sums of money each year to ministries and missions. The pastor has held several key positions within the denominational life of the church. Surprisingly, in such a large church, the members really try to make everyone feel welcomed; however, they do not always succeed.

Marquee Church Characteristics		
POSITIVE IMAGES	EMERGING TENSIONS	NEGATIVE IMAGES
High-energy church.	Successful image.	Tend to promote the church over the Christian faith.
Members are driven at times. Enthusiastic.	Too large, too rich, too noisy.	Religious corporation with layers of bureaucracy.
Efficient and well run.	People can be overlooked.	Feeling of emptiness in spite of all the religious activity.

Broadway can be a driven church. It tends to hide from problems and cover them with rhetoric of success in other areas. It believes it is the best church in town, and scarcely acknowledges sister churches who may not be as successful as it is. It is corporate in its organization, with lavish offices and a large staff. The wealth of the church and its historic status in town makes it difficult for members to identify with those who are not as confident in their religious life.

Wings—Neighbors

Type 3, the Marquee Church, also has some neighbors. The wings of type 3 are type 2, the Giver Church, and type 4, the Romantic Church.

When type 3 is influenced by type 2, it can become preoccupied with the way in which others perceive it. The church can become quite outgoing, but may also be focused on gaining attention. When type 3 is influenced by type 4, it can increasingly focus inward and concentrate on reaching its own goals with little consideration for those on the outside.

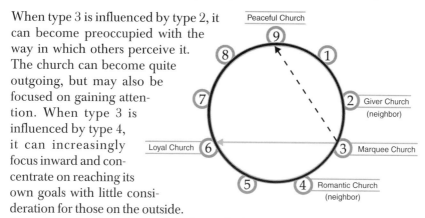

It can become obsessive with tasks, and take positions that isolate it from sister churches or the community.

Directional Arrows

Type 3 can move in the direction of type 9, the Peaceful Church, during its most stressful times. It depends on loyal members for support even when they are insecure about goals or programs. When under stress the church can lose momentum and energy and may even decide to ignore problems, hoping they will go away.

In the best of times, type 3 draws strength from type 6, the Loyal Church. They take pride in their denomination or tradition. They are unshaken in their confidence that they have the resources to solve most any problem. They will join with others in their tradition for a cause that is worthy. They become supportive and encouraging, but under stress can avoid reality and choose to immerse themselves in activity.

Broadening Type 3's Personality

Type 3 can broaden its personality by taking the best from types 9 and 6. The Marquee Church is defined by its efficiency and is very image conscious. However, it needs to properly assess that image in terms of the community. The type 3 church must learn to ask difficult questions from the community and take seriously how community members view the church. The church must be willing to let its true image emerge, even if it is not consistent with what the church might want to portray to the community, to be more authentic. It should learn to adopt some modest goals and cultivate those aspects of the church's personality that are positive within the community.

Type 3 churches should learn to become supportive of other churches in the community and less concerned with their own image, being willing to join hands with various organizations for the good of the community, even if the Marquee Church does not get the credit.

Is Your Church a Marquee Church?

The following statements may help you determine whether your congregation is a type 3 Marquee Church.

❑ Yes　❑ No　It is very important for our church to appear successful.

❑ Yes　❑ No　Even if we are not experienced in a particular program or ministry, we will try it.

❑ Yes　❑ No　We feel we are very efficient in how we conduct the programs of our church.

❑ Yes　❑ No　We have great organizational skills that others could learn from.

❑ Yes　❑ No　We try to accomplish as much as we can, even if it means that our church members are stretched a little.

❑ Yes　❑ No　Some people have characterized us as self-promoting or wrapped up in ourselves.

REFLECTION:　Based on what you know of your church, what other characteristics might point to Marquee Church tendencies?

Church Type 4: The Romantic Church

■ A PARABLE: To the outsider, Camelot Church certainly fits into the neighborhood. It is a beautiful building with ivy growing along the walls, though well-manicured for just the right effect. The grounds are peaceful, with benches under the trees and fountains. Inside, the church is adorned with rich carpets and fine woods. Canvasses from the masters line some of the hallways. The pipe organ is obviously a classic and the chandeliers drip with sparkling light. The Sunday order of worship reflects the history of refined church music and the liturgy is uniform and poetically written.

Scott had been wounded years ago by his home church and had been searching for one that was different. A friend had told him about Camelot, so he made his way through the wealthy neighborhood to find the church. He sat alone, and no one spoke to him. He was caught up in the beauty of the service and the pastor's sermon, "A Christian Response to Ecological Need." His veil of melancholy began to lift. He began to anticipate each Sunday as he attended more and more. This church seemed to be ideal—that is, until his feelings of longing and emptiness emerged once again. "I just miss my home church," he thought to himself. Although he had attended Camelot for several Sundays, no one knew his name. ■

Camelot Church is a type 4, a "Romantic Church." People who attend the church are often attracted by its beauty and its sensitivity to issues. It looks like the ideal church in a Norman Rockwell painting, but it can be a cold and lonely place.

Romantic Church Characteristics

POSITIVE IMAGES	EMERGING TENSIONS	NEGATIVE IMAGES
Aware of its beauty and prestige.	Can be overly sensitive to its image.	Self-doubt in spite of its image.
Passionate about issues.	Can focus exclusively on its stance on issues.	Can be eccentric with regard to the world around it.
Can be a caring church.	Members can be inwardly focused.	Can overlook individual needs in favor of global issues.

Camelot Church is a Romantic Church. It is very self-aware and is impressed with the fact that it is not a church for everyone. It is authentic in its passion for global issues such as world peace, ecology, and justice. Members are proactive as they carry their religious views into the community to advocate for humanity. In many ways, through its art, music, and theology the church is preoccupied with the philosophical meaning of life. But Camelot tends to be somewhat aloof with regard to its views on the issues. Its people often feel that they have the best approach and sensitivity to greater concerns. The church can launch into dialogue with other faith groups, but will largely do so in order to understand the other, rather than out of a desire to speak about the uniqueness of their own faith. As such, their desire to dialogue is for the greater good of the community, race relations, inclusiveness, and peace.

Camelot can face negative reactions in the community because it lacks evangelistic passion, not caring much about its neighbors or visitors. It can be less attractive to those who do not enjoy a "high church" tradition. It can give the appearance of cliquishness that caters only to the highly educated or refined in the community. It can be lonely and may find more affinity with churches outside its tradition than those within.

Wings—Neighbors

The wings of type 4 are type 3, the Marquee Church, and type 5, the Analytical Church. When influenced by the Marquee Church, type 4 churches can be quite energetic regarding issues they care deeply about. They are highly motivated to make contributions that are uniquely reflective of who they are. When they are influenced by the Analytical Church, they can waste a lot of time learning more and more about the issues and actually doing less about them. They can hold onto their understanding of the world as a commodity and think that they know the answers.

Directional Arrows

In their best moments, type 4 churches move toward the positives of type 1. Their high moral values and commitment give them the confidence that they can achieve anything they are passionate about. But when type 4 churches find themselves in conflict, they move toward the negatives of type 2, the Giver Church. They can become overly idealistic and overly concerned about what others will think of them. They can soon doubt their place in the community if they feel they are passionate about an issue that the community doesn't value.

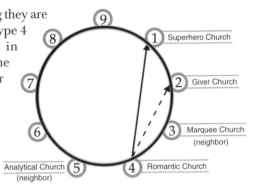

Broadening Type 4's Personality

Type 4 can benefit by observing type 1 and type 2. The Romantic Church needs to take the evils of the world more seriously. It should not hesitate to be more aggressive with ministries that may not be refined, or cultured, but earthy. Although type 4 is a concerned church, it should demonstrate compassion to the needy and not be afraid of including those who are needy in all that the church does. It should become more objective about the needs of the community, less theoretical, and not be afraid to dream large.

Is Your Church a Romantic Church?

The following statements may help you determine whether your congregation is a type 4 Romantic Church.

❑ Yes ❑ No We are a refined, cultured, and sensitive congregation, often oriented toward life's meaning.

❑ Yes ❑ No We are constantly monitoring our own spiritual experience.

❑ Yes ❑ No Our church takes its life very seriously. We are passionate about spirituality.

❑ Yes ❑ No Sometimes it appears that we are a bit sensitive, if not moody.

❑ Yes ❑ No We have a strong sense of the beauty of faith and the beauty of our church.

❑ Yes ❑ No We may seem a bit dramatic to those on the outside.

REFLECTION: Based on what you know of your church, what other characteristics might point to Romantic Church tendencies?

Church Type 5: The Analytical Church

■ A PARABLE: University Church is located about a mile from the largest research university in the state. Many of the members are professors, students, and staff of the university. The pastor is a distinguished preacher and theologian, and is in great demand on the speakers' circuit. The church takes great pride in this fact, and when he is away, they always bring to the pulpit an equally distinguished guest speaker.

Susan, a manager of a local restaurant, comes from a small town in Ohio. She has never been very religious, but her boyfriend, Tom, is a member of University Church and has been urging her to attend services with him. Tom, a doctoral student at the university, is reserved and quiet, while Susan is very outgoing. After several months it became apparent that Susan was unhappy with the church. She told Tom that Sunday after Sunday it was like being in school–too philosophical, probing, and scholarly to suit her. After all, he was the student; she loved being with people who knew how to laugh, not pondering theological axioms. ■

University Church is type 5, the Analytical Church. At first glance, University Church is quite attractive. Stately and reserved, it offers an intellectual approach to faith.

Analytical Church Characteristics		
POSITIVE IMAGES	EMERGING TENSIONS	NEGATIVE IMAGES
Insightful to spiritual issues.	Faith may be too analytical.	Faith can seem quite abstract.
Always learning more and more.	May become too focused on issues that do not matter.	Can exhaust people with subject.
Confident in its ability to solve nearly every problem.	Hesitant to rely on help from sister churches or persons with opposite viewpoints.	Can become resentful that others are not as insightful as they are.

The services each Sunday at University Church give the members an insightful look into the world of faith. They probe the issues of faith deeply. Advanced courses are offered to members who wish to know more, and they are usually taught by an expert in the field. The church seems wise in all things. Its people prefer to think about issues and faith rather than expressing emotion. When the church faces difficult decisions, it tends to bring in experts and analyze the problem over and over again. Usually, their approach to problem solving seems detached from everyday life, and, at times, from even the community itself.

It is not unusual for the church to spend great amounts of time and resources researching how to best solve its dilemmas. They prefer to decline help from anyone who is not an expert in the matter. No matter how much they learn, they are still anxious to explore issues in further detail.

University Church has often been accused of being Analytical by those such as Susan who cannot abide the seriousness of the church week after week. Such people might feel that the church seems out of touch with reality. University Church does not draw many returning visitors.

Wings—Neighbors

The Analytical Church surrounds itself with types 4 (the Romantic Church) and 6 (the Loyal Church). When the Analytical Church is influenced by the Romantic Church, it sees beauty in learning, but can be so focused that it has trouble working with persons outside the group. It has an idealized notion of how to solve problems, but within this can be very imaginative.

When type 5 churches are influenced by type 6, they can be unshaken by their conclusions and approaches to problems. They are able to draw conclusions from lots of input and are disciplined enough to be creative in problem solving. They are anxious to do things right as far as they see the issues and they draw their strength from within.

Directional Arrows

Type 5 can draw its strength from the characteristics of type 8, the Growth Church. It is driven to be the best and to appeal to the highest levels. It is creative and insightful. The church can be outgoing, especially toward people who appreciate its educated approach to faith.

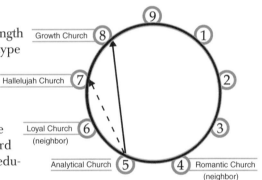

Type 5, when it faces times that are stressful, tends to move toward type 7, the Hallelujah Church. It is confident, always looking for a positive spin on things, and can be very imaginative. It can become interested in a variety of issues. Members can be disappointed when people do not seemed as fulfilled as they are. But if the church faces severe difficulties, members can become impatient and frustrated that their solutions aren't working.

Type 5 tends to have members who stay a long time and make lasting friendships. But they can also be cold and withdrawn from a community that doesn't appreciate their style of learning.

Broadening Type 5's Personality

Type 5 can benefit by enlarging its personality. It needs to take the best from types 7 and 8. Because type 5 is an Analytical Church, it will often focus inward and preoccupy itself with learning more and more, and fail to act. It can benefit by becoming more outgoing and assertive. Type 5 should not keep what it knows of God from the world. It should view its strengths as a gift to offer the world around it.

The church should learn to translate what it knows into actions that focus on ministry to the world. It should become confident and optimistic that its message is one worth hearing. It should set goals for growth and develop programs that are attractive to the community and that meet the community on its level.

Is Your Church an Analytical Church?

The following statements may help you determine whether your congregation is a type 5 Analytical Church.

❏ Yes ❏ No We are concerned that people join our church who have a view of faith that is like ours.

❏ Yes ❏ No We are probing into the issues of faith. We want to learn more and more.

❏ Yes ❏ No We prefer to be known as a thinking church rather than an emotional church.

❏ Yes ❏ No Our approach to living the Christian life is based on insightful approaches to faith.

❏ Yes ❏ No We prefer to be our own type of church. If others do not agree with us it is fine with us. We are who we are.

❏ Yes ❏ No Some in the community have said that our approach to faith is much too analytical or theological.

REFLECTION: Based on what you know of your church, what other characteristics might point to Analytical Church tendencies?

Church Type 6: The Loyal Church

■ A PARABLE: Charles is pastor of United Church in a medium-sized town. His church is small but is thrilled to have the young pastor serve them. Recently, however, the denomination turned up the heat in its rhetoric against the ordination of women to ministry. Charles, who just finished the seminary, has not decided what he thinks about the issue. Since coming to the town, he has met Cindy, who pastors another church in the area, and he is quite impressed with her skills in ministry.

Charles recently received a letter from a civic organization in town. They wanted him to come and speak about women in ministry today. They had even chosen the title for his speech: "Why Some Churches Won't Ordain a Woman for Ministry, and Others Will." Charles was uncomfortable about the invitation. He knew that if he declined the invitation, some of his members would take offense that their pastor refused a chance to represent them and their denomination about the issue. He suddenly realized that he needed to take a position on the matter. If he represented the views of his denomination, the church might be pleased, but what about Cindy? Without an opinion of his own, he did not want to create a problem for ministers like her.

After much deliberation, Charles accepted the invitation. The speech went rather well, with several probing questions afterward, but on the whole it seemed positive to him. Driving home, though, he remembered his feelings on the way to give the speech. He had been angry. He hated being put in such a spot. "I wonder if all that anger came through?" he thought.■

United Church is a type 6. It is a church that enjoys being identified with the long history and religious tradition of its denomination. But in recent days, since Charles has arrived, and especially after his speech to the civic club, some in his church wonder if he is indeed as loyal to the denomination as they thought him to be. They realize that he is young and they understand they are a small congregation, but they do hope to grow one day. They haven't thought what it might mean if Charles tries to change things.

Loyal Church Characteristics

POSITIVE IMAGES	EMERGING TENSIONS	NEGATIVE IMAGES
Pride in their denomination.	Tensions in denominational life cause them to be unsure of who they are.	They may choose to fight others who threaten them.
Cooperates with other churches.	May find it harder to work with others when disagreements arise.	Can be insecure and withdraw.
Unshaken in their beliefs.	May be suspicious of those who do not share their beliefs.	Can be overly dogmatic and oppressive of others.

Type 6 churches depend on group identity. They are loyal to their tradition, at least as loyal as they can be. They are pragmatic, however, and will do what they believe suits them best. They are cooperative with churches in their tradition, but usually do not cross denominational lines.

Loyal Churches, such as United Church, have a theological position that is representative of the long history of their denomination, and they will often modify that position if the denomination modifies it. They want to be part of the whole and have difficulty thinking of themselves as not being included. Against the world, they believe there is safety in numbers.

But because of this, type 6 tends to gather security from the outside. They are never sure on the inside if they are doing their best. They can project these fears onto other churches and wonder if they are as spiritual as they should be. They like guidelines, often from the denomination, and they know the risks of not complying. They are often conflicted with the decisions they make.

Wings–Neighbors

Type 6 is associated with type 5, the Analytical Church, and with type 7, the Hallelujah Church. When a type 6 church is influenced by type 5, it can be rather intense and disciplined. It can be almost passionate about theological correctness or ethical and social beliefs. It can, however, become quite competitive with other churches and critical toward others who do not cooperate with the denomination the way it does.

When they are influenced by type 7, type 6 churches can become sociable, playful, and eager to fit in. They can become outgoing and active enough to share their faith with great flair. They can celebrate their strength in numbers and take pride in the way they see the world of faith. At the same time, they can become quite anxious and blame others for their troubles.

Directional Arrows

Type 6 in the best of times can draw strength from type 9, the Peaceful Church. When it is at peace with itself and the world around it, it feels secure. At these times, when members are at peace and are often optimistic about their future, the church is more inclusive of others. It invests in modest goals and programs that tend to satisfy the membership. It depends on the faithfulness of its members and celebrates long tenures of pastors.

But when there is conflict, type 6 churches move toward the pitfalls of type 3, the Marquee Church. They become task-oriented and dedicated to fixing the problem, even if it means changing leadership in the church. They worry about how they are being perceived and feel threatened if they go against the authority of their denomination. They may even hide from their problems and try to cover them with theological rhetoric fashioned to convince others of their faithfulness.

Broadening Type 6's Personality

Type 6, the Loyal Church, can broaden its personality by taking notes from type 9 and type 3. The Loyal Church will often hesitate to move out unless its authority approves. However, there are times when the denomination or church tradition is at odds with the community around the church or the needs that are to be found there. Type 6 must understand that it is a kingdom-focused church and it should be aware of what God is doing in its community and the world at large. It should be ready to respond without waiting for approval from someone on the outside. The church needs to become more trusting of its own vision. The church should strive to know itself but to be open to other views and supportive of those views in order to engage in meaningful dialogue and witness.

Is Your Church a Loyal Church?

The following statements may help you determine whether your congregation is a type 6 Loyal Church.

❏ Yes   ❏ No   We are proud to be part of our denomination or tradition and this pride has an important place in our church life.

❏ Yes   ❏ No   We depend on our sister churches to partner with us in our missional efforts.

❏ Yes   ❏ No   We are unshaken on theological matters, especially when our denomination or church leaders agree.

❏ Yes   ❏ No   We do not like to be in the spotlight as a church, we only wish to be known as loyal and faithful.

❏ Yes   ❏ No   We really do not like change, especially when it comes to the basic way we have always been a church.

❏ Yes   ❏ No   Sometimes people on the outside say that we are too traditional or even rigid.

REFLECTION: Based on what you know of your church, what other characteristics might point to Loyal Church tendencies?

Church Type 7: The Hallelujah Church

■ A PARABLE: Joan's business trip to Chicago on Friday did not go so well. The client she had been working with for over a year, and who was due to sign a contract that would surely garner her a big promotion, suddenly backed out of the deal. Joan had been savoring the idea of a promotion. She had grown tired of constantly flying around the country and being away from her family. A new promotion would give her nine-to-five hours in an office not far from home and would provide more stability to her life. But now, all those hopes were up in smoke. She worried about explaining the failed deal to her boss.

Joan did not feel much like going to Sunrise Church this weekend, but she worked with the youth and did not want to disappoint them. Besides, her church would cheer her up; it was such a happy place. The music was loud and upbeat when she walked into the sanctuary. Her friends greeted her. Already, the Chicago disaster seemed manageable. She had her friends, her church, and a loving family. The sermon was just what she needed. The pastor preached on "Staying on Top When the World Knocks You Down." She joined in the smiles, the singing, and the upbeat atmosphere of her church. Joan would make it now. She had renewed energy for the meeting with her boss on Monday morning.

Driving out of the parking lot with her family, Joan knew that God was going to take care of her. Tomorrow would be a better day. ■

Sunrise is a type 7 Hallelujah Church. It is a happy place and concentrates on the Christian life as victory over the world.

Hallelujah Church Characteristics

POSITIVE IMAGES	EMERGING TENSIONS	NEGATIVE IMAGES
Optimistic spirituality.	Disappointed when others are not as optimistic as they are.	Faith may not be taken as real.
Praise and worship are high on the agenda.	Worship styles can be impulsive.	Worship looks too much like a production.
Ability to plan and execute large-scale events.	Follow-up is often not done well.	Outreach plans seem intrusive to the community.

The type 7 church is upbeat, full of enthusiasm, optimistic, and always ready to take on any challenge. It is a praising church. Everything is centered around praising God, no matter what happens in life. The church is always planning large events at which people can gather and celebrate their faith. Crusades, evangelistic block parties, and special musical concerts are regular fare. Members of the church have Sunrise stickers on the back windows of their cars with the inviting slogan, "Follow me to watch the Sunrise." Members of the church do not talk about problems in their lives, just opportunities to give God the praise. Many of the members of Sunrise come from nontraditional churches, and it is not unusual to see hands raised during prayer times or during the music of worship.

Rarely do church members stop to evaluate what they are doing. They just move from event to event and from service to service, focused on getting more and more people involved in the celebration of their faith. However, there are things that seem to be missing in the life of the church. They generally feel that needy people are a drain on their spirituality, and as such they do not do much to help with the poor, homeless, or ill. Sometimes they are not very good at following up with people when setbacks do occur.

There are some in the community who view the members of Sunrise as trying to escape from the world with an unrealistic view of life. They are turned off by the hype that seems to come by way of their radio commercials, billboards, and members who seem always to be smiling. They think that Sunrise would be a good church if they would not ignore all the hurt around them.

Wings–Neighbors

The wings of type 7, the Hallelujah Church, are 6 (the Loyal Church) and 8 (the Growth Church). When type 7 is influenced by the Loyal Church, it strongly identifies with other churches that are praise oriented. They tend to gather confidence that the churches that are growing are the ones with a "sunny spirituality." The ones that are not growing, they conclude, are the ones that are too formal, too stiff, and too preoccupied with the world.

When type 7 takes direction from type 8, the Growth Church, it tends to be obsessed with its desire to be the center of attention in the world of faith. It is creative in ways to draw people to itself and prides itself on varied programs and activities. Generally it has a staff of extroverts, and leaders are often inspired by the drive of their mentors.

Directional Arrows

Type 7 relates along two lines. When the type 7 church is going strong, it takes inspiration from type 5, the Analytical Church. It can become somewhat smug, pleased with itself, knowing that it is a unique church and that others do not view the world with the enthusiasm its members display.

They focus on life's meaning, which is centered in praise and worship; this is a retreat from the world, a place of safety. The problem, however, is that this church can become so removed from the realities of life that it offers no practical help to its members. The community can view the church as not being very real. It can turn people away who are not as perfect in their spirituality as the type 7 church appears to be.

When type 7 churches face difficult times, they tend to move toward type 1, the Superhero Church. They become very attuned to the high goals of the life of faith and set standards that can be impossible to reach. They can be obsessed with making the world into the image they envision. They can tend to retreat away from the world.

Broadening Type 7's Personality

Type 7, the Hallelujah Church, should inform its basic personality by relating to types 5 and 1. Because members of type 7 tend to focus on personal spirituality, that energy should be directed more in the direction of mentoring others. The facts of faith should be taught along with the celebration of faith. The church should become more aware of the evils in the world and see them concretely and not simply spiritualize them. That is, the church should work to rid communities of drug houses, advocate for those with AIDS, become involved in the fight against prejudice, and develop programs that offer physical as well as emotional help to victims.

Type 7 should offer educational opportunities to members and those outside the church to learn skills that will improve lives. Rather than holding onto its spirituality, the church should seek to partner with other organizations that encourage people and seek better lives.

Is Your Church a Hallelujah Church?

The following statements may help you determine whether your congregation is a type 7 Hallelujah Church.

❏ Yes ❏ No We are an optimistic church that looks on the sunny side of things.

❏ Yes ❏ No Praise and worship are high on our agenda. We are emotional in our faith.

❏ Yes ❏ No We tend to prefer to do big events and celebrate our successes.

❏ Yes ❏ No At times we can be a little unorganized and may not follow through on our plans.

❏ Yes ❏ No We have trouble connecting at times with the realities of life's ups and downs.

❏ Yes ❏ No If we are honest, some people might accuse us of not living in the real world.

REFLECTION: Based on what you know of your church, what other
characteristics might point to Hallelujah Church
tendencies?

Church Type 8: The Growth Church

■ A PARABLE: Donna is the pastor of Mill Valley Church on the south side
of town. Her congregation is educated, older, and loving in their ministry
to the community. Growth has been slow, however, because the church is
traditional in its worship style and because it lacks monetary resources at
times.

Just about two miles away is a large, thirty-acre complex that at one
time was a sleepy little church in the countryside. Green Fields Church
had called a very high-energy young pastor who worked day and night to
grow the church. He brought to his staff people who were like him and, in
the course of eight years, grew the church from a membership of just over
one hundred to more than fifteen hundred.

But Donna has noted that area churches are suffering. It is not unusual
to hear her fellow pastors complain that they have lost members to Green
Fields. Not long ago, Donna happened to bump into the pastor of Green
Fields at the grocery store. After pleasantries were exchanged, the pastor
noted that a young man from Mill Valley had just recently moved his
membership to Green Fields. Donna wasn't aware that this had happened
and commented, "Well, I am sorry to lose him at our church, but I am sure
you will enjoy getting to know him." "By the way," she said, "I've noticed
that quite a few of our smaller churches seem to be losing members to
Green Fields. Are you concerned that some people might grow critical
and accuse Green Fields of stealing sheep?" The pastor responded, "They
can think what they like, I suppose. We are not stealing anyone's sheep.
But we are growing greener grass on our side of the fence." ■

Green Fields church is a type 8 church, Growth Church. These kinds
of churches often grow at the expense of others around them. They give
the image of success, but can lose members as fast as they gain them if they
aren't careful.

Green Fields Church is obsessed with growth. Every program is
critiqued in terms of whether it contributes to the overall growth of the
church. Staff are often challenged to personally enlist people to join the
church. The leadership press programs that are outreach-focused in design.
They are a church that carefully controls its image as being the fastest-
growing church in the area, and they wish to present a successful image to
anyone who examines the church. They are protective of their status,
especially in denominations that highlight growing churches as the model
of faithfulness. They are always looking for recognition of their efforts and
will challenge any critics of their approach to growth.

Growth Church Characteristics

POSITIVE IMAGES	EMERGING TENSIONS	NEGATIVE IMAGES
An aggressive and assertive congregation in terms of church growth.	Can be accused of taking members from other congregations.	Sheep stealers.
Set high goals to be the best.	People are pressed to be aggressive with church growth goals.	Growth can outpace ministry to people.
Very attractive programs, multilayered staff.	Activities can crowd calendar and take on a life of their own.	Church may appear to be too large and may want to grow just to be larger.
Can raise large sums of money, especially for building programs.	Competition for budget by different programs.	Constant emphasis on giving to the church for new buildings or programs.

These churches are usually highly evangelistic, at least in rhetoric. They tend to be conservative with regard to values, and may go to excess in taking a stand against what they perceive is wrong with churches that do not grow as fast as they do. They depend on focusing on demographic growth sectors, and may relocate where they believe growth will be ensured due to migration patterns of cities.

Growth Churches can be domineering to their sister churches in the area. They can intimidate them by their success. When involved in controversy, they mobilize large groups of people and money to support their cause. Pastors of this type of church can become dictatorial and exhibit dominance over others. Some grow large enough to become denominations unto themselves and feel little to no responsibility for cooperation with other churches.

Wings—Neighbors

The neighbors of type 8 are type 7, the Hallelujah Church, and type 9, the Peaceful Church. When type 8 churches are influenced by type 7, they tend to relish their success and see it as God's confirmation of their efforts. They become even more energetic, charismatic, and aggressive in their efforts. They can become so confident in their blessings that they run over more vulnerable churches and barely notice.

When they are influenced by type 9, the Peaceful Church, they can become more steady and develop quality programs and outreach using the vast resources they have available. They can build programs that are comprehensive and minister to members from the cradle to the grave. They can bring vast resources to solving any issue that may confront them; at least, they have the confidence to do so.

Directional Arrows

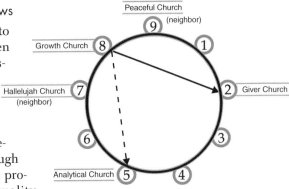

Type 8 is related to types 2 and 5. When things are quite positive, type 8 can draw strength from type 2, the Giver Church. In spite of type 8 churches' largeness, they can, through their comprehensive programming, offer quality ministry to people who have need. They can feel sympathy toward people and exhibit great concern for the larger issues of life in the community. When affected by type 2, type 8 churches are confident and satisfied with the kind of church they have chosen to be. They can contribute large sums of money to victims, causes, and ministries for the benefit of their own members and the community at large.

When things are difficult, type 8 churches move toward type 5, the Analytical Church. They may retreat from cooperation with other people of faith and focus entirely on themselves. They can become quite critical of other churches who do not take evangelism or outreach as seriously as they do. They will analyze problems carefully when impacted by type 5 and move in the best interest of their self-image.

Broadening Type 8's Personality

Type 8 can learn from types 2 and 5. It needs to lessen its emphasis on growing just to grow, and seek to be more giving. It needs to develop intimacy with newcomers and develop relationships with people in the community for the sake of friendship, not membership alone. It needs to display more humility even as it is successful and growing. The church needs to develop a listening ear to the concerns of other churches that feel victimized by its growth, and seek to aid them in their growth.

Type 8 churches should always measure the impact of their growth potential and focus on discipleship as a means to help those who join. They should be willing to give themselves away to struggling churches that need resources both here in the United States and across the world.

Is Your Church a Growth Church?

The following statements may help you determine whether your congregation is a type 8 Growth Church.

❏ Yes ❏ No We are a church that is serious about growing larger than we are.

❏ Yes ❏ No Our church wants to be the best one around and we plan accordingly.

❏ Yes ❏ No We are an active church that demands faithfulness of our members.

❏ Yes ❏ No Some might say that we take members from other churches nearby.

❏ Yes ❏ No We are constantly in need of resources, money, and people to fuel our growth.

❏ Yes ❏ No Sometimes our emphasis on growth outpaces our ability to minister to others.

REFLECTION: Based on what you know of your church, what other characteristics might point to Growth Church tendencies?

Church Type 9: The Peaceful Church

■ A PARABLE: Frank is pastor of Harmony Church, located in downtown. It is a historic church full of senior citizens who constantly talk about the good old days of its past glory. Once the church was a powerhouse of influence and had been home to pastors of national fame. But the community, the city, and the times changed; when people moved away from the downtown, the church withered. The suburbs and their churches offered people an opportunity to escape the city, and only the faithful stayed in the aging community around the church.

Frank is a young pastor who hopes to turn the church around, but he knows that the community has changed so much that to have any kind of future at all, the church will have to undergo some drastic changes in its self-identity. Frank is not a fighter, but he has a vision. He wants to minister to the singles who have moved into the renovated loft communities in the downtown, but they have lifestyles that are problematic to many traditional folk. There is a large community of gay and lesbian people nearby that Frank knows needs ministry. Reaching them will raise eyebrows.

At first, the congregation seemed interested in the prospect of growing, but they soon grew overwhelmed when Frank talked to them about the challenges of ministering to mostly single people and persons with alternate lifestyles. This is a peaceful church that has learned how to cope with problems in the past. They have valued the notion of holding on to one another through tough times. Though the congregation did not want to say no to Frank, it was clear they were having trouble saying yes (to the idea of reaching such different groups of people). Frank could see the challenge, but he could also see the enormous potential of embracing such a change. "Small steps," he kept thinking. "I'll just have to take small steps." ■

Harmony Church is type 9, a Peaceful Church. It knows what the challenges are, but facing the uncertainty of the future could cause its world to fall apart. What if they try to change and it doesn't work? Right now, staying the course looks most appealing.

Peaceful Church Characteristics		
POSITIVE IMAGES	EMERGING TENSIONS	NEGATIVE IMAGES
A very harmonious church.	Can be indecisive about the future.	May be paralyzed by doubts.
Goals are not difficult to achieve.	Goals are not set very high.	Goals for the church make little difference in the long run.
Historic, stable congregation.	Low-key satisfaction with their fate.	Selfish about the future.

The Peaceful Church wants to maintain harmony at all costs. It has a hard time rising to meet new challenges because it is often paralyzed by fears that it may end up being worse off. The church often wants to blend into the scenery when it comes to conflict within its tradition or denominational life. The congregation is happy with itself and its modest goals. It is an attractive church to people who are tired of controversy or pressures from work. The church tends to expect little more than attendance from its members. It is an unassuming church that is generally a happy place.

But the church can be hindered by its indecisive nature. It will often put off decisions, hoping the problem will simply go away. It wants to make sure that everyone in the congregation agrees as much as possible about decisions that are made. Harmony is essential.

If people on the outside comes to know the church for what it is, they might see it as trying to live in isolation from the real world. They might see the members set in their ways, choosing to die rather than to change. Behind the smiles of the members is a very protective nature and suspicion of anyone who might want to change things.

Wings—Neighbors

Type 9 is surrounded by type 8, the Growth Church, and type 1, the Superhero Church. When type 9 is influenced by type 8 it can become sociable and inviting. It can be very down to earth and gracious to those who may choose to visit. Its members can be charming and inviting, especially if they believe that others who are like them might join the congregation.

When influenced by type 1, type 9 can be restrained and idealistic. It can become complacent and choose to bask in the memory of days gone by rather than living up to the challenges of a new day. It can feel isolated as the last bastion of historic values that have served to shape the church's worldview.

Directional Arrows

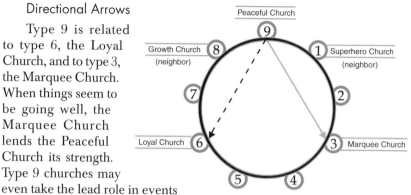

Type 9 is related to type 6, the Loyal Church, and to type 3, the Marquee Church. When things seem to be going well, the Marquee Church lends the Peaceful Church its strength. Type 9 churches may even take the lead role in events such as hosting a conference in the community. They may even be willing to enter into debates within their tradition and can serve as mediator for both sides since they view both sides so well.

But when pressed or when faced with troublesome decisions, type 9 churches tend to adopt some of the weaknesses of type 6, the Loyal Church. They can become stressed and anxious when things change. The church can react critically and defensively and increase its dependence on its sister churches to help it along. It will look to others within its tradition for affirmation and value, and trust what they have to say as long as it is positive. When they are stressed, Type 9 churches will try to keep the rules of their tradition no matter what, even if it puts them in an uncomfortable position with the community around them.

Broadening Type 9's Personality

Type 9 is the Peaceful Church. It can broaden its personality by adopting characteristics from type 3 and type 6. As a Peaceful Church, type 9 is reluctant at times to take chances in ministry. It needs to understand that its opinion does really matter in the world. It has gifts that it can use to bring people together and should not hesitate to develop programs that are visionary. The Peaceful Church should see itself as partner with God in all that God is doing in the world, and be confident in its ability to reach goals. It should also learn to partner with other churches in order to enhance its ministry.

Is Your Church a Peaceful Church?

The following statements may help you determine whether your congregation is a type 9 Peaceful Church.

❏ Yes ❏ No We are a historic, stable congregation.

❏ Yes ❏ No Harmony among our members is a priority with us.

❏ Yes ❏ No We tend to be good at peacemaking since we can see both sides of issues.

❏ Yes   ❏ No   Our goals are not difficult to achieve.

❏ Yes   ❏ No   At times we can be indecisive as a congregation about issues.

❏ Yes   ❏ No   People on the outside are unsure about our stance on issues that face the community.

REFLECTION: Based on what you know of your church, what other characteristics might point to Peaceful Church tendencies?

Remembering the Triads

As noted earlier, the Enneagram's nine points are divided into groups of three, called triads. The triads are composed of a dominant personality type and the associated "wings," or those types that immediately surround the dominant one. It is not unusual for one of the wings to be stronger than the other. But each wing contributes to the overall personality type.

Some church types function instinctively in regard to the world around them.[9] This triad is formed around types 8 (the Growth Church), 9 (the Peaceful Church), and 1 (the Superhero Church). Churches in this triad may have a tendency to see the world as receptive to them and what they have to offer, as with the Growth Church. Other church types have a feeling that the world may view them as insecure or lukewarm, as with the Peaceful Church. Still other churches believe the world expects them to perform or display themselves, as with the Superhero Church. Churches' responses will depend on how they feel about the world around them.

A second triad includes those churches that relate to the world emotionally. These usually gather along types 2 (the Giver Church), type 3 (the Marquee Church), and type 4 (the Romantic Church). These churches often respond emotionally to new situations and may respond before they fully analyze the situation. For example, the Giver Church will tend to see the community as in need of their ministry and will be emotionally involved with ministry to a broken world; the Marquee Church is emotionally tied to performance and promoting a positive image; and the Romantic Church often relates to the world in terms of its sense of the value and beauty of faith. Because members value the refined and cultured aspects of faith, they feel that others would also.

The last grouping of types includes the thinking or contemplative ones, which are usually grouped along types 5 (the Analytical Church), 6 (the Loyal Church), and 7 (the Hallelujah Church). These churches respond to the world around them with certain ambivalence, caution, or even suspicion. The Analytical Church may respond to the community by probing what the community thinks about an issue and will want to respond in ways that to it seem authentic and well-reasoned. The Loyal Church is sometimes suspicious of the community's confidence in them and thus may doubt the authenticity of faith statements made in the community. The Hallelujah Church believes it has found the meaning of life in its vision of faith as celebration, but it is often not confident that the community understands the depth of its optimism.

Understanding the triads can give insight into how the church moves toward the community. The first triad (types 8, 9, and 1) moves in their witness to the world by choosing to stand firm in their position. They just know, deep down inside, that they are right in their view of the world. They are sometimes surprised when they have expectations based on instincts that prove to be the opposite of what they actually find in the community.

The second triad (types 2, 3, and 4) functions on feelings. They will move in their witness to the world outwardly. They will often advance toward the world and respond out of a sincere emotional attachment before they have really thought about the implications. They are often similar to caregivers who want to be needed and will sometimes be overbearing to help when others actually do not want their help at the time.

The third triad (types 5, 6, and 7) move cautiously into the world around them. They are not sure that the world is a very friendly place, and have to do their research before they move into action. They will move in their witness to the world with reservation. They may test the waters and retreat if they find certain kinds of ministry too threatening or difficult or not aligned with what they perceive themselves to be.

Every church has a certain personality type. Finding your type should not be a difficult process. Most church members have a sense about the church and its ministry that may resonate with the types discussed above. None of these types are in and of themselves negative or positive. It is not the goal of a Marquee Church to suddenly change and become a Peaceful Church. Human personalities are what they are. But we learn over the years to modify our personality traits in ways that make it possible for us to relate to others without offending them or in ways that make us more complete. If a person is an overachiever, for example, she can learn to be more supportive of others and less concerned with her own prestige.[10] We learn ways to relate to the world around us and to function within communities so that life becomes not a wrestling match, but more like a waltz. We move with life instead of always fighting against life.

Churches, likewise, can choose to either fight against the world and run the risk of not being taken seriously, or they can learn to converse with the world in ways that give them a chance to lead occasionally in the waltz of life. The witness of the church can become much more effective when we give the community a chance to hear what we are saying. Often, giving them that chance means that we must modify our personalities in order to be heard. No one is suggesting that the message of the gospel is to be modified, compromised, or watered down. The gospel has its own integrity and power. But what churches must learn to do is to communicate the life-giving message of faith in ways that enable the community to hear. This can be done when we know who we are, who the communities around us are, and what we need to do to help them know us better.

6

Facing the Obstacles
The Ones on the Inside

Churches are groups of human beings gathered together to be the body of Christ in the world. Therefore, churches both reflect the best of humanity and sometimes the worst as they become entangled in the problems that are common to humanity. They often resist change, especially the older and more established ones. Corporate churches that view themselves as institutions are the ones that have the hardest time making changes: they often want to send the proposals for change through committees and study the issue to assess the impact of any changes. Other churches have the opposite problem: they jump from one new thing to another and often tire members who long for some sense of normalcy. Denominational churches are bombarded from headquarters with program upon program, and often send mixed messages to the church and the community regarding the priorities of their ministry.

With so many interpersonal and organizational dynamics, it is no wonder that there is often some conflict. There are those who will immediately embrace change because it promises them relief from the concerns they have had all along. Others will resist change because they like things just as they are. The most difficult kind of change is from the inside out. With every proposed change, obstacles will pop up. Each one has to be addressed in order to move forward.

Change is often defined as the ability to assess the current state of the situation, to look for viable alternatives, and then to move toward action that will modify the original situation or problem. Not everyone will be able to manage the changes that might be called for. Some may choose to leave the church, while others will stay but not remain quiet. They may choose to silently work against any change that the congregation wishes to make. These are certainly liabilities, but a greater question still remains: "Why Can't Our Community Hear What We Are Saying?" If your church is serious about engaging that question and about becoming an authentic witness of the gospel to the community around it, changes will likely be worth all the struggle.

Change does not always have to be traumatic. When approached with sensitivity, education, and prayerful direction, change can happen with minimal fallout. In his book, *Good to Great*, Jim Collins says, "under the right conditions, the problems of commitment, alignment, motivation, and change largely melt away."[1] It is up to the leadership and membership of each church to take seriously their commitment to change in order to be faithful to the Great Commission, to align to what God is doing in the world, to be properly motivated as people of God who care about the community and the world at large, and to change from an institution of corporate religion to a kingdom-focused church. The process will demand facing obstacles from the inside.

Facing the Obstacles for Change

One of the first obstacles to be tackled on the way toward the kind of change that will move the church into the community, and perhaps the most intense stumbling block, is the nature of the local church. Over the years, churches tend to settle in and narrowly define themselves. Each has a distinctive way of relating to the congregation and to the community around it. Either they seek to enhance the religious education level of the church and community, or maybe they define themselves according to their denominational heritage or tradition, or they take seriously the role of change agent in the world. In all cases, they seek to change the people inside the church and then move outward to change the world.

Churches that define themselves by trying to pass along religious education to the community are in constant competition to garner the interest or desire of the community for learning about faith in the first place. We live in a world in which the Internet has made it possible for people to learn about nearly every subject. Much of the culture approaches learning about faith on a personal level. That is to say, they will either read the latest book on spirituality, research a particular faith on the Internet, or dialogue with a coworker about his or her faith. Rarely do most secular people look for a church for the specific reason of learning about the Christian life.

Those churches that are intent on defining themselves along their denominational lines face a huge obstacle with the community. Most people today care little for denominational labels. I was asked by a friend who pastored a Methodist church to come and conduct a seminar related to church and community life. His church had a small sign in front of the building that identified it as a Methodist church, but inside when I asked the congregation about the church, several of them indicated that being Methodist was the last thing they were interested in. What attracted them to the church were the outreach ministries of the church and the spiritual emphasis of the church. There were folks in the church from almost every tradition. The pastor told me that tradition or denominational affiliation did not matter to the congregation anymore: what mattered was trying to be faithful to what they understood the gospel message to be.

Churches that focus on what they believe God is doing in the world have a chance to be more creative and less encumbered by either tradition or competition for the minds and hearts of people. Herb Miller tells of a pastor in Pennsylvania who believes congregations that are transformed are those that meet the gospel message at the crossroads of life's hard knocks. "Concepts like grace, forgiveness, love, reconciliation, prayer...are not static concepts. They communicate growth...creative expression...and an invitation to a new "changed" way of living."[2] If change is going to occur, it will be at the very heart of the church and the way it defines itself in terms of its calling to the community it serves. This is why it is so important for every church to understand its personality and how it is viewed by the community. Each church will need to engage the positive and negative nature of that personality and be ready to redirect itself for more effective witness. One way to begin is by asking a few questions:

1. Given the personality of your church right now, how do you relate to the community around you? Do you try to educate the community about faith? Do you approach the community from a denominational point of view? Base your answer on the number of unchurched persons from within the community who have been ministered to in the last year by the church. How many have joined the church and why have they joined?

2. What has your church found out about how it is viewed by the community at large?

3. Who are you currently reaching with the ministry of the church?

4. Who is being overlooked?

5. Why are they being overlooked?

6. Do you assume anything about your church that has been largely disproven in the larger community? For example: you assume that your church is friendly, but when you interview people in the community, they say that the church seems cold and unresponsive to them.

7. What are the programs you currently invest in that are focused almost entirely on the membership?

8. During the week, how accessible is your church to the community?

9. What are the religious demographics of the community, its ethnic makeup, and its age span, its socioeconomic position, and what are the common lifestyles of the people?

10. Are you willing to reshape your ministries in order to minister to what you have found?

Contextualization

A second obstacle to be encountered is the challenge of contextualization of the church's ministry within the community. This is an evaluative process by which the church seeks to initiate change in a holistic manner for the benefit of the community. It is also the assessment of change within the limits, scope, and expectations of the church's overall mission. It will suggest changes to the vision of the church (what the church understands the ministry of the gospel to be in terms of its context); to its function from Sunday to Sunday (less focus on activities that point inward and more emphasis on ministries that suggest themselves from the community itself); and to the influence of the church (a movement away from status among religious people toward vulnerability as it ministers within its context).

When the vision of a church changes in terms of its sensitivity to its context, several things begin to happen. Instead of offering religious faith to a community, the congregation has the potential of seeking the true meaning of Christian faith lived out in the world. When this begins to happen, each member will take seriously his or her role as minister.

I worked with a church in Leesburg, Florida, that had caught a vision of ministry I have not found in many churches. The church is defined by an approach to the gospel that is ministry-based. They have scores of ways to minister to persons: pregnancy care, shelters for abused persons, drug rehab, homeless ministries, ministries to wealthy persons, and dozens of others. Spending a couple of weeks at the church and observing how they communicated the gospel was truly amazing. I interviewed member after member by asking a simple question, "What do you do here at the church?" Time and time again, without any coaching, members would reply, "I am minister to singles." "I am minister to seniors." "I am a minister to homeless persons." "I minister to young girls who are pregnant." None of those persons were staff members. They were church members who understood that *they* had been called to ministry and they did so gladly as the extension of their church life. What was apparent to me in this church was the fact that the ordinary church member had taken seriously the call to kingdom-focused living, and their ministry to others was the measure of their faithfulness to that vision for life.

There is a church near our university that has also taken contextualization seriously. It is near Buford Highway in Atlanta, a corridor where thousands of people from ethnic backgrounds that encompass the world live. This church has long been a traditional, white, middle-class congregation in a nice neighborhood. But as the demographics began to change toward a multi-cultural reality, the church had to redefine itself. It faced a change-or-die decision. Tim, the pastor, began to lead the church toward a process of reaching out to migrants who needed help with food, shelter, and language skills. Over a period of time, the church changed its personality to one that no longer identified itself as middle-class Baptist, but a church that identified itself as a haven for people in need. The church has been a place where my students have worked each semester as a part of their mission immersion class. Their case studies and verbata tell the story of a church that knows its community and is seeking to provide both physical and spiritual help in ways that make it vital. The church is growing again, but this time as a reflection of its community, not exclusively white and middle-class, but multicultural and socioeconomically diverse. What makes this church a study in the ability to contextualize itself to the needs of the community is the contrast that is offered. Just a mile or two away is a sister church that has refused to accept the challenge of the community around it. Soon they will sell their property unless they change. If a church is to grapple with the task of being more contextual in terms of the community, a few questions will have to be asked as well:

1. How willing are we to reshape ourselves in order to make the church more accessible to those in the community? Do we need to change worship times, music, or weekly activities that will provide more access? Are we willing to minister to people who are not like us?
2. What kind of language do we need to use to converse with the culture around us? In other words, how can we talk about spiritual issues in a way the culture understands and avoid church language?
3. Does our community need educational opportunities, job training skills, medical aid, or other social needs that we can provide?
4. As we change to meet the community where it lives, how will we communicate the gospel in new ways?
5. Are these ways consistent with our tradition or does our tradition make it difficult for the community to hear us? How can we overcome these issues?

Transformation

Another obstacle from within to be overcome is the serious engagement with transformation. The ability of the church to examine carefully the "why" behind every program or approach taken toward ministry and mission is critical. Not every church member is going to be comfortable in examining why the church does what it does week by week.

Transformation is never easy. It means changing old habits and assumptions. It means testing new ideas and opportunities. Transformation can be an obstacle because most church members grow so comfortable with the routines of church life that they lose touch with the motivation behind their actions. They can lose touch with theological truths as well.

A couple of years ago, I served a church as interim pastor for about fifteen months. I kept preaching Sunday after Sunday about the character of the kingdom of God. I kept emphasizing the need for every church member to listen to what God was saying to them and to join God in God's redemptive work. I remember one Sunday speaking about leading others to faith in Christ and challenged the membership to form friendships with people and mentor them toward Christ. I also suggested that if they did lead someone to Christ that they should have the opportunity to baptize them and to continue to disciple them in their new faith.

Several church members challenged me that only the pastor should baptize people. I asked one of them to show me in the Bible where that was true. He could not, of course, so I preached on Phillip and the Ethiopian and again challenged the church to consider what could happen if members saw themselves as ministers. A few weeks later a young man made his profession of faith during the close of the service. He told me that he had been led to faith by a member of the church. I decided to test the church's willingness to consider what I had been preaching in recent days. So, I approached the church member and asked him if he would baptize his friend. He said he would have to pray about it, so I waited.

A couple of weeks passed and I called him to ask for a decision. He said he would be glad to but did not know how. So I told him I would tutor him so he could do it with confidence. On the Sunday of the baptism I sat at the front of the church and watched a layperson enter the water, explain to the church that he had been influential in his friend's conversion and then baptize him. A lot of eyes in the congregation were no longer dry, including my own eyes.

This simple transformation of a theological assumption created a firestorm of conversation and interest in the meaning of baptism, how ordinary Christians could participate, and a newfound vigor for evangelistic witness. It was not without criticism. But the church as a whole celebrated a step out of its traditional assumptions toward newer insights about partnership with God in the matter of witness.

When church members seriously examine the "why" behind their assumptions of what it means to be church, tension grows. People have to come face to face with assumptions they once considered biblical, but when examined find out they are cultural or simply a matter of tradition. The real test is whether or not we are willing to step out of our comfort zones and test new ideas and practices in order to energize the church and transform it. If a church is serious about changing its personality or its traditional way of doing church in order to interface more effectively with the communities around it, creativity will be demanded.

A church on Atlanta's south side had tried the usual outreach programs suggested by its denomination, but most had failed. The community was deaf to nearly every offer the church made for participating in the services and the opportunities the church afforded. However, a church member offered a suggestion during a business meeting that slowly changed the church's approach. The church had a sanctuary that was multipurpose in design. Chairs were on the floor instead of pews, so the whole sanctuary could be arranged for any function.

The church found out that the nearby school had grown so much over the last few years that it no longer had space to host families during graduation exercises. The school was in a panic about the upcoming graduation, so the church member suggested the church offer the sanctuary to the school for its graduation at no cost. This was the first time the church had ever offered its building to the community for any nonreligious use. It was more than adequate for the graduation. There were a few church members who objected at first, but the offer soon paid some dividends. The church was publicly thanked for its generosity, thus changing its image in the community, and families who did not attend church got an opportunity to meet some of the members and to begin forming friendships. As a result, the number of visitors from the community increased because they were influenced by a church that did not mind giving its facilities away to the community.

Later in the year, this small step opened the way for the church to try another community event with more confidence. It hosted a July 4 fireworks display. It cost the congregation quite a bit of money to put on the display, but to their surprise hundreds of people from the community attended who otherwise had never stepped foot on the campus before. Each person who came was given refreshments and invited to visit the services. Again, the number of visitors increased. This simple transformation–making the church more available to the community–has led to greater conversation with the community at large. The community now knows more about the church because they have seen the church in action on Saturday and on Thursday, instead of just on Sunday.

When a church learns to ask, "Why do we do what we do?" it will gather insights that will clarify the vision of the church and thus lead to renewed commitment, or it will be willing to modify itself to be equipped for more creativity in its ministry. Transformation within churches will require:

Leadership That Is Freed to Serve

Most leaders in churches, especially lay leaders, serve with great commitment. But these leaders often lack imagination and freedom to color outside the traditional lines of expectation. Leaders that are transformative are those who are willing to take risks, to step out in faith and test new ideas. They tend to think from the outside in as it regards the mission of the church. If leaders are to be set free to imagine and envision new possibilities, there needs to be a welcoming climate for visionary leadership within the church. Jim Collins says that creating a good climate develops the place where the truth is heard and the brutal facts are confronted.[3] Sometimes leaders are held back by a lack of expectation for growth or creativity, or even by a subtle insistence that followers be somehow shaped in the image of the leader. Followers try to meet the low expectations of the leader. The brutal facts are before most churches today. The communities around many churches aren't listening to what the churches say. And, furthermore, they aren't that interested. Unless leaders are encouraged to color outside the lines of traditional religious expectations, not much is likely to change.

Leaders Who Are Gift Oriented

Linda is an executive in a Fortune 500 company in Atlanta. Every day she makes decisions and manages budgets in the millions of dollars. She is a student of mine hoping to one day become pastor of a church. In a conversation one day she told me that with all her experience and ability, the most her local church has allowed her to do is to work with other women in the church. She is stereotyped by her church; they cannot see her potential or her gifts to serve.

When a church seeks leaders, often there is a disconnect between the gifts they use every day and what they are asked to do on Sunday. Laypersons should be encouraged to use the gifts that come naturally to them in the service of the church. Otherwise, they may struggle with effectiveness. Learn to ask, "Why is Susan working in the nursery when she is a wonderful high school teacher?" Try to connect people to their strengths.

Passionate Spirituality

A lost discipline in many churches is the personal testimony. Seldom do church members get an opportunity to hear of the spiritual journey of their fellow church members. A church that wishes to transform itself must take seriously a commitment to deeper spirituality and one that is shared. A note of warning needs to be sounded here. There are some people who do not understand the difference between authentic spirituality and simple religious addiction. There are some people who will cloak their spirituality in a guise of designer religion. That is, they will mix a little New Age, a little Christianity, a little pop culture, or any number of other ingredients, and call it spirituality. Some of them are trying to escape painful memories of a religious past. I once had a church member who chastised me every Sunday because I did not preach on the Holy Spirit. She was preoccupied to the extent that she told me once she saw spirits daily. Religious addicts' lives can spin out of control and define spirituality 180 degrees away from reality. They will tend to throw all the passion of former addictions into their spiritual life, and they can become quite disruptive to a church trying to take spirituality seriously.[4] The journey toward authentic spirituality needs to be monitored lest it get out of control in the hands of people who are religious addicts.

Worship is a corporate experience as well as a personal one. If it is true that the secular world is interested in spirituality, then churches must address those issues publicly. There are many people who never step foot inside the church who maintain a rigorous spiritual discipline in their lives.

I visited a warehouse in New York that had been converted into a Buddhist center. I attended a session during which issues of spirituality were talked about by the leader. After a period of meditation and chanting, the subject that was addressed by the spiritual leader had to do with the spiritual disciplines of life. It was amazing to me to look out over the "congregation" and note the large number of young and old alike. I interviewed several of the people there about their lives. I met one or two who had adopted Buddhism as their religion, but some who said they were not Buddhists but found in the weekly sessions what their churches never emphasized. They were eager to get in touch with their inner selves and the center gave them that opportunity.

The power for spiritual insight suffers when the spiritual journeys of church members are assumed and never spoken of. People want to participate, but most worship services leave little opportunity for spiritual participation except during periods of music or prayer. And then most of that time is simply routine. The Buddhist center in New York may have touched on something very vital. It is an opportunity for people to get in touch with their spiritual needs and to connect those spiritual insights to daily life. Passionate spirituality needs a creative outlet in most churches today.

Worship That Inspires

One of the most significant moments for worship for a lot of people occurred not in church but at the movie theater. Mel Gibson's film *The Passion of the Christ* took both Hollywood and the nation by storm. It became the eighth highest-grossing domestic film of all time. It improved the sinking revenues at many movie theaters, but mostly it brought renewed emphasis on faith for a lot of people. According to the Barna group:

> Four out of ten adults (41%) said that within the past two years they had seen a movie that had caused them to think more seriously about their religious faith. Not surprisingly, it was the people who were already most inclined to think about faith matters who said this, such as evangelicals (68%) and people with an active personal faith (65% of those who pray, read the Bible and attend a church service in a typical week).
>
> When asked to identify the movies that had led them to ponder their faith, *The Passion* was the only movie to be listed by more than 5% of this segment. Overall, six out of ten adults who had reflected on their faith in response to a movie (59%) identified *The Passion* as one of the movies that caused such reconsideration.[5]

What is interesting in the research that the Barna group conducted was their observation that 18 percent of the people surveyed indicated their religious behavior had changed because of the movie. Barna said, "about 13 million adults changed some aspect of their typical religious behavior because of the movie and about 11 million people altered some pre-existing religious beliefs because of the content of that film."[6] What's more, Barna said that the poll indicated that about 4 percent of the nation's agnostics and atheists said they attended the film.

People are interested in faith. Worship that is inspiring has to move beyond methods and gimmicks and beyond the worship wars that pit traditionalists against those with contemporary tastes. An elitist position with regard to worship will draw to it only those who are interested in elitism. Whatever its form and style, worship has to touch the deeper questions that people have about God and address who they are in terms of their relationships with the Creator. Marva Dawn is exactly correct. Worship needs to reach out to people, but doesn't need to be dumbed down.[7]

Intimacy in Small Groups

People need time and an opportunity to process their spiritual journeys. Those who are religiously oriented will tend to find small groups a refreshing addendum to their typical diet of Sunday school. Groups held in homes, for example, provide a safe place for people to discuss their doubts and questions outside of the "holy campus." When around the picnic table at someone's home, they feel less ill at ease that somehow they are disappointing God with their questions.

Most of the megachurches that have continued to thrive have been those in which small groups provide identity, companionship, and learning on a weekly basis. These groups are where the growth really occurs. Friends invite their friends to the group, and they introduce them to Christ in a nonthreatening setting. We need to fully realize how damaged a lot of people are by religion.

Scott, who lived across the hall from me in college, turned out to be a person wounded by religion. Forty of us lived on the hall during my freshman year. Thirty-eight years have passed, but I can still remember the taunts I received from some of the guys on the hall because they knew I was a Christian and I went to church each Sunday while they slept in, often trying to get over a raucous Saturday night. I came in one Sunday evening from having preached in a small country church. I was still in my suit and tie. They grabbed me and tossed me into the shower. They regularly short-sheeted my bed, and otherwise poked fun at me all the time. They tried in every way to rattle me and hear me let go with a string of expletives so common to their vocabulary. But I never did. I was no saint, but I understood that they were just having fun at my expense.

Last year, I was to speak in a church in suburban Atlanta. Before the service, I was sitting down front in the first pew and a fellow, now bald, came up and sat beside me. He looked familiar, but I could not place him. He knew my name having read the bulletin and made a connection to thirty-eight years ago. "You don't recognize me, do you?" I said, "No, I'm sorry, I do not." He then introduced himself to me as Scott, the fellow who lived across from me during my freshman year. We laughed, caught up, and enjoyed a few minutes together. Then he said, "I have always hoped that I might run into you one day. Remember all the hell I gave you in college?" I smiled and said, "Yes, I do." "Well, you never retaliated against me or any of the other guys on the hall. That has stayed with me all these years. You really lived what you claimed to believe. Last year, I became a Christian also," he said. "I had been brought up in a Christian home, but at an early age I learned to hate religion." "In fact," he said, "religion was always shoved down my throat until it made me gag. I was constantly criticized during my teen years because I did not act like church people thought I should act. So, when I got to college I gave up on God. But you proved to me that people of faith are not like the ones I grew up with. I just wanted to thank you," he said. Scott reminded me that there are probably countless numbers of people who have been damaged by religion, and some haven't survived the damage.

Small groups can take seriously the issues that people have, based on their past experiences with religion. If the small groups are willing to be understanding, supportive, and caring, they can help a person find authentic faith without all the baggage associated with painful memories. Even then, small group work can be a slow process. It will not always succeed in reaching those who are terribly wounded. Mary Tuomi Hammond tells the story of how her husband once offered a study group on "How Can I Believe Again?" He put out flyers in the neighborhood and hoped for the best, but few attended. But in conversations around town it became apparent that the flyers had stimulated interest in the subject. She interviewed a couple of persons who said that they had wanted to attend but that the prospect of facing spiritual questions was just too painful given their experience of religion. Hammond said, "These posters seemed to pry a few hearts open a little bit, though not enough to risk participation in a group setting. Through the experience, I realized that ministry among the dechurched encounters much deeper resistance that I ever imagined."[8] Small groups can hold promise, but they will generally face an uphill challenge to enlist those who have been dechurched. With prayer and consistent caring, however, they hold promise to create a place of safety for those who want to explore again what it means to believe, but who are cautious. Small group leaders must take seriously that secular and dechurched people are not orthodox in their faith. Faith for them is a confusing issue. Every small group needs then to take seriously the metaphor of a journey in terms of faith. It has a starting place, not always comfortable, some bumps in the road, but the journey can offer surprises along the way toward authentic Christian faith. Do not give up just because the starting point may be difficult.

Ministry-based Evangelism

When considering what the culture thinks of religious faith, we need to be honest. In nearly every outreach tool I have seen, the assumption is that people are religiously oriented in the same way church people are. The truth is that unchurched people do not care about the language of salvation, nor are they proficient with it. Many of them have had experiences in which they have been treated as objects by those intent on witnessing to them. When all that is communicated to unchurched people is concern about their eternal destiny, most of them could care less. They want people to care about them, not just their souls.

I was on an airplane flight from Chicago one summer and I sat next to a young man who was well-dressed and polite, at least at first. I had scarcely gotten through my peanuts and soft drink when he turned to me and asked, "Brother, have you been born again?" I told him that I was indeed a Christian, but he doubted my word and proceeded to whip out a tract and read it to me. I kept saying to him that it was not necessary, but he continued. He was determined to get me saved again! I am a patient person, but this guy really rubbed me wrong. He paid no attention to what I had said to him about my faith and insisted that I hear the gospel once again. If I got agitated and upset about this fellow, think how unchurched people feel. No wonder they feel abused by religious zealots who ignore them for who they are and simply want to meet their quota of salvation conversations for the day. Unchurched people can smell evangelists from miles away, and they do their best to avoid them.

If I read the Scriptures correctly, Jesus never invaded a person's life the way some evangelists do. He respected people, even to the extent of letting them walk away, such as in the encounter with the Rich Young Ruler. What I see in Jesus' life was a sensitivity to people and the deepest needs of their lives. He practiced ministry as the foundational concept to all he was about. Years ago, I wrote a book that dealt with evangelism from a ministry perspective.[9] I am convinced that authentic ministry to persons will open the doors to their hearts. They will invite us in for coffee with their innermost being. We simply have to develop the skills that are needed to listen to their lives and respond in sensitive ways.

Eduard Thurneysen speaks of the value of listening in ministry to others. "If any instruction at all is valid in this area, it would be that one must be prepared to be a listener—a patient, concentrated, attentive, alert, and understanding listener and nothing else."[10] Ministry-based evangelistic witness takes place when we carefully listen to a person's story and the needs he or she shares with us. We learn to minister to the whole of the person in the whole of his or her circumstance and life. During the process of authentic and caring ministry in which we are willing to be vulnerable, we have a chance to express little snippets of spiritual insight that soon begin to build to a crescendo of questions about God. It is *not* a five-minute process. It can take weeks, months, and even years with some people. Time is needed in the process for people to assess our ministry to them and what God is saying to them about the care they are receiving. It takes time to fall in love. What makes us think that we can get people to fall in love with Christ with a canned speech? We have to introduce them through our caring responses to a person who loves them more than we do. We do that by our actions. They have the potential then to develop an ability to see in us the Christ we claim to know and then, at some point, they no longer have to work so hard at it. Christ's love penetrates their hearts through our very presence with them.

Years ago in a research project, I contrasted churches that practice evangelism without ministry and follow-up with those that approach evangelistic witness from a ministry base. The findings were just as I suspected. One year later, the people who had been reached in ministry were still involved in faith discovery and growth, whereas the churches that practiced a "soul only" kind of evangelism lost touch with the ones who had been evangelized. One church in the Atlanta area that I researched had baptized nearly 500 people in one year, but only a few of them were still around a year later.

Ministry-based evangelism holds the promise of never using people for religious goals. If it is practiced authentically, the key will be on ministry. Ministry will always be the priority, whether that ministry is for adequate food, shelter, and clothing, or whether that ministry is focused on detoxifying people from a religious faith that abused them at some point in their life.

Helping people come to personal discovery of the Christ who cares for their total existence is the goal for evangelism. My friend Malan Nel says that the question for most people is not whether there will be eternal life in heaven but whether there will be life here on earth. For a lot of people today, that question is vital to their survival. Knowing that a person can live a truly authentic and full life here with God is far more valuable than asking them to just hold on for some promised reward in eternity. People who are abused, tired, or lonely need the assurance that there is a fullness of life to be gained here and now. The good news of the gospel is that Christ is interested in them becoming fully human and partaking in the life that he offers for living today.

Agape Love

Churches that face transformation will have to center all that they are and all that is done on the principle of agape love. This will be a shock to the system of most corporate churches. Most of them want to be loved in return. They call it faithfulness. Agape love gives with little thought of return. It gives because giving is the essence of this kind of love.

Several years ago, I pastored a church in a small town. I had preached often about the principle of agape love and had illustrated that the church had to get in the habit of giving itself away to the community and to the needs of people around them. One Sunday proved to be a parable. I arrived at the church early for Sunday services and noticed a body under one of the trees on the church campus. I walked over to see and discovered a man just waking up from the night's sleep. He was homeless and had sought a soft place to sleep for the night.

I helped him get his things together and invited him to come into the church building for some coffee and doughnuts. It was apparent to me that he had not eaten in some time and needed further help. I called into the office one of the church deacons and introduced the man to him. I asked if the church could help him. Before the deacon could answer, I suggested that we take some money out of the general fund and get the man into a hotel so that he could rest and clean up. Since the service was about to start, I invited the man to come inside and worship with us. He sat at the back and after the services my wife and I took him out to lunch. Then I took him to a hotel so that he could have some privacy and tend to his needs. I checked back on him for the next two days and took him food and spent a lot of time with him talking about his life. He had been a successful businessperson who had become homeless after his divorce because of addiction to alcohol. Since that time he had been wandering from place to place. He claimed that he was a person of faith and that he only wished to someday get back on his feet again.

I contacted a businessperson I knew and asked him if he had a job the man might take to help him reestablish himself. Graciously, the business friend said he would find him something to do. I hurried back to the hotel to tell the man the good news, but he had checked himself out and was long gone. The person at the desk said he had no idea where he had gone.

On the next Sunday, I was confronted by the deacon, who said to me, "You see, preacher, I told you we would get burned if we helped this guy. He just took advantage of us." It seemed as if the deacon was correct. Yet I remembered that we were not accountable for making this man into our image of success. We were, however, responsible for helping him along the way. We learned how disappointing it can be when we minister to people when the end result is not what we had expected. We had honestly seen to his needs, shared our spiritual journey with him, encouraged him, and sought to invest in his future, but he turned away. We understood what Jesus must have understood when the Rich Young Ruler turned away. Loving with a kind of love that is vulnerable enough to expect nothing in return is difficult. But it is what we are called to do in the business of ministry to others. I have to believe that our loving efforts did not go unrewarded by God. Somewhere along his journey, I have to hope and pray that this man will remember kindness and will turn to the God we tried to portray for his every need.

Practicing agape love to the community will mean that the church is prepared to give and to provide services to others when they have nothing to give us in return. We cannot insist on their membership in return for our care. All we can do is continue to love them for Christ's sake and celebrate those times when we see them fully embrace the love that God offers them through us.

Embedded Nature

Ironically, this is not necessarily a negative concept. Taken in one direction, embeddedness can be an obstacle to growth and creativity. Someone once said that the last dying words of any organization are, "We've never done it that way before." Taken in another direction, the concept can provide insight and help for future days. An embedded nature is actually necessary for change because it forces any organization to examine those qualities of its calling that are unique, unchangeable, and essential. If a church is to transform itself, its personality, and its overall ministry, it has to get in touch with its gravitational center. Most churches believe that their gravitational center is Jesus Christ. Somehow, that is not always the case. It becomes clear that the church may actually work against the spirit of Christ when its status quo is threatened. During the civil rights era of the 1960s, for example, there were churches that actually posted people at the entrances to avoid being integrated. These actions certainly did not reflect the spirit of Christ. The gravitational center for a lot of churches are their history, tradition, denominational affiliation, underlying theology, or corporate status. It cannot always be assumed that every church centers itself on Christ and Christ's kingdom.

Three questions need to be explored in order to figure out where the gravitational center is and how embedded it is in the life of the church. These have to be answered with honesty. They need not be "spiritualized"; instead, they should reflect a sober look at reality.

1. What is it that is absolutely essential to the nature and calling of our church that cannot be compromised in any fashion?
2. What is it that makes this church distinct and that we are unwilling to change no matter what?
3. What is the one mandate for the future of this church that is non-negotiable?

The answers to these questions reflect the embedded nature of the church, its gravitational center. If a church wants to be transformed toward a kingdom-focused church, then Jesus Christ and his kingdom will have to be at the gravitational center. This will have to become the embedded nature of the church: to live as Christ lives, to reflect the qualities of the kingdom of God, to partner with God in redemptive mission. These are but a few of the essential qualities that have to be found at the center. In some cases, churches—if they are willing to be honest—will find that instead of the qualities of the kingdom, they reflect the qualities of institutionalization and religious bureaucracy to the community around them. Instead of reflecting the living presence of Jesus Christ, they might reflect only a story about one who lived two thousand years ago. Whatever the findings, the exercise will help any church to elevate its priorities and name its weaknesses.

This process will take courage. It is not for the faint-hearted church. It can lead to innovation in the way the church ministers to the community around it. In some cases, the church will have to shift the paradigm of its essential identity and claim another identity, one focused not upon a religious corporation but upon a living kingdom presence in the community. What does it take to shift the paradigm? How can the church become innovative?

Thomas Kuhn wrote about the scientific community and found that even scientists with their focus on research and the facts of discovery will at times deliberately skew the data they find in the direction of their expectations. So, we hear in the news that chocolate is good for you one day and will ward off cancer, and the next day we hear that chocolate is a health risk. The data is always being "adjusted" to support preconceived expectations. This happens all the time in churches. They will skew the feedback they receive from the community and believe they are being effective when, in reality, the community may be telling them it isn't listening any longer.

Churches ought to pay attention to Thomas Kuhn. He said that innovation happens upon the willingness to shift the assumed or familiar paradigm that is currently functioning to what might be imagined. "The one who embraces a new paradigm at an early stage must often do so in defiance of the evidence provided by normal observation."[11] What Kuhn found was that paradigm pioneers,[12] as Joel Barker calls them, are people who do not rely on everyday assumptions, but rather imagine new possibilities. Normal observation might lead most church members to believe that their church has value in the community or that their ministries are effective, whereas the paradigm pioneer might have a notion that all is not as it seems and envisions approaches and possibilities that, as far as she knows, do not exist yet anywhere.

When the visionary dreams, he exercises faith that goes beyond what many think of as faith. Kuhn puts it this way, "There must be faith that the new model or approach will succeed with the large problems that confront it, knowing only that the older model has failed with a few. A decision of that kind can only be made on faith."[13] If a church is serious about helping the community hear what it is saying, it must embrace visionaries and dreamers who can see what others fail to see. Every significant change within the culture has taken place at the edge of the culture's expectations. When a congregation truly makes a commitment to authentic ministry in a community, it will not be accomplished by just engaging in another program or minor changes in form. It will happen as a result of a complete commitment to being a different kind of church than in the past. The church will need to measure its new vision and commitment on two levels: First, "Will the shift in our identity and purpose be a true change of direction based upon what we have found within the community?"; and second, "Will this new direction or new vision bring the kind of commitment we need to effectively be on mission with God in our community?"

Learning to face the obstacles on the inside of the church can lead to new discoveries about the world around the church and can lead to a renewed commitment on the part of the church to become innovative and creative with God in the world.

Facing the Obstacles
The Ones on the Outside

It is not a natural tendency for most churches to look at themselves or their ministries from the outside in. Church members usually think in terms of carrying the gospel to the world, implying that the gospel is a commodity that the world needs and that the church has to share. Therefore the process becomes one of moving from inside the church to objects of concern on the outside. There are obstacles to the church's message that originate outside the doors of the church and factor into the receptivity potential of the church's message to the community.

There are two levels of obstacles. Level Ones are the most serious that the church will encounter in trying to get its message out. Level Twos are less serious, although still significant. Level Two obstacles are enough to discourage many churches from trying to get their message out to the world. It might be helpful to look at Level Two obstacles first.

Level Two Obstacles

A Level Two obstacle that is deep within the American value system is that of privacy. Americans value their privacy and do not appreciate when people or organizations impinge on it. When Congress made it possible for people to be added to a "do not call" list, the numbers were staggering. More than 60 million Americans rushed to sign up when the opportunity was opened to them to keep their telephone numbers private and out of the hands of telemarketers. The list has continued to grow.

I was asked to come to a church in North Atlanta to help them with a conference on understanding their community. Upon arrival at the church, the thing I noticed immediately was that across from the church was a very large subdivision. Great potential for the church, some might say. But the subdivision was not only gated, it had a ten-foot wall that ran the length of the highway. It was a clear symbol that this subdivision wanted to isolate itself from the world around it. When I asked the church members what outstanding characteristic they noticed about the subdivision across the street, none of them mentioned the wall. They had ignored the message of the wall, the gates, and the isolation that was suggested.

Privacy matters make it difficult for churches to communicate with individuals in their communities. The idea of going door to door with the gospel has long since vanished as an outreach tool. As the world grows more and more dangerous, people are tending to value their homes as sanctuaries or refuges from the world's problems. People seem to be more suspicious when they see a car in their driveway they do not recognize, or when they notice people in the community who do not seem to belong there. The one sure way a church can offend the community around it is to devalue the desire for privacy.

A second obstacle is to be found in the schedules by which people live. People do not work only from nine to five. People in communities work around the clock. Many sleep during the day and work at night. Many work odd shifts, on three days and off two days, on four days, off three. Many stores have figured this fact out and are now open twenty-four hours a day.

Yet many churches have not caught on. We still have services based on the agricultural clock. That is, the 11:00 hour was chosen because farmers could get their milking and some other chores done early on Sunday morning before heading to church.

I served in Bardstown, Kentucky, in a small church where most of the membership had farms. They were dairy farmers for the most part. It was a small church, and several of the men in the church would come to the services in their cleanest overalls. They knew that the church service was just a break in the routine of their daily chores and they wanted to come to church, eat dinner (as they called the noon meal), and then go into the fields. They did not want to change clothes. Time is precious to a farmer. It was not unusual for the fellow who led music to simply wipe off his boots and come to the service straight from the milking barn. However, not too many city folks even know why the services are at 11. Few, if any, have ever milked a cow. Seriously, though, many in the community work on Sunday morning, and it makes it impossible for them to attend at the time the church chooses to hold its services. For years Catholic churches have offered Mass on Saturday, and many Protestant churches, particularly megachurches, have added Saturday or weekday evening services. The idea of the 24-hour church may need to catch hold and grow even more.

Community values also function at Level Two. They can be beneficial, or serve as a hindrance, to the ministry of churches. Churches usually remain in a location for decades. But communities are always changing. What might have been a middle-class community in years past might now be a run-down community with crack houses on every block. Economic factors play a significant role in the way communities change. As communities grow more affluent, values tend to follow an affluent lifestyle and expectations, but as communities decline, the value system may also change. Declining economics can become a breeding ground for crime, homelessness, and depression in the community. Crime also exists in wealthy communities, but they tend to have more resources with which to cope than do declining communities. Facing a change of values in a community can be a formidable challenge to a lot of churches. Some do not cope with the changes at all and simply choose to move the church when a community declines. Seldom do they move if the community suddenly becomes affluent!

Some churches will stay in their location, no matter what. Even if the community changes from a family-centered community to a business and industrial district, some will remain. Thanks to the ease of travel in this country, people have no problems commuting to their favorite church. But what is troubling is to find a church located in an area where the community has changed from what the church has always assumed. In many towns, primarily white churches are located in communities near the city center, which has changed to African American or Latino, or has simply grown run-down and poor. It is not unusual to have a thriving church in such an area. But it is thriving because people drive in from their suburbs to the church in town. When a membership analysis is done in some of these churches, virtually none of the members live anywhere near the church and its changed community, nor do they reach out to the community. The people who live in the shadow of the steeple almost never bother to visit the church just across the street. They know who attends, what kind of cars they drive, and how well they dress. For a person in a poor or transitional community, this can be a significant obstacle. It is not unusual for these churches not to have a single member within a mile radius of the church–the area represented by the changed community–but rather to have members who attend from five to fifty miles away.

These obstacles are apparent. There are certainly others that your church may have noticed. But there are other obstacles that are not so apparent to churches that wonder why the community cannot hear what they are saying. I call these Level One obstacles.

Level One Obstacles

Level One obstacles are the most serious, though they are seldom noticed by churches. They function to keep the community deaf to the message of the church. The reason that they are seldom seen by the church is because they are so tightly connected to the church itself and the way it functions. What is often taken for granted, or is "business-as-usual" or normal operating procedure can confuse the community around the church and keep the church in isolation.

The first of these kinds of obstacles relates to the kingdom-building syndrome. Many people on the outside of the church are quite savvy about the church and its mission. Many of them know and understand, sometimes more clearly than church members, that the church's mission is to reflect Christ's mission. They are quick to sense when the church is existing for itself and building its own version of the kingdom. Most unchurched people care very little about church growth. What they do care about, and are surprised when they find them, are churches that are willing to sacrifice their comforts for the benefit of others.

It may seem quite natural for a church to want to grow, build large buildings, have recreational facilities, and be clothed in affluence. But people on the outside, the dechurched, as Mary Tuomi Hammond calls them, have the image of Jesus as a poor man. Somehow, the image of a cathedral doesn't make sense considering the one who had nowhere to lay his head.

The kingdom-building syndrome doesn't limit itself to bigger and more elaborate building projects. It is amazing how many people on the outside know what is going on in the life of a church they never attend. A few years ago, the church I grew up in became embroiled in controversy. I do not attend that church any longer because I live elsewhere. But I have family who are still in the church. It seems the church called a pastor who had a reputation for trouble wherever he went. As it turns out, he proved to be intent on whipping the church into the kind of church he wanted it to be. He literally told the membership one Sunday that if they did not believe as he did, they were probably lost. He actually invited people to leave who did not agree with him. Needless to say, this caused quite an uproar in the church.

I went back to my hometown while all this was going on, and I was having lunch at a popular restaurant there. I heard people in the next booth talking about the problems at the church. One of them remarked, "Well, I don't go there, but I hear people talking about the problems at such-and-such church all over town." The word had gotten out. Such-and-such church was in tumult, and folks all over town knew it.

The kingdom-building syndrome can be most destructive when leaders in a church try to make the church into their image instead of being faithful to the image of the kingdom of God. When that happens, the community learns of it. And when they learn of the troubles, they confirm what they have always suspected about church people. This becomes a significant obstacle to overcome. No matter what you tell some people, they will not believe and they will not hear because they have seen too much dysfunctional religion and kingdom building all around them that is not consistent with what they believe Christianity should be. The lesson to be learned is simply this: Just because people do not attend your church, do not think for a moment that they are ignorant to what goes on. They are constantly forming opinions in regard to what they see. If a church truly wants to change its personality, its image, and its mission to be conformed to Jesus Christ, it will have to prove it to those on the outside over and over again.

Another Level One obstacle that comes at the church from the attitudes of those on the outside is the church's track record of community involvement. If you care to notice, nearly every company today touts its track record of community involvement. Many companies have in their mission statement a goal of community improvement. Companies want to be good neighbors. Unfortunately, most churches don't. This may seem harsh to say, but given the resources that most churches take in each year, only a small percentage of those resources ever wind up in the community in tangible ways.

Some churches are actively building Habitat houses, helping with the Red Cross blood drives, and aiding victims of flooding or fire. Many churches will give money to homeless persons who come by the church, and at Thanksgiving and Christmas churches will prepare food baskets and the like. These are notable and helpful to the community. But the fact still remains that many Christians have forgotten that it is the job of the believer to care for the widows and orphans.

I have often used this analogy in church consultations. "Suppose that tonight a terrible storm will hit your town. The only damage, however, will be right here on this spot. A giant tornado will sweep down from the heavens and wipe this church and all its building off this block. Nothing will be left, just an empty lot. How would the community react? Would people in your community drive by and remark, "What used to be on this corner before last night's storm?" Or would an army of persons from the community be here bright and early the next morning rebuilding the church because they know the community cannot live without it?"

How vital is your church to the community? Is the church a place where the community can gather to improve the educational level of the children or adults? Is it a place that will stand in the gap for abused persons in the community? Is it a place where lonely senior citizens in the community can have the quality of their lives enhanced? Is the church a community of believers who embody the ethics of the kingdom, the love of the kingdom, and the hope for the kingdom? If your church is passionate about these things, the community will be impacted. Kingdom values will become the true core of the church. They will never be compromised or abandoned. "Only those values about which you are so passionate that you would never, under any conditions, give them up qualify as truly core."[1] Without the core values of the kingdom, it will be impossible for any church to change what it is in the eyes of the community at large.

A pastor in a small town called me recently. I had worked with his church over the years and encouraged their attempts to interface with the community through ministry-based efforts. The pastor had received a call from the local bank and was asked to have the church trustees at the bank for a meeting on a certain Tuesday. He had no idea what the problem was, but they all appeared with the bank's board of directors to hear what they had to say. The president of the bank said to the pastor, "We have $20,000 in our safe here that was given some time ago by an estate for community benevolence. It has been here ever since and our auditors want it removed from our records. We do not know how to use this money, but we know your church does. Will you take this money and use it in your ministries to the community?" The pastor was stunned. Of course they would. How many banks want to give a church money free and clear? But this church had a reputation in town for consistently caring for the community and town. Even the bank noticed.

If the community doesn't think well of your church's track record with regard to community involvement, it will pay scant attention to what your church says, no matter how passionately the church may express its concern for the well-being or salvation of those in the community. Without a repeated track record of actions that are valued in the community, and that reflect the core values of the kingdom of God, the community will remain deaf.

A third Level One obstacle, the kind that is serious enough to keep the message of the church from being heard in the community, is single-issue tunnel vision. People on the outside of the church are turned off by churches that constantly rail against personal sinfulness. Most people do not have to be reminded of their personal sin. They live with the knowledge of it day after day. That is, they live with the knowledge of the kinds of sin that churches tend to rail against. They have heard for years Christians condemning smoking, drinking, dancing, and a whole laundry list of things. People who are unchurched can rattle off all kinds of sins. They only have to turn on the television and watch a television evangelist with a stern look pointing a bony finger at the screen telling the audience that it will go to hell if it doesn't quit sinning against God, and then naming the sins for them. People who are unchurched don't pay much attention to these condemnations because long ago they admitted they are not perfect. And many of them have made peace with that notion. They know they will never live up to the ideal that Christians seem to embody, so they have learned how to manage. But they pride themselves that they do not commit grave sins, the kind they see on the nightly news. People will acknowledge sin. They recognize it readily, especially when they are on the receiving end of wrongdoing.[2] But people can also justify their behavior and ignore their behavior.

Sin is real. But the characterization of sin by preachers, the media, and popular culture has seldom arrived at the devastating reality of it. It almost takes a horrific event such as the bombing of the Murrah building in Oklahoma City or the attack on the World Trade Center buildings on September 11 to bring the reality of sinful behavior to the forefront of most people's thinking. People can ignore what they believe to be the minor sins of individuals, the ones that many Christians are so vocal about, but they have a difficult time dealing with evils that are shocking, global, political, or cultural in nature. This is where the culture becomes insecure.

Just after the events of September 11· a few religious people almost celebrated the event as an opportunity to compel people back to God. This was the event they had been looking for that would shock the nation into recognition of its sin and force it back to God. They relished the idea that the news media reported on the large number of people who were flooding the churches in New York City. Surely, they thought, revival was on the way. But scarcely two weeks after the attack, the churches saw declines in the number of people who came there to pray.[3] Americans were not on the road to revival. Most of the ones who crowded into the churches went there for solitude to think and to pray for the victims. They did not go to church, by and large, to get right with God before the end came. They just wanted a place that was a sharp contrast to the violence they had encountered. They needed to feel secure again.

A church that focuses much of its attention on what the culture sees as "minor sins" of the individual will largely be ignored. Today there are actions that some Christians call sin that the culture would not consider calling sin. For example, shopping on Sunday is not a sin to the community at large or even to many Christians today. Many people do not see as sin choices people make with regard to sexual behavior, such as living together without marriage, or gay or lesbian lifestyles. Relativism is the foundational building block of postmodernism. In the postmodern mind, all things are relative, and what is good for one is not necessarily good for another.[4] Nothing is absolute.

In the 1960s, a book appeared on the scene called *Situation Ethics: The New Morality.*[5] It became a sort of "bible" to a lot of emerging postmoderns looking for a way out of the strictures of their upbringing, though most of them had no idea of the tenets of postmodernism at the time. Fletcher argued against the idea of any absolute right or wrong, and said that what was right was based on the choices that a person made. All that Fletcher required in his ethic was that no harm be done to another. As Harry Lee Poe points out, "For Fletcher, the standard was love. He would ask simply, 'What is the loving thing to do?'"[6] Much of the thesis of Fletcher's argument is in full flower in the larger culture. Libertarians today have the same kind of philosophy as Fletcher. As long as no one is deprived of life, liberty, economic well-being, and so on, Libertarians do not see much that would be classified by most people as sinful behavior.

But when Christians adopt a single issue, such as homosexuality or gambling or drinking, and condemn it time and time again in their churches and in the media and elevate it to grave sin, much of the culture turns a deaf ear. If homosexuality, gambling, or drinking doesn't affect them, they do not worry about it. Gay and lesbian marriages, for example, may not directly affect their marriages, so they may not care about what others do.

They tend to see Christians as making an issue out of something that for them is not an issue.

Many unchurched people are also quick to see inconsistency. They may hear of a congregation condemning a certain lifestyle or action as sinful, but they may also notice a large number of obese Christians struggling to walk out of the church building. They may see church members pass by homeless persons on the corner. They might hear prejudiced attitudes toward people of other ethnic origins. They notice these sins. Of course, not all Christians do these things. There are great hosts of sensitive Christian people who do demonstrate care to the needy in tangible ways, who do live lives that are consistent with what they believe and who are not prejudiced toward others. However, those who are inconsistent tend to represent a norm for a lot of people who are deaf to Christianity or who have been wounded by churches.

If a church really wants to engage the community on the issue of the devastation of sinful behavior, it has to do so with an approach other than mere condemnation. I interviewed a young man who was living with his gay lover. I asked him what he thought about churches and if they had helped him in any way. Tears welled up in his eyes, and he said through a choked-up voice, "I have needed love all my life. I was raised by an abusive father and often beaten. A friend took me to his church, and I felt better for a while, until they found out I was gay, and then they kicked me out. I don't believe churches want people like me around."

Instead of single-issue tunnel vision, especially in the arena of human sinfulness, the church that wishes to engage the community must offer people a resolution to the problems of sinfulness in their lives. One of the most common by-products of a lifestyle of sinfulness is the feeling of emptiness that so many mask with alcohol and drug abuse. Many people have suffered losses of marriages, friends, finances, and self-esteem as a result of their lifestyle. Here the church can offer a sympathetic ear and a helping hand. Christians have to remember that they too have been rescued by Jesus Christ from potentially destructive behaviors. Understanding that it is only the grace of God in our lives that separates us from so many who are caught up in sinful behavior ought to be instructive to a caring congregation. People need help processing grief, loss, and insecurity. Pastoral care is vital for hurting people.

In many cases, people are going to need consistent, long-term care to overcome the demons in their lives. Cultivating friendships that do not judge people, but care for them as Christ cared for the woman caught in the act of adultery, is vital. When a community senses that a congregation is actually willing to accept people where they are in life and love them into a relationship with Christ, they will respond.

For a lot of people who are outside the church, the most meaningful gift a congregation can provide is the opportunity to find purpose in their lives. It is anecdotal, perhaps, but can be easily observed by any casual student of the culture, that many young people are simply wandering from job to job, from apartment to apartment, from one group of friends to another. Those who have been victims of substance abuse are the ones that seem to wander the most. They can have a very difficult time getting their lives back on track, especially after losing jobs, savings, and, in some cases, marriages.

There are precious too few halfway houses in communities that will help facilitate entrance back into wholeness. There are few churches that have ministries in this area. But it is vital today given the availability of drugs on the street. And it is a problem that is affecting families that have always been a part of church life. Drug abuse and alcoholism is no respecter of persons.

Matt was brought up in a Christian home, but got hooked on prescription drugs as a result of an automobile accident. His cousin John, also brought up in a Christian home, got addicted to crack cocaine. Both boys found help through the Penfield Christian Home in Georgia. But the home is one of only a few, and they are limited in the number of people they can help. Churches that want to minister to people who are caught in sinful behavior or destructive lifestyles should consider sponsoring a home like Penfield. There are enough churches in every county to have at least one or two homes that can be dedicated to helping people get off drugs and offering them a fresh start in life.

Money is not the problem. Most churches, especially larger ones, have enough money to build elaborate buildings or to sponsor expensive mission trips for their members, but they need to consider also the needs of people within their own Jerusalem. A drug recovery program that is effective can go a long way toward changing a community's image of a church. They can be assured they will never run out of people with whom to minister.

If a church is willing, it can overcome the negative obstacles that are hurled toward it from the outside. It will overcome these obstacles by naming them for what they are and setting in place a response to them. If a church realizes that it is justly being characterized from the outside as a self-centered kingdom builder, one that cares little for community involvement, or one that is guilty of single-issue tunnel vision and condemnation, it should work to put into place a proactive response to turn opinions around. Instead of being self-centered and building the church for the comfort of the congregation, the church would do well to focus resources that it would spend on itself toward ministries shaped for the community. It could plunge into the community and insist on being related to the ethos of the community. It will become an active good neighbor to the community, sponsor community events, and advocate for the community when necessary. And instead of being the church known for blasting others because of their sins, it will become a hospital for sinners. It will be the place where the community understands the church to be in the business of repairing damaged lives, and restoring wholeness to broken people. Nothing will be so effective in the long run as counteracting the negative images of the church that come from the outside with a vision for greater ministry that proceeds from the inside. Every criticism of the church from the outside is an opportunity to adjust its personality and its ministry in terms of the ones who need it the most.

8

How to Listen to the World around You

This book has put a lot of emphasis on paying attention to the culture. Unfortunately, most church members have seldom been exposed to the importance of the culture's point of view. It is not that church members are callous to the culture. Rather, it is that not much emphasis has been placed on listening to it instead of speaking against it. Good listening skills are essential for working among those who are not part of the church culture. Those who are outside the fellowship of churches have often endured years of prodding and invitations from friends and family to be a part of the Christian community. Yet they remain outside. The goal of learning to listen to the unchurched is not the development of a method to bring them in. It is instead a serious engagement with people outside the church on the basis of respect for them and care for them as human beings.

Part of Jesus' ministry was invitation. He invited people to come and observe what he was doing. "Come and see," he would often say. It was an approach to people that encouraged questions. Anytime we encounter something that is new to us, we naturally have questions. The problem with the perception of unchurched people is that they do not think that churched people want to answer their questions. Much of what we need to do with the unchurched is to give them an opportunity to ask questions, to probe deeply into the questions that surround Christianity and faith in general.

It has always been problematic to me that it was not until I arrived at the seminary that I encountered people who were not taken aback by some of my questions. I was often frustrated as a child in my home church when my Sunday school teachers did not seriously attempt to address my doubts and my questions about the miracles, the resurrection, the violence in the Old Testament, and a host of other questions I had. At one point, a Sunday school teacher told my parents that I was disruptive because I asked too many questions and did not simply accept what I was told to believe. I was raised in a very conservative church that expected people to simply believe what was being said, not to question what was being said.

Unchurched people already tend to believe that church is the place where they are invited to not think.[1] It is quite normal for people to be skeptical when they hear stories that do not make sense in terms of their everyday experience. Step back a minute and put yourself in the shoes of a person with little to no religious orientation or upbringing. Someone tells her the story about the burning bush and Moses' experience. She will tend to ask the same questions that Moses must have asked. How can a bush burn but not be consumed? How can a voice come out of the bush? None of the story makes sense. It is as fanciful as any fairy tale in her thinking. She may be told that it was a miracle and that God could do whatever God chose to do. God could make a bush burn and not be consumed. God could speak in an audible voice to Moses. What is there that is so hard to believe about that? But most likely, she has already decided the answer. She has decided, since her experience of life demands a more practical explanation to things that are out of the ordinary. Moses just thought the bush was burning because the leaves were perhaps golden and the sun was bright and reflecting off of them. Maybe a slight breeze was rustling the leaves and causing the sunlight to be refracted in ways that almost looked like flames. The voice he heard was probably a result of being too hot in the midday sun or maybe a hallucination. There might be other conclusions that she would bring to the story that made more sense to her than the account recorded in the Bible. How can she believe such a fantastic tale when her everyday experience disproves all of it?

The problem she has is not unbelief. The problem she has is there are often too few Christians who will engage her doubts and who would be willing to dialogue with her about what the story can teach us by way of parable or metaphor. Most faithful church members may themselves be too insecure to venture the possibility that the story might be a work of fiction in order to tell a greater story. Unchurched people who are invited to not think about what they are told or about the stories they read in Scripture are in effect told to not struggle with matters of faith. They get the message that to struggle to believe is somehow wrong. Most of them have had to struggle all of their lives to believe certain things: hard work can bring rewards, people are for the most part good and not evil, love is a positive experience between two people, or things work out in the end. They struggle because they do work hard and are not always rewarded, they meet people who are not good but sinister, they suffer a divorce, and, in the end, things often fall apart. Yet people often continue to struggle to believe in the positive in spite of the negatives in their lives.

Unchurched people have a suspicion that emotion, mood, or feelings are devalued in most church settings. That is, they have the sense that Christians have to be always smiling and that when they are depressed, angry, or sorrowful, Christians are not free to express their true emotions. Unchurched people have seen too many "artificial smiles" on the faces of Christians, especially in the Christian media, and grow weary of them trying to put a positive spin on things. "Scripture verses are often used to buttress this insistence on expressing only positive feelings,"[2] according to Mary Hammond. Unchurched people do not buy for a moment that Christians are always happy. They suspect that when they are away from the church, they throw fits, use language that is not "praiseworthy," and can be as depressed as anyone else when things go badly. What they want proven to them is that Christians are honest enough to confront their feelings, emotions, and moods in ways that suggest they have a hidden source of strength even in the worst of times.

Those outside the church also have figured out that most of the time church members seem to them to be like little children following the Pied Piper. They view many religious leaders as those who mesmerize others to follow their way of thinking. They have witnessed, especially among television preachers, the scandals of the PTL Club, the constant emphasis on prosperity religion, and the swarms of people in giant healing crusades and they are deeply suspicious. They doubt that a person confined to a wheelchair can be slapped on the forehead and suddenly get out of the chair and walk. Such an action makes no sense to them. They simply figure out that either nothing was really wrong with the person or that someone has been dishonest.

Gene Scott, a television preacher who died recently, had a vast empire that covered the globe with his church services. He lived a lavish lifestyle, smoked cigars while he was preaching, rode motorcycles, traveled in limousines, and reportedly gave large sums of money away to area causes,[3] but by some estimates took in over one million dollars each month[4] through his ministries. Unchurched people sit back amazed that so many could be "duped" by these religious leaders.[5] They will often project those feelings into local churches, especially those who have pastors who are always in the news advocating for certain types of behavior, or who are politically vocal on issues like abortion, prayer in the schools, and other hot button issues.

Unchurched people including those who have given up on church life, want the freedom to follow their own dreams, convictions, and insights without having to be led by someone else. They do not want their test of faithfulness to be that they never complain about what they are told, or what they are asked to do. Freedom is important to many postmoderns today. A church that offers freedom of expression and free thinking is much more likely to not be cast in the mold of the Pied Piper syndrome.

Learning to Listen

Most of the time, the reason why the community cannot hear what we are saying to them is that we are too busy talking, and not listening. The sermon is a prime example. Church members come each Sunday to hear a sermon. Everything tends to lead up to the sermon or homily. It is the responsibility of the faithful church person to sit back and take it all in. They are not encouraged to talk back, or to dialogue with the one giving the sermon. In many African American churches and some conservative churches in the South, it has long been the custom to say, "Amen," when the congregation agrees with something that is said from the pulpit. This is often the extent of any feedback that is given by the congregation. But it is not dialogue.

The unchurched person senses that churches are always about giving sermons to the community. They feel they are expected to sit up straight and listen. I once counseled a fellow minister who was having a few problems in his marriage. I knew the person very well and I knew that he was normally very sensitive to his wife's needs. But he told me that she often accused him of preaching to her or giving her a sermon whenever he offered her advice or even when she asked for his advice. He became more and more frustrated to the extent that he was afraid to say anything to her for fear of being accused of preaching. As it turned out, his wife had grown up under a dominant set of parents who were always scolding her, and had been a member in a fundamentalist church in which the pastor constantly shouted at the congregation each Sunday. No wonder she projected those same expectations on her husband when he tried to give her loving advice. She saw him as a preacher and could never separate his preaching from his conversations with her.

The unchurched often have expectations similar to this wife. They are always prepared to hear a sermon. And for many of them the sermon is seldom expected to be good news. One of the reasons the community cannot hear what the churches are saying is they have little to no expectation of being able to respond, to dialogue, or to have someone really listen to them.

If churches are to be seriously engaged in listening to the culture around them, they have to overcome some habits that are deeply ingrained in their attitudes toward unchurched persons in the community. One of those attitudes is that unchurched people are people we do not really want to have conversation with in the first place.

There is a hidden surprise here. The unchurched person will often be far more receptive than we believe when we want to discuss matters of faith or church life with them. When they find out that someone is truly interested in what they have to say, they can provide us with a fascinating view of the world we rarely see. I believe that one of the reasons the New Testament is so detailed with the encounters of Jesus among all kinds of people is to reflect Jesus' own fascination with the varied lives of people. He really wanted to know what lepers thought, how the rich lived, what the Pharisees believed about God, and what motivated the person living in flagrant sin. There is no way that Christians can hope to minister to the community and be on target with their needs until we take time to know them. Dialogue is the key.

Dialogue is essential to the process of understanding why the community cannot hear what we are saying. Dialogue is a two-way street. It is not a license for the Christian to defend what she or he believes. Dialogue is an open invitation to get to know someone else at deeper levels. It may lead to authentic witness and faith sharing, but the first goal is to honor the other person as having something to say to us, to have opinions, to have value. A way we project to others that we value them is to be willing to dialogue.

Dialogue is like a dance. The best dancers are the ones who, when they dance together, the observer cannot always tell who is leading. Two people are simply moving together in rhythm and painting a flowing picture. Have you ever noticed a heated discussion between two people? The volume increases. Faces grow red. The casual observer is immediately struck by the fact that neither of the two in a heated discussion is listening to the other. Rather, what they are doing is blasting their opinions forward. It is simply the case of two people who are being monological. They just happen to be staring at each other while they are delivering their monologues.

But have you ever observed a couple of lovers over dinner? Both of them tend to be leaning into each other, speaking softly while gazing into each other's eyes, eager to hear what the other is saying. There are usually periods of silence, with smiles. It is clear they are thinking about what is being said. They are often completely oblivious to the sounds of clinking dishes around them and other conversations. They are in their own world, two people who are as one.

This is what has to happen when we truly have dialogue with others in the community. There might not be the intimacy of lovers, but there certainly can be the attitude of vulnerability to the other. It is the kind of vulnerability that invites others to explore with you, to give you new insights, and to benefit from your own thoughts. Silence is critical to dialogue. People become very weary with others who just ask them question after question and wait for response. That is not true dialogue. Dialogue is never forced. It flows. People need time to consider what the other has said. They need time to reflect. They need time to demonstrate that what the other has said has struck a chord of truth. This is often done in those times of silence. "Times of silence, pauses in the encounter, can slow the pace and cause us as witnesses really to look at the person, to consider her life, to value her as a person, to feel compassion."[6] Do not be surprised as you learn to dialogue with others that they have deep levels of faith and commitment. What the unchurched have to say to us is worth hearing. It just may be that they are hearing from God in ways we do not hear. But we will never know if we do not take time to invite them into the living room of our lives.

One of the most significant ingrained habits is selective listening. Most people selectively listen. If we did not, we would go crazy with all the sounds that impact us. Right now, as I write this chapter, my ears are being assaulted. The rattle of the keyboard as my fingers fly across the keys, the aquarium bubbling in the corner of the room, the whirr of the hard drive, the birds singing just outside the window, and the air conditioning clicking on and off. But the sound I am listening to the most is the voice between my ears. If I am to finish this book, I cannot listen to all the other sounds.

Selective listening is foundational to what we want to hear. We want to be encouraged, so we listen for encouragement. We want to be loved, so we listen for loving words. We don't spend our time trying to selectively listen to people who say negative things to us. We try to ignore those words and those people. Often when we listen to someone, we listen to what we have already decided we want to hear.

If we approach the community with selective listening, we will do our best to hear the positive things others have to say about faith. We won't bother to listen to the nuances of their language that might suggest a struggle to believe, or hidden anger. Church members should be encouraged to talk less and listen more. Give people an opportunity to explain at great length what they feel about Christianity. Be sure that your body language is inviting to them. Lean toward them as they speak and look them in the eyes. Don't become distracted by other sounds. Concentrate on what they are saying. Smile and nod, don't frown. Give them every evidence that you are truly fascinated by what they are saying.

When they suggest a response from you, don't be so eager to defend. Ask them to further explain what they mean. Keep giving the people you talk with an opportunity to fully talk about what they believe. Don't take notes. Note-taking intimidates some people, and they will be hesitant to really be honest. Simply listen, be authentic, caring, and loving toward them. Let them know by your facial responses, body language, and eye contact that you find what they are saying interesting and that you are learning from them.

As you listen to people, learn to face your own prejudices. We all have them. Prejudice is nothing more than our tendency to prejudge things. We do it all the time. Prejudice can be helpful. We prejudge that electrical wires that have fallen in an ice storm are dangerous, so we do not go near them. But prejudice can obviously be a crippling reality. If we view the community around us, having prejudged them, as people who do not care about spiritual things, we will miss the fact that research indicates overwhelmingly that most people are highly interested in things spiritual. Or if we believe that the community around us prefers to live in rebellion against God, we will miss the fact that most unchurched people read the Bible, pray, and talk with their friends about their spiritual lives. Most Christians work hard to not be prejudiced against people because of race, ethnic origin, or economic status. But prejudice can be strong against the lifestyles of the unchurched.

A few years ago, a church decided to overcome its prejudice against NASCAR racing. The church was located near one of the largest of the NASCAR tracks in the South. Every time a race was conducted, the streets around the church became clogged with people going to the races on Sunday, and the church members could not even get to their church for services. So they decided that when a race was scheduled, they would move the services to Saturday. Then they went beyond. They went to the race on Sunday to set up booths to provide water to the campers at the racetrack, to provide medical help for minor injuries or heat-related illnesses, and to use golf carts to transport people who had difficulty walking, all the time wearing T-shirts with their church name embroidered on them. It provided opportunity for conversation, practical ministry to people, and created a positive image of the church in the community and at the racetrack. Soon they began to notice visitors in their Saturday services who had come early to camp out and attend the race on Sunday.

Another church is in a community with a large dirt track, where sometimes more than 10,000 people will attend the races on Saturday nights. The church has become so involved that the racetrack officials asked the pastor of the church to be the chaplain of the track, and he rides the pace car and has prayer before each race. These churches have overcome prejudice against this one particular lifestyle and sought to find ways to minister to people who love racing.

An effective listener will also work to overcome point-of-view blindness.[7] This "blindness" occurs when we become so preoccupied with our view of something that we cannot see another person's view. Have you ever heard anyone, especially in a moment of frustration while trying to explain something to another, say, "Why don't you understand? It is as clear as it can be." Yes, it is clear all right, to the person speaking. But the other person just doesn't get it. Have you ever told a joke that grips you with laughter only to find out that another person has no idea why you think it is so funny? Puns illustrate point-of-view blindness beautifully. The intention is to take what one person knows and to twist the meaning, but to never fully reveal the hidden meaning.

People who are experts in any area of life develop point-of-view blindness. It is natural. This is because in order to be experts, they have to concentrate energy, learning, and skills toward mastery. In effect, their world becomes, for example, golf, physics, or cooking. Professional golfers master their skills so effectively that they are absorbed with golf. No two golfers have the same stroke. Each has developed a unique approach to the game that works for her. They cannot explain how they are able to know instinctively which club to use, how hard to swing, and how to direct the ball. It comes as a result of years of work toward mastery. They become one with the game. They can show an amateur how to address the ball, how to keep the swing square to the ball, and how to read a green, but the amateur will not become a professional after one conversation with a pro. The amateur will have no idea of the thousands of balls the pro has hit out of the bunker in practice sessions. The amateur has a point of view about the game that is blind to the years that it will take to shoot like a pro. He may have an idea of the years, but until he has spent the years of practice, he will not fully realize what it will take. Likewise, the pro has developed skills to such an effective level that she cannot adequately instruct an amateur to avoid the slice. She can explain the mechanics needed to avoid a hook or slice, but her muscles are too well trained. The only time she will hit a slice is when she wants to do so. How can she tell an amateur just starting out what that is like? Her point of view is that of a professional who has a mastery over the game that the amateur can only dream about unless he is willing to spend decades of work and energy.

Those of us raised in church can have a point-of-view blindness regarding others who have no idea what church life is about. We must never assume that the unchurched person understands our church language, illustrations, or emotional attachments to faith. Many committed Christians have not lived in the world of the unchurched community in quite a long time, if at all. Therefore, we will have to begin where the unchurched or perhaps dechurched persons begin in their journeys and learn along with them. The unchurched person will learn new things about faith as we dialogue together, and we will refresh our memories of experiences long forgotten in the journey toward faith.

A few years ago, I served a church near my home as interim pastor. It was a joyful fifteen months, during which Sunday after Sunday I tried to encourage the members to identify with those in the community who were not Christians or who were not members of a church community. One of the members told me that she had been working with a young man in the community who simply did not understand baptism. She had exhausted her convictions about baptism, and he still did not understand. She had blindness to his point of view. Her own conviction of baptism's importance had blinded her. They were just two people blindly stumbling along on two different paths, neither traveling on the other's.

I decided to help the church remember baptism in a way that would give them a new range of emotion about it and perhaps new spiritual insights. I preached about baptism knowing that many in the congregation had been baptized ten, twenty, or even thirty years ago and had long since forgotten what it was like for them. I went over the significance of baptism, our Lord's baptism, and what the church believed about the sacrament.

Prior to the service I had done quite a bit of preparation. I had instructed the people in charge of the sound system that I wanted a certain piece of music to be played at a certain time in the service. I picked out three women and two men in the service to help me. I asked them to be ready to join me at the front of the church and to hold bowls of water.

At a certain place in my sermon, I called for the "ministers" to come forward. The five church members came forward with their bowls filled with water and faced the congregation. I then asked the congregation to be in an attitude of prayer and to come forward two by two and go to one of the five ministers with the bowls of water. As each of two persons came to the ministers with the bowl of water, they were asked to put their right hands into the water. They were asked to feel the water and to gather up the water and pour it onto the hand of their partner. They were to baptize each other's hand.

The music that played over and over again as the people came down to the front of the church was Alison Krauss's "Down to the River to Pray" from the film *Oh Brother, Where Art Thou?*[8] As the music softly played, the church members were asked to quietly remember their own baptisms, to live them once again. Then they returned to their seats and remained in a spirit of prayer. It was a moving service though which, probably for the first time, many church members relived what it was like to be baptized and pondered baptism's significance to them.

The church member who had been stumbling along in her conversation with a young man who did not understand baptism told me that the next week she related the experience of the service with him. It led to other questions, and the discussion provided him some insight to what she had been trying to say to him. She had gained new images with which to explain what baptism meant. He now had a clearer understanding of the symbolic nature of baptism.

Learning to truly listen to others results in demonstrating to them our true love and appreciation for who they are. Every opportunity to listen to the unchurched community around us is an opportunity to explore together thoughtful insights of each other's spiritual existence. We are enabled to travel into each other's worlds and to explore regions that have been foreign to us. One of the most important things to remember is that authentic listening helps us to avoid placing ourselves as Christians in spiritual authority over others. Postmoderns have a difficult time with authority from any direction. We are not likely to be effective if we come across to them as spiritual masters. Being willing to listen to others, to be vulnerable to their questions and insights, places us on level ground. It avoids any notions of superiority.

Using Listening Skills (Individual to Individual)

The communities in which we live are full of people who want to be listened to. We all value people who seek us out in order to listen to us.

People who want to hear what we are saying are placing value in us and expressing confidence that what we have to say is worth hearing. Learning to be redemptive as we listen to others is a skill that can be developed and viewed as a positive approach to faith sharing.

One of the first things that must be done is to learn to sense the religious orientation of others. Listen carefully, over time, to what they speak about. How much of their normal conversation is laced with spiritual overtones? How much of it seems to be angry speech or prejudiced speech or loving speech? Even the negative overtones that are picked up can inform us as to whether or not people have likely been injured by religion or by religious people, or if they are simply not aware or are confused about the dynamics of Christian life.

Learn to communicate genuine interest in another human being.[9] As Christians we need to be encouragers of others and to do so in a way that communicates their value both to us and to God. We live in a world in which people are often devalued. How refreshing it is when we meet someone who really does value us.

My students had to work for ten weeks in a missional setting among the homeless, abused, or neglected people in our community. It became more that just an assignment for them. In reading their verbata, I saw the development of genuine interest on the part of my students in the stories of people who had become homeless. I found homeless persons who said that they felt more human just because someone bothered to listen to them and not just hand them food or clothing and send them on their way.

Christian hospitality was a key method of witness in the early church community. Christians opened their lives up to the community, to the traveler, to the homeless, to the sick, and those who needed a friend. "Tertullian depicted a universal union of Christians evidenced by their peaceful communion, title of brotherhood, and bond of hospitality."[10] It was even the case that later on the Christians had to develop some safeguards in terms of their practice of openness and hospitality to all. "Generosity toward strangers prompted the churches to search for some safeguards, for they soon experienced the deceptions of false prophets and charlatans, a consequence of deliberate naivete."[11] The point, however, is clear. Their spirit was one of openness to strangers and that of hospitality toward all, so much so that some were taken advantage of, but that fact did not seem to stop the practice.

A second step follows the sensing of people's religious orientation and the communication of genuine interest in them as human beings. It is simply that we give feedback on the person's story.[12] "I had no idea you were once a university professor. I have always known you as a businessperson. When did you teach at the university?" is a confirmation that you have learned something about another and that you were really listening as that person told his or her story. It is an opportunity to reinforce the value of the other person's life and experience. It can lead us into opportunities to discuss the gifts that God gives to us and the gifts that we can give to each other.

A third step is exploring together religious concepts.[13] When the other person hints at or directly addresses a spiritual issue, take time to ask what the person thinks and explore how the matter impacts the person's life. Be prepared to explain how the issue impacts your life too. In some cases, the person will want to know more. This is an opportunity to provide helpful materials and to begin a study of the concept together. Remember, this kind of occasion opens the door for education and for mentoring, so don't miss these opportunities. I had a student who told her small group that she had had such an opportunity, but she had frozen up and did not address the person's comments. If seminary students have a difficult time with this process, it is probably something that happens to all of us. Listen carefully. Don't manufacture a religious discussion. Let it arise naturally, and when it does, go further with it.

Fourth, make sure that experiences of faith are kept simple and yet personal. Show how God has met your needs, not with religious jargon, but with everyday illustrations. Ask if the other person has had similar experiences, especially in times of crisis. It never hurts the conversation to ask the other person, "Does what I am saying make sense to you?" Or, "What did you just hear me say?" Clarify what the other person has said to you by saying, "I think I heard you say…"

Fifth, if the other person responds positively to your testimony of what you have experienced in faith, ask how you might be helpful in probing the issues of faith more deeply. Move slowly. Don't push, but allow the person to test the waters. Keep listening to questions the topic raises in the other person and to his or her responses. Tell stories from Scripture that might illustrate a point. "Your task is to help the lost (or unchurched) person become aware of the movement of God in his heart."[14] The person is learning to drive the car, and you are there to encourage him or her and to help navigate the journey. Sometimes you will need to clarify, sometimes amplify, and sometimes introduce new concepts. If the person says something that sparks new insight in your own life, be sure to say so, letting the person know that you have learned together.

A sixth step to remember is silence. Give God time to work. Let the words you speak and the encouragement you give be like dough that needs time to rise. Be available and be an honest friend. Be vulnerable enough for the other person to tell you any doubt or any emotion. Keep understanding the other person, keep praying, and keep sharing insights into the world of faith from your experience. You will be the kind of witness who may not know all the answers, like the blind man whom Jesus healed. He said he did not know much about the controversy over Jesus but that what he did know was that once he was blind, but now he could see. As a witness, you do not have to know all the answers, just tell others what you've seen.

Using Listening Skills (Church to Community)

A church that wants the community to hear what it is saying must learn to listen to the community. There are three steps in the process of learning to listen to the community. Unless a church makes a deliberate effort to work these three steps, it will not likely succeed in convincing the community that it is seriously interested in what the community has to say.

Step One

The church has to be absolutely willing to take input from the community and to take it seriously. To do so, the church has to focus its *collective attention* on the community, the way individuals focus attention on another when listening. Does your church have a Web site? It makes little difference how small a church might be, it could always use a Web site. The reason is simple. Most people, especially those under the age of thirty, do their research on the Web. They have learned the enormous power of the Web. People are shopping more and more on the Internet. Two companies that research Web activity place the amount of yearly commerce on the Web at nearly 350 billion dollars.[15] Some estimate that there may be as many as 180 million people on-line in the United States and Canada and millions more worldwide.[16] This number will continue to grow as innovations on the Web multiply.

People will visit your church via the Web before they ever step foot inside the building. The Web site needs to create immediately in the mind of the visitor an openness to the community. There needs to be a feedback section on the Web site where people in the community can comment on what they find by way of ministries offered, times for services, and the like. Invite Web visitors to suggest actions the church might take to meet a need in the community. Provide an opportunity for people to register, if they wish, to receive the church newsletter or other communications. Be sure to let the visitor know that you will only visit them in person if they request a visit. Develop a chat room where not only members can converse but visitors as well.

Publish on the Web materials that are helpful to the community. Resources that link to service agencies for job training, dealing with addiction, financial planning information, recreational activities, etc., should be on your site. Make the Web site as interactive as possible so that information can be gained not only about your church but about its partnership organizations. For example, if your church works with Habitat for Humanity, be sure to link to their Web site. Publish helpful materials for individual Bible study, sermons that speak to issues in the community, and other resources that make it possible for people to get a sense of the spiritual atmosphere of the church. Having a Web site is not a luxury. Budget for it. It is a necessity today.

Another step in focusing the collective attention of the church on the community is to encourage church members to pay attention to the community's conversation. At work, at school, at the grocery store, throughout daily life, the community is speaking. Are the members of your church listening? Encourage church members to take note of issues that surface in everyday conversation. Then ask them to report what they hear to someone in the church who will take responsibility to gather information from week to week.

In a church I served, we formed a committee whose responsibility was to gather information from the community from week to week. Six people were on the committee and their phone numbers and e-mail addresses were published in the church newsletter. Church members would call them and e-mail them whenever an event happened in the community, or an issue was developing in the community that might be addressed by the church community. The committee chairperson had the responsibility to forward the information to the staff. This input covered a wide range. At times, we learned of a home that had burned in the community, or that a business had been burglarized or that an issue had developed in the school system that had people talking. We also learned of other needs, such as sickness, death, or tragic accidents. Each event that surfaced in the community was addressed in some way. We prayed for the people involved, carried groceries and clothing to people who had lost a home, visited families in the hospital who had a teenager who had been involved in a car crash, or sent encouraging letters to community leaders who were dealing with troubling issues, letting them know that our church was praying for them. The issues also served as content for sermons that made the church more aware of the needs in the community. A simple listening committee or a hot line to the church office will keep the church focused on the community and keep its vision turned outward.

Step Two

The church has to *clarify its missional purpose* as it responds to the community. When churches begin to focus their collective attention on the community and really listen to what the community is saying, they will be overwhelmed with the input they receive. First, remember that no single church can redeem the world by itself. Churches and Christians are partners with God in God's mission, therefore each church needs to function in response to the way it hears God speaking. Second, each church has a unique personality and will need to use the strengths of that personality for effective outreach to the world. Using the Enneagram will also help churches more effectively utilize the strengths of personality as they move toward the community. If a church hears of a particular need in the community and the church knows that it cannot respond adequately to that need, it should network with other churches and agencies to help the need to be met. Utilize every resource. Don't simply give up on a need in the community because your church feels overwhelmed. Help the community to have confidence that your church is really trying to respond to what it has heard.

Whenever a church listens and responds to the community, it should do so knowing that its mission is to be redemptive. The church should not seek to replicate or try to become any other service organization. The church cannot be the Red Cross, for example. It can minister to people with compassion the way the Red Cross does, but it cannot do what the Red Cross does so well. Nor should it. The church in its compassion and care for the world is charged with announcing the good news of the kingdom. It should never forget that is its purpose.

A church can confuse those to whom it ministers in the community if it serves well but does little to help people address spiritual needs in their lives. The larger community expects the church to offer spiritual help, therefore it should not be timid in doing so. But its announcement of the good news of the kingdom needs to be done holistically. The missional purpose of the church is to minister to the complete experience of persons. In keeping with its missional purpose, every church should move outward into the community in ways that minister to the wholeness of persons, the wholeness of relationships, and the wholeness of the community. It is a large task, but one that is accomplished though the goals that are set for each ministry done by the church as it listens and responds to the community.

This was best illustrated to me when I visited Cuba a couple of years ago. I went to a town where a local church began to really listen to its community. A section of the town had been ignored for years. Businesses had moved out, homes had fallen into disrepair, and crime had moved in. Poverty was a significant issue.

The church in the center of town listened to the stories of persons who lived in the neglected community and found that it once had a baseball team that used to play all over the island. So, the church went into the impoverished community and began to form a baseball team once again. They helped to restore buildings that were run down, helped people plant gardens, cared for sick and needy people, and hauled off trash from the streets.

It held Bible studies in homes in the community and helped people who did not have transportation to come to church in town. Several church members worked with other baseball teams across the city to have the district included in the schedule of games. It was not long before the once-neglected community began to rally around its memories of their once-proud baseball team. Over time, the team improved to the extent that it won games and began to be recognized. The community began slowly to restore itself. This district regained its pride, its sense of history, and many of its traditions because a church in town sought to minister to them in holistic ways. They now have a new church in the district and people are beginning to come to faith who had once been ignored.

When a church clarifies its missional purpose, it learns to announce the good news of the kingdom of God in holistic ways. It never deviates from its calling to redeem in ways that are complete. When a church responds to a community's voice the way that church in Cuba responded, the gospel has more authenticity and those affected are enabled to see Christ living through the church in ways mere religiosity can never explain.

Step Three

The third step in helping the church to listen to the community is *simple availability.*

People trust organizations they can reach and talk to easily. Today, we depend on voice mail. Have you tried to call a large organization lately? You will never talk to a living person. You will be looped into cyberspace by endless menus that frustrate your simple question. And all the time, the recording is telling you how important you are to the company. Most people just slam the receiver down in disgust. But those companies that still answer the phone with a living person have a better image. This is one reason why some small companies, the ones that actually focus attention on the customer, are growing and larger companies that believe they have a hold on the market are seeing their market share decline.

As I travel across the country, I find most churches locked during the day. Sometimes only one door will be open. Unless you are a member of the church and you know the rules, you would never know how to gain entrance to the building. I walked around one church for thirty minutes trying every door to see if I could get in. And I had an appointment! Finally, in frustration, I called the church on my cell phone to get someone to come to the parking lot and let me in.

If I am frustrated with such behavior by churches, think what it says to the community? It sends a message loudly, "We are only open when we want to be open (Sundays) and we do not want to talk to you except at our convenience." The community that finds the church locked up tight during the week gets the impression that it does not want to be available to hear community needs.

There are security concerns, to be sure. Some of the buildings might need to be closed off to save energy when not in use. There are plenty of legitimate needs to lock some doors. But to leave the community with the challenge of trying to find the elusive unlocked door is foolish.

Years ago, the faculty of the School of Theology at Mercer made a decision. It was a simple one. We would be accessible to our students. When I went to seminary, that was not the case. Lowly M.Div. students seldom visited their professors' offices. Nor were they encouraged to do so. But at our place, we decided to keep our doors open. Most of the doors in professors' offices are wide open. It causes us some difficulty from time to time as we try to prepare lectures or to write articles, because students will often just pop in to say hello. But the policy has changed the ethos of our school. Students know that the professors are always available. The image of an open door demonstrates to the students that we trust them. They have learned that if our doors are closed, we are not there. But if the door is open, they can come on in.

Closed doors do not invite conversation. But the issue of unlocking the doors of churches during the week needs to be a decision that is made in the context of the church's location, its safety concerns, and its priorities. Regardless of how many doors the church locks, signs should be posted that let the community know which door is open. People in the general public are not turned away when they go to a business, to city hall, or to a bank and a sign on the door that directs the customer to the proper entrance. Likewise, churches need to take seriously the simple task of letting the community know how to enter the building.

It is not just about locked doors, however. Simple availability is communicated when appointments are kept, phone calls are returned quickly, e-mails are responded to, and when church members do in the community what they have said they will do. Nothing is as discouraging to the community as promises made by churches that go unfulfilled. Since the church is a voluntary organization, it has to rely on the faithfulness of the membership to carry out its ministries. Rather than motivating people with guilt or pressure to minister to others, the church has to change its vision. It has to stress the importance of being a partner with God in God's redemptive mission. Every member has to be set free to use gifts that are unique. One of the real problems that church leaders have is that they become so concerned with having every slot filled that they will often pressure people into jobs that do not suit them. People never become passionate about things they do not love. Create an opportunity for the congregation to discover the tasks they love to do. This will, of course, mean that some of the ministries that your church might want to do will not be realized–that is, until people begin to rise to the occasion out of love.

Learning to be available to the needs of the community means that the congregation is invited to respond to what they hear God saying to them. And then it means that the leadership of the church invests trust in what the people in the pew are hearing. I once heard a story about a person who ran around asking others if they had seen his group. He was frantically trying to find what direction they had gone in. Finally, someone pointed in a direction and the frantic person said, "Thanks a lot, I have to catch them; I'm their leader." There is a lot of negative connotation to be found in that illustration. But there is also a positive one. Often leaders can so dominate the group that it lacks creativity of expression. At times the leader may need to step back and then catch up when the new direction is apparent.

Then, rather than trying to get the group back on the course the leader might envision, he too can catch a vision of new possibilities. Being available to the community might just mean that the leadership of the church needs to step back a little and let the community lead.

Restructuring Your Church

Those of us who rely on computers know that they can be a blessing or a curse. I would hate to think what it would have been like to write this book on an old-fashioned typewriter. I remember term papers in college being written on a typewriter and how frustrating it was when I made mistakes. Remember trying to make corrections on carbon copies? But today's computers not only allow us to type with ease, simply hitting the backspace key to fix our errors, but they fix our spelling, format the page, produce multiple copies, and remember what we have typed.

But if you use a computer long enough, it is going to crash on you. It will just freeze up at times, for no apparent reason. Actually, it happens when the computer either doesn't have enough memory to process all we are asking it to do, or when it gets confused with multiple tasks being routed through the processor. When this happens, it will just lie down and die. No matter how many keys you push, the cursor will just not move. The only solution is to reboot the machine. And if you did not save your information, you're out of luck. You will have to start all over.

Every now and then churches need to be rebooted. They can get so confused with all the demands and expectations of the congregation that they freeze up when it comes to life according to the kingdom of God. Churches freeze up when in conflict. They freeze up when membership begins to decline. They can freeze up when leadership changes or when denominational troubles occur. They generally freeze up more often when they forget who they are in God's great mission.

Churches are like other organizations in many regards. They function best when the organization is healthy, purposeful, and visionary. The church is most healthy when people are willing to contribute to its well-being. This contribution comes when people naturally form networks with others who have a similar vision. Friendships bond, and identity builds. They work together to accomplish goals. When people are in an organization together, they develop feelings about the work they are doing. Members of a healthy organization–in this case, a healthy church–work together to allow different ways of doing tasks that are in concert with the feelings that people develop about the work that is being done. When the networks become sick or freeze up it is generally because somehow little regard has developed for the feelings that people have about the work that is being done, or networks have been devalued in some manner. Then the whole organization has the potential to become dysfunctional.

One of the most important concepts to remember is that the health of a church can be enhanced by putting the most gifted and energetic people in charge of the creative ministries of the church. It is often the case that the most energetic people are the ones who get tagged to solve problems in the church. Problems need to be addressed, to be sure. But gifted people are not usually problem solvers. They are dreamers who imagine what is not there but could be. They throw vast quantities of energy at their dreams. Problem solvers often look at the facts, the here and now of the situation, and they work toward a manageable end result. Your church will need both. President Kennedy was a dreamer who envisioned humankind walking on the moon. He had no idea how to do it. He just dreamed about it and laid the challenge before the country. Yet it took thousands of problem solvers to even get the rocket off the ground. Make sure that you get the right people in the right slots–let dreamers dream and problem solvers make the dreams come true. But make sure they are on the same page.

If a church is going to be all that God intends, it also has to have a sense of its purpose. I once heard a story about someone who passed by a building that was under construction. The passerby stopped and asked the construction workers, "What are you doing here?" One construction worker said, "I'm building a cathedral." Another shouted back, "I'm earning ten bucks an hour!" Purpose makes all the difference. Church members need a clear understanding of what God has called them to do. We should never assume that the purpose of the church is understood, embraced by all, or even functioning. Every major company constantly reminds its workers of the goals and purpose of the company. It puts the mission statement or a goal-inspired slogan that reflects the purpose of the company on office posters, coffee mugs, pencils, and in the break room. It never assumes that the company mission statement or goals for the future is a given. The company works hard at keeping its purpose in front of everyone. When members can clearly see, even in the small details of church life, the greater purposes of God in action, they are more able to work with unity and commitment toward achieving the mission of the church in the world.

Vision is the other key. It is the food that sustains the church toward its future. The biblical writer was correct, "Where there is no vision, the people perish" (Prov. 29:18, KJV). So it is with churches. Churches may hold onto the membership and sustain themselves for years going through the motions of worship, committee meetings, and youth activities. But vision may not be there. There are hosts of churches that are fixtures in communities, but the community cannot point to one single contribution, other than providing a place for worship, that the church has made to community life. The church, in the opinion of the community, has not advocated for the poor. It has not worked against social injustice. It has not built homes for the homeless. It has simply held services for the membership. And most of these churches have also been ignored by the larger community around them.

Vision gives the church the ability to touch the future. Vision dares to dream what might be. Churches need to envision what God envisions for the world. There is no sin in dreaming great dreams and not achieving all of them. The great sin is not dreaming at all. One of the most important visions for the future that can occur in a church is the vision of being kingdom-focused instead of merely religiously focused. This chapter will concentrate on how to restructure the church from a corporate religious community toward a kingdom-focused, ministry-based community of faith. If your community cannot hear what your are saying, it is most likely because they are hearing a lot of things you may be saying about religion, but not much about the kingdom of God. It may be time to reboot.

What Is Your Church Architecture?

This question has nothing to do with the buildings. It has everything to do with how the church manages the individual components of its internal environment and processes them for its mission to the world. Architecture encompasses certain standards of expectation that are often historical, traditional, Scriptural, or cultural, but most often a mixture of all. Architecture holds the church together; creates order, loyalty, or fidelity to its self-identity; alignment of the membership to its purpose; and offers the promise of the sustainability of its mission. The architecture of a church can be open or closed in terms of the world. Understanding this reality is the first step toward becoming a ministry-based kingdom-focused church.

Generally speaking, a church is closed in terms of the world if its internal components—worship, music, prayer life, business—all function to serve only the members who are there on Sunday morning. Worship, for example, should serve the members who are present, but worship has two dimensions that are critical. First, worship adores and glorifies God. That is its highest function. Christians draw strength through the worship of God. Worship builds community life and forms a strong bond of encouragement for Christian living. Second, worship provides us with insight into the heart of God. Worship helps us to see the world in the way Christ sees the world. Therefore, worship has an end goal of turning us toward the world and commissioning us for service to the world. Isaiah has a case in point that illustrates the problems of worship in only one dimension:

> To what purpose is the multitude of your sacrifices unto me? saith the LORD: I am full of the burnt offerings of rams, and the fat of fed

beasts; and I delight not in the blood of bullocks, or of lambs, or of he goats. When ye come to appear before me, who hath required this at your hand, to tread my courts? Bring no more vain oblations; incense is an abomination unto me; the new moons and sabbaths, the calling of assemblies, I cannot away with; it is iniquity, even the solemn meeting. Your new moons, and your appointed feasts my soul hateth: they are a trouble unto me; I am weary to bear them. And when ye spread forth your hands, I will hide mine eyes from you: yea, when ye make many prayers, I will not hear: your hands are full of blood. Wash you, make you clean; put away the evil of your doings from before mine eyes; cease to do evil; Learn to do well; seek judgment, relieve the oppressed, judge the fatherless, plead for the widow. (Isa. 1:11–17, KJV)

This particular passage is in the context of a rebellious nation, but the lesson is still appropriate for us today. Worship that is not faithful to God's mission in the world is not pleasing unto God. Notice the contrasts. God cares little for the solemn meeting, for sacrifices, for holy days. What God does care about is a pure life, advocacy for the oppressed, ministry to the fatherless, and concern for the widow. In the book of Luke, there is an ever-present theme, and it is a preferential option for the poor.[1] Matthew 25 should be foundational to our understanding of God's concern that we care for the world. Worship exalts God but turns the church outward. A church whose worship is closed is one that omits the second dimension, thereby rendering its worship incomplete.

If the church's music is merely entertainment for the membership, it is closed. If it is missional, it is open. There is a lot of contemporary music today that omits the second function of worship. This music may have its place when used to glorify God. But it needs to be balanced with action toward the world. Many of the old hymns did this well. The first verse or second verse usually glorified God in many respects. The verses worshiped the beauty of God's holiness. But very often, the third or fourth verses focused the task of the believer to the world. The old hymns may be old and out of style in some churches, but the writers understood worship.

If the church's prayer life is concentrated entirely upon the members of the church and their families, it is a closed church. Listen carefully to the prayers of the church. You may find that the majority of the prayers are focused on our illnesses, our needs, our salvation, our goals. When was the last time your church engaged in serious prayer for the outreach of the church into the community? When were the members encouraged to carry in silent prayer the names of their unchurched friends, neighbors, and coworkers before God in intercession? If the church prays with God for the world around them, it is open.

The business of the church is closed if it serves only the religious corporation. It is open if it serves the community around it and if it focuses toward the world. One of the best ways to examine this reality is to look at what is spent by churches to maintain the buildings, provide for internal church activities, staff costs, and building projects, and how much is spent for outreach to the community. Every year churches spend more on mortgage interest payments for their buildings than they spend on the mission of God in the world around them.

There are many churches that give a tithe of their budget for "missions." Most often this money is sent to a mission organization or denominational clearinghouse for mission. Some churches believe that they have done what is needed to support God's mission to the world by giving the tithe to mission. Often, the balance of the budget goes to the needs of the local church. One of the first items to be cut in some church budgets is its missional giving, especially when there is a budget crunch or a building project. Of course, this is not the case in every situation. There are many, many churches that give to global mission causes and who budget for serious engagement in the community, but the warning must always be heeded. How a church chooses to use its budget reflects whether it is an open system or one that is closed.

When a church is a closed system, it spends its energy in ways that dissipate rapidly. An example will aid our understanding. I have always loved clocks, especially antique clocks that you have to wind up and that have pendulums and chimes. I have a wall clock that ticks for seven days before it needs to be rewound. I can hear it chiming all through the house, but on occasion I suddenly realize that I have not heard it chime recently. Then I find out that it has run down. I forget during those seven days to wind it. Only when it quits and stops chiming do I remember that I need to wind the clock.

That clock will run as long as tension is on the spring. When the tension dissipates, the clock stops. It constantly requires a renewal of its energy. "This tendency to run down is called increasing entropy, a term borrowed originally from thermodynamics."[2] Closed systems often function until they run down. Then the keepers of the system scurry about trying to renew it again. Revivals used to play the same kind of role in churches. The church revival was held each year in many churches to get the members fired up again and to give the church a push when it sagged. The problem that exists in closed churches is that the church is endlessly trying to find some gimmick or program that will inject energy back into the life of the church since it is always suffering from increasing entropy or the tendency to run down. Perhaps one of the reasons pastors and staff members have such short tenures in these types of churches is that they just grow weary of continuously winding the clock.

Open systems also suffer increasing entropy. They tend to wind down at times, but they are constantly being renewed with new or additional sources of energy from new believers being discipled into the life of Christ and his church. The spring is being constantly renewed. Like a self-winding watch, each time the arm moves, the watch is being wound. If the ideal could be imagined this type of clock would never stop. Always in motion on a person's wrist, no friction to wear the gears–the clock would tick forever because it is always being renewed.

The open system church is always being renewed by the Holy Spirit as people are energized in worship; it is being renewed as members interface with the community in ministry; it is always being renewed as new challenges are found and plans are laid to meet those challenges; and it is always being renewed as its members hear for themselves what God is doing in the world and provide insights, creative notions, and energy for the accomplishment of the church's mission.

One of the most critical reasons why the community cannot hear what some churches are saying is that these churches are closed systems. They are not open, creative, and being constantly renewed by interaction with the community around them under the leadership of the Holy Spirit. The church is a living body. If it is being heard by the community, it is usually an open system and seems very alive. If not, it is probably a closed system and, as far as the community is concerned, that church is dead. It has lost its ability to speak in ways the community can hear.

What Color Is the Sky?

Of course, this question has little to do with meteorology. But it has everything to do with moving from a corporate dispenser of religious services toward a missional church that embodies the characteristics of the kingdom of God. Every church needs to understand how it reflects its climate to the community. Is the climate one that is gray and overcast, or is it bright and sunny? In other words, does your church reflect to the community a potential of threat or opportunity? If the church is imagined in the community as a collection of religious rules and regulations, it will be a threat to most people who have little regard for what they believe to be the constraints of religion on their lives. But if the church is imagined by the community as a place where people can explore their spiritual insights, it will likely become inviting and certainly on their radar of consideration when they have questions of a spiritual nature.

The question is, How do we develop inside the church the ability to project a climate that brings to the community the potential for invitation? There are at least four critical steps that are necessary.

First, make every effort to avoid the perception that your church has all the answers to life's problems. Unchurched people have the idea that Christians, by and large, really do believe that every problem of life can be solved if they just trust Jesus. Those of us who are Christians do place our trust in Christ to help us with every problem we face. But being a Christian does not exempt us from the troubles of life. Some Christians still die from the ravages of cancer, no matter how much they place their trust in God. Unchurched people are plagued with enormous questions about why good people suffer, or why there are wars in the world, or why their marriage failed. They need the opportunity to meet Christians who have an honest faith who have also failed in their marriages, have been ill or injured, and who still struggle with issues of prejudice in their lives. Nothing is so powerful in witness as the occasion when an unchurched person views the authentic struggles that a Christian constantly works to overcome and when that Christian explains the help he or she receives from God in dealing with the struggles. The task of the church that would be missional in the world is to dialogue with the troubling questions, not provide easy or glib answers. The missional or kingdom-focused church is interested in communicating to its unchurched community the questions the congregation has in their quest to be people of God and how the gospel helps them to answer some of those questions. But its first task is to create an opportunity to invite the community around the church to explore those questions with its members.

Focus on engaging the community with questions and issues that are common to all people. One of the most powerful ways a church has to influence the community is to emphasize that its Christians are seeking to find solutions to the questions and habits that plague them. Listening sessions in the community that invite the sharing of questions about God and the challenges of everyday life can lead to new opportunities to address contemporary concerns. I once saw a sermon title advertised that had the potential to attract people who struggle with addictive behavior. It read, "How to stop doing what you keep on doing, but just can't stand doing." That sermon title raised an issue common to most everyone and had the potential to engage people who wanted to break the cycle of dysfunctionality in their personal lives.

I talked to a pastor in a large, innovative church in Chicago who told me that he had difficulty really understanding the troubling issues that the unchurched community faces in everyday life. He was constantly surrounded by church people and needed a different view. He would leave his office each day and spend two hours visiting in town, having coffee at a popular hangout. He would meet people and invite them to just talk about what troubled them. He would seek every opportunity to understand the questions or issues that bothered people who never attended church. He needed to step outside the normal kinds of questions he encountered that Christians asked about faith, and hear from non-Christians who were trying to grapple with faith. It gave him a different view of the world. One of the most telling indictments that unchurched people often make concerning churched people is that they do not understand the real world. They may be right.

Second, don't be afraid to engage controversial questions. There are a lot of questions that Christian people just don't want to ask in church. They are perhaps afraid that the questions might point to a deficiency of some kind in their faith. Unchurched people are not as concerned about what others think about their faith or lack of it. They really do not care to question whether or not there was a real Adam and Eve. That question doesn't really matter to them. But they would like to know the issues that drive debates over abortion, the war in Iraq, terrorism, or capital punishment. Unchurched people have their opinions. Most of the time these opinions are formed without the benefit of any input from persons of faith. Sometimes those who are unchurched are not sure whether their opinions are correct. I have met many who have told me that they would like a chance to debate with Christians in a fair and honest way about issues that trouble them. They want to explore what the problems are and what the solutions might be. But they often have a difficult time finding an opportunity to discuss their concerns without hearing some people lace the discussion with religious language they don't understand in the first place. A church that wishes to take seriously the questions of the community around it will not dodge an opportunity to engage issues that the unchurched community raises, even if the opinions of the community are somewhat shocking to the sensitivities of churched people. Christians have to learn to be patient, loving, and caring enough to take people where they are and to nudge them toward the ethics of the kingdom.

In our state, the adoption of a statewide lottery to fund education was a hot topic a few years ago. Churches came out against the lottery on ethical and moral and religious grounds. All the religious rhetoric was there. Several politicians, including the governor, came out in favor of the lottery as a way to enhance the opportunity for affordable college education, especially for families who could not afford to send their children to college. It was a way to raise revenue for an overburdened educational system. Nearly every church and church member seemed to have an opinion on the divisive issue. Likewise, those not in churches had an opinion. But to my knowledge, I witnessed no interface between the two, certainly not around my area of the state. I am sure that the churches debated internally what they felt about the impending lottery. I am sure that people in the marketplace debated it as well and some may have even dreamed about what they would do with all the money they were going to win. What a great opportunity for both parts of the community to have conversation and to explore all the pros and cons of the issue. Many churches missed an opportunity to seek with the communities around them any alternatives that could have been discovered to fund educational needs. Further, the churches probably missed the opportunity to talk about state-promoted gambling in intelligent ways that were beyond simple religious rhetoric railing against it. The topic was a perfect opportunity to address with the community what the church believes about life according to the kingdom of God, a life that is concerned about societal structures that are built which oppress people rather than liberate them. Many unchurched people were also against the lottery. They could have been encouraged and supported. The lottery passed.

Remember this important concept: don't blame the community for the questions that haunt them. I once heard a friend of mine say that you can't really blame lost people for what they do. It is not that they are bad people. They just don't know the (Christian's) rules. They really don't. Christians seem to know the do's and don'ts that they believe makes a good Christian. Most try to avoid those actions that are negative. But unchurched people are liable to say or suggest any possibility, or question most any sacred cow.

If it is true, as my teachers often said, that there are no stupid questions, then our churches should reflect the kind of climate of learning that invites questions that may not be sanctified. If it is the truth of the gospel that the church wishes to convey, it will not communicate that truth by insulting people who ask troublesome questions.

Third, keep a lookout on the horizon. Watch for the storm clouds that might be brewing due to an insensitive response to the community or lack of response to a critical issue. One of the storm clouds that can arise in the relationship between church and community is the use of speech that is not sensitive. Church members need to be careful in their speech when it comes to issues of multiculturalism. We live in a pluralistic world in which people from all cultures are represented. Learn to be sensitive to the kinds of speech that offend persons. The church needs to educate itself when working with multicultural groups to find out how they like to be related to. Learning the language of ethnic groups in the community can pay dividends. Encourage those who speak Spanish, for example, to bring their concerns to the church. Likewise, offer as many opportunities for events to be multilingual as possible. The language of people is important to them. Honor that language, honor the customs of all people. Be sensitive.

Watch for breaks in the clouds. A church that wishes to create an open climate toward the community will be its own worst critic at times. Members will question why the church took a certain position and how it failed to be redemptive. At the same time, it will celebrate breaks in the clouds of suspicion toward the church that might occur in the community. Jim Collins says that all major companies that grow from good to great conduct autopsies without blame. He says that in doing so, they go a long way toward creating a climate in which the truth is heard.[3] Most churches need to evaluate every outreach effort or ministry conducted by the church toward the community and focus on correcting any problems that might have hindered the quest for communicating the truth of the gospel in ways that can be heard in the community. The church needs to build on those positive attributes that have been the most effective in telling the story of the gospel to the community around the church. How did the community respond? Build on the strengths of those positive responses. Keep watching the horizon.

During the Olympics that came to Atlanta a few years ago, I heard about a church that looked toward the horizon and saw an opportunity. The church was located far away from Atlanta, and they knew that most people in their community would not drive hundreds of miles for the events. So the church decided to host its own Olympic events during the same time period as those held in Atlanta. The church opened the events to the community, took out newspaper ads, and announced the events on the local radio station. It was a huge success and was a gift to a rural community far removed from Atlanta. The community was able to celebrate the spirit of the Olympics in its own context.

Fourth, make sure the witness of the church is in High Definition. Have you seen High Definition television yet? It brings details to the viewer that cannot be experienced on regular television. The Atlanta Braves baseball organization installed the world's largest High Definition scoreboard to kick off its new season. The scoreboard is a 5,600 square-foot screen made by Mitsubishi. It is 71 feet tall and 79 feet wide and weighs 50 tons. The scoreboard has more than five million LED lights. It boasts over 400,000 watts of light power and cost 10 million dollars. Players were cautioned to be careful on the field because the fans could now see details they may have never noticed before. Fans can actually read the player's lips when they get into a spat with the umpires!

In creating a climate that is welcoming to the community, the church needs to realize that it cannot merely provide information about the Christian life. It has to do so with creativity–in High Definition. My sense of Jesus' ministry is that he used the dramatic as a way of engaging people with his message. He walked on water, fed thousands with a few fishes and loaves, turned over tables in the temple, and touched lepers. He did what was unexpected. He illustrated the kingdom of God in story and in drama.

I saw the impact of such storytelling in a church in Kentucky. At Christmastime, the church decided to tell the story of the birth of Jesus with some flair. They set aside their large recreational building as the venue. They covered the floor with tons of dirt and built Bethlehem inside the building. Church members played the part of beggars in the street, merchants, and ordinary citizens. The church members dressed in period costumes. Roman soldiers were there. Sheep ran through the town. People were cooking, buying, and selling on the street, and the whole place looked like a scene from a Hollywood movie. There was an inn with the keeper outside turning people away because it was full. Visitors who walked through Bethlehem made their way through the streets toward the inn and then outside to the cold December night where on the lawn of the church were campfires of families who could not find a room at the inn. And then they saw a manger with animals and the Christ Child, and even witnessed the star that hung over the city. It was a giant production put on by a church of about 500 members.

The first year they had over 600 people who signed cards indicating they would like more information about the church. The next year, word had gotten out and the state patrol had to be called in to direct traffic. People waited over an hour in traffic just to walk through Bethlehem. Thousands of people have attended the production each year. This church learned to tell the story of the birth of Jesus in High Definition.

It is not enough today to simply provide information. We live in a world today in which anyone can get access to any subject on the Internet, including everything a person ever wanted to know about religion, faith, or specific details of Scripture. But the creative church can promise what the Internet cannot, it can promise community. One of the most important and most attractive aspects of a church on mission is its ability to create the kind of community that is not only creative in the way it handles the story of the gospel, but the way it handles life's story as well. The High Definition church brings the same creativity toward creating a welcoming community as it does in telling the gospel story with drama. Love, acceptance, inclusivity, mutual respect, peacemaking, reconciliation, and celebration are all done in the High Definition of the Spirit of God.

Moving to a Ministry Base

Virtually no church can move beyond corporate religion unless it is committed to becoming ministry-based as an expression of its commitment to the kingdom of God. What does it mean to be a ministry-based church? It means that everything the church does is focused outward as an expression of its commitment to the Great Commission. A church realizes that its highest form of worship occurs when the church is face to face with the community living out the gospel, speaking the gospel, and ministering the holism of the gospel to human need. There are a lot of churches that assume this is their character. The honest appraisal called for in this book would challenge those assumptions.

A church that wants to restructure itself along kingdom-focused lines will have to engage its most difficult critics: those within. Because it is not the nature of most Christians to think in terms of the kingdom of God and ministry to the community as fundamental to the existence of the church, every effort will need to be made to bring people along on the journey. Preaching needs to be focused on the essential character of the kingdom.

I served as interim pastor at a church at which I began to preach about the kingdom of God as an expression of the essential character of the church. At the end of a year and a half, a lady came to me and said that she finally understood. It had nothing to do with her ability to grasp the principles, nor my ability to speak about them. It is just not second nature to most who have lived their lives under the umbrella of corporate religion.

Every effort must be made from the pulpit to embody the principles of kingdom living. The pastor has to embody inclusiveness, reconciliation, forgiveness, peace, justice, and love, to name only a few of the characteristics found within God's kingdom. Much of the success of moving a church away from a corporate vendor of religion to a missional church will be the responsibility of the leadership. They will have to carefully mentor others along the way. Leading a small group study is helpful. Teaching the principles is a must. But avoiding the traps of the corporation is the hardest.

The pastor will often be loaded with responsibilities for committee meetings, budget meetings, business meetings, program meetings, and so on. The most difficult thing a pastor will have to face is the temptation to attend them all. Remember what was said earlier about people who are visionary? There are trusted leaders who can handle the details of running the everyday corporation. The visionary pastor has to spend his or her time mentoring and molding others for the work of the kingdom. Leading in ministry to the community is essential. No pastor can talk about ministry to the community without being involved in that ministry personally.

A second notion of transforming a church away from a religious institution toward a ministry base is to back up the ministry of the church with the budget. Suppose that a young couple comes into your office and the following proposal is made:

> "Pastor, my husband and I have been talking and we would like to start a ministry out of this church for after-school tutoring. We teach high school and we have noticed a large number of our students are constantly behind. They simply do not have the skills to perform well. A lot of them live in the community around our church. Can we begin working with these students a couple of nights a week, with some volunteers from our church here, and help these kids?"

Any pastor would say yes. But the pastor might say yes with little thought given to the fact that materials will be needed, kids will need to be transported, some will need to be fed an evening meal, and so on. It will take budget allocation. Is your church willing to budget money for a dream? What if it fails? Remember what was said before: "To dream and to fail is not a sin. To fail to dream is the sin."

Once a ministry begins, elevate it so that everyone in the church can see it. A ministry to kids who need extra help in school needs to be recognized in a way that will not embarrass the children who take part but in a way that affirms the work of those involved with the kids. Likewise, when the ministries grow, if there are people who make the decision to become Christians as a result of the ministries, give the leaders of that ministry an opportunity to baptize the new believers.

Every time a new ministry begins, publicize it for the church to notice. Keep illustrating that the church is called to minister to the community. If the ministries develop to an extent that there are ten or more, have a ministry banquet at which people of the church are asked to attend, to celebrate the work, and to give to it. Have testimonies from those for whom the ministries have meant much.

Begin a potential ministry leader class. Give people the opportunity to learn how to do ministries. Enable them to work alongside those already involved to learn what is needed. Keep the challenge before the congregation to listen to what God is saying to the church about the community. Encourage the church to envision creative ways to meet the needs they have heard about in the community.

Each ministry director should be charged with developing, along with a team of ministry leaders, guidelines for the ministries. In some cases, legal matters will be involved. The church should pay for legal counsel, especially when it comes to providing safe homes for abused women or children, or for pregnancy care and other matters that might involve matters of the law.

Each ministry needs to be holistic. It needs to minister to the physical, emotional, and spiritual needs of the people who are involved. Every effort should be made to invite, not coerce, those to whom ministry is focused to walk with the leaders in spiritual discovery. Don't rush the gospel witness. Give time for love to do its work. Give time for care to be realized. Give people permission to question anything they wish about Christianity and what it means for one to experience salvation. Help people to understand their commitment to spirituality and discipleship.

The ministry-based church will emphasize that every person in the congregation is a minister. Each person should be encouraged to find some small way to live out ministry to others. Celebrate each one, no matter how large or small. Develop visitation teams that will go into the community, not to hunt for potential church members, but to dialogue with those in need. For example, suppose that you notice in the newspaper that a family has lost its home due to fire. Do some research. Find out where the people are living as their home is being rebuilt. Care for them and encourage them to contact your visitation team for needs that may arise. Another possibility is to have a contact in the hospital emergency room who can call a designated person in the church when someone is brought into the hospital as a result of injury. Soon after the person is moved to a room and is stabilized and can receive visitors, take a care package. Get to know the person and begin ministry. Let this person know that your church has been praying for him or her ever since the accident.

Dream, imagine, test the waters, and be proactive so that everything your church does is done in response to what it hears from the community. When the church gathers for worship on Sundays, always have a prayer time in the services for the ministries of the church. Speak frequently about what the ministries are doing in the community and keep the congregation focused on its essential mission of embodying the kingdom of God to the world.

These are but a few steps toward turning a church away from an internalized religious body to the body of Christ in the world. Don't be afraid to develop a dream team to imagine the possibilities. Vision is everything.

10

What Tomorrow Brings

I have fond memories of my grandfather. He lived to be nearly ninety years old. We would often sit together on his front porch and he would tell me stories of his youth. He grew up in a poor rural family with little access to education. The world he was born into had no radio, no indoor plumbing, and people did not travel through the skies; in fact, his entire world consisted only of neighbors within just a few miles of his home.

In my grandfather's lifetime, he not only saw the development of all of the above, but witnessed even more astonishing events–such as two World Wars, the Depression, the civil rights era, the Korean and Vietnam conflicts, and the missions to the moon. He was subjected to a world full of changes beyond his wildest imagination, yet he survived all the changes to his world and lived a long, productive life. He adapted by learning to save his money, something he did not have during the Depression; he worked to help the country sustain itself through the World War II, and he learned to use modern-day inventions, drive an automobile, and travel to far-off states. All of our grandparents and their grandparents before them learned to adapt to the changing world.

It is very interesting that some churches have changed very little since the 1950s. They have made some minor shifts, but they have remained the same in terms of their vision for what God is doing in the world. Other churches have changed with the times and have found the cutting edge of ministry shaped toward the diversity of their context. They have heard God speak clearly about mission and they have become creative and visionary as they have joined God in ministry to the world.

The choice is before each church today. It can either move ahead and seek to become more kingdom-focused as it senses the mission of God in today's world, or it can choose to remain static and leave its community deaf to the life-giving message of the gospel. As we look ahead to what the future may bring, it may be helpful to look in times past for inspiration. I have chosen to end this book in terms of inspiration and hope. I fully believe that if Christians can look to the history of the early church, with all they faced, then nothing in our future will intimidate us as we seek to partner with God to reach today's world. What better example of how to focus on what God is doing in mission today than by looking back at what God did in the New Testament period? How did the early Christians challenge their world? What might their example teach us about ministering in our world today?

Looking Back

In many ways, the ancient world of the New Testament Christian is analogous to our contemporary world. Potential for opportunities as well as hostilities were evident in the New Testament world. The New Testament Christian lived in a polytheistic world with a powerful government structure, and amid both affluence and poverty. Today's world exhibits similar characteristics. Neo-paganism, secularism, various world religions, racism, poverty, and powerful government forces all combine to place Christians today in a similar context. While the *Pax Romana* made it possible for the Roman Empire to tolerate various religions, including the Jews and Christians, today's culture tolerates all religions but pays little attention to them. Indeed, the postmodern era with its inherent fragmentation is more like the ancient world than the modern world with its systematized structures.

Kenneth Scott Latourette demonstrates that the early church's successes were due to the efforts of ordinary lay Christian missionaries.[1] Latourette says, "The chief agents in the expansion of Christianity appear not to have been those who made it a profession...but men and women who earned their livelihood in some purely secular manner and spoke their faith to those whom they met in this natural fashion."[2] He continues to explain that travelers and slaves, merchants and professional people made constant contact with the general population and spoke of their faith. Latourette quotes Origen as support for the work of individuals in the spread of Christianity. It was Celsus who criticized the spread of Christianity by "workers in wool and leather and fullers and uneducated persons who get hold of children privately and of ignorant women and teach them."[3]

E. Glenn Hinson has suggested, however, that while individuals did play a significant role in the expansion of the early church, their institutional life also made possible the mission of the early Christians to attract and enlist converts.[4] Latourette's assertion that individuals were the primary component to the success of Christianity addresses a significant problem that many church members seem to avoid—that is, individual accountability to be on mission and to be proclaimers of the gospel. Almost no Christian today would admit to avoidance of personal involvement in mission, but it is clear from statistics that the sharing of the gospel by individuals in churches is a low priority. Many factors contribute to this problem: among them is the idea that the church body is able and will do the work necessary to evangelize the culture. Therefore, it becomes easy for the average Christian to simply focus energies on worship and work within the church and feel that she or he is on mission. Evidence in the New Testament indicates that individual Christians did take personal responsibility for carrying the gospel to others within the context of their daily lives, and that they did not depend on the corporate church to do the work for them.

Reports in the Scripture of individuals who seized opportunities for mission outreach are evident. Many of these encounters were not focused on the establishment of any church but instead the focus seemed to be on the individual convert or groups of individuals. Glenn Hinson explains, "In some instances it is probable that individual witnesses, especially laypersons, secured conversions which did not lead to the formation of churches or to church affiliation."[5] Phillip and the Ethiopian, Peter and Cornelius, the witness of Stephen, the Philippian jailer, and the witness of Paul are a few examples. Hinson also indicates, "Soldiers, sailors, merchants, artisans, and travelers of all kinds scattered the word all over the ancient world."[6] Many evangelistic monks of the late fourth and fifth centuries went from place to place making converts. Prior to the establishment of churches in a locale, individuals were at work sharing their faith all over the Roman Empire of the first century. There is evidence in places such as Damascus that Jewish Christians were already in the cities prior to the formation of churches. Martin Hengel notes, "Luke presupposes that there are already Jewish Christians there, and he mentions just one of them, Ananias, by name, additionally describing him as a pious Jew."[7] Luke even avoids the term *ekklesia* in Damascus when describing Paul's visit, there obviously not wishing to suggest that a church was in place. It is rather possible that Luke is describing a community of believers in "the way," as seen in 9:2, to indicate that the community had not organized independently from the synagogue community. According to Hengel, "Presumably it met in one or more private houses as a kind of 'Messianic conventicle,' but at the same time it presumably also attempted to exercise influence on those who went to the synagogues."[8] This is precisely why Paul had been given letters to go to Damascus in the first place. These members of "the way" had been disturbing the synagogue with their witness of Jesus and Paul was given letters of authority to go to the synagogue at Damascus to try to bring order and rebut those causing the disturbances. So, evidence is apparent that individuals functioned in the cities at first, then, as they found others of "the way," joined together in the synagogues to share their faith. They met in homes to support their fellowship and their mission, but remained primarily attached to the synagogues.

The combination of good roads, peace, and tolerance enabled people to travel and visit points of the Empire far removed from Jerusalem. Through their travels, people carried the gospel witness as they traded and as they relocated from town to town. Later, Paul benefited as a traveling missionary from the *Pax Romana,* which guaranteed citizens relative freedom. The relative ease with which Paul could move from city to city led to a positive attitude toward Roman rule which can be seen in Paul's writings in Romans 13:1–7. It is entirely possible that prior to the establishment of churches the Empire had numbers of individuals in the cities discovering others, in relative freedom of worship, who had become believers, thus preparing the way for the gospel to evolve into larger groups of association and into churches. The importance of the emerging community cannot be overlooked as individuals linked themselves together and sought to make converts.

Not only did individuals contribute to evangelistic and missional outreach, but it is apparent that the early New Testament community functioned as a vehicle for the gospel. As Christians moved within the culture, they had opportunity to speak to others about their faith to the extent that "most converts became acquainted with it through casual contacts."[9] Thus, the earliest Christian "missionaries" formed "small conventicles with their followers; one might even call them 'special synagogues' with offensive Messianic doctrines."[10] The Christian communities were constantly vying with Judaism and the mystery cults to win converts to the faith. It is possible that the typical convert heard about Christianity by chance. Perhaps it was "a word dropped by a friend or neighbor, witnessing a martyrdom, overhearing a conversation."[11] No matter the case, the attraction to Christianity within the larger community was apparent. Persons in the various communities could not help but notice the love of the Christians for others. Charity was offered, according to Hinson, "without expectation of return or consideration of merit; fellowship opened to all social levels–masters and slaves, men and women, young and old, rich and poor."[12] The range of their love was evidently broad. They cared for widows and orphans, for the sick, for prisoners, for slaves, those unemployed, and victims of calamities. The fellowship that the early believers shared openly with others was a powerful attraction.

The Christians' steadfastness in the face of persecution, their high moral standards, their assurance of victory over evils, and their assurance of salvation to come, were all factors that were noticed by the culture at large and contributed to the spread of the faith in this period.

Christian behavior within the larger communities was also noticed. Pagans would often scrutinize the Christian moral character. In his letter to Trajan, Pliny reported a morally favorable impression of the Christians based on his investigation. Although he faulted Christians' "inflexible obstinacy," he found nothing "socially harmful in their meetings."[13] Galen, the physician, criticized Christianity for its philosophical naiveté, but expressed appreciation for Christian courage in the face of death.

Wherever persons traveled, they found hospitality from the Christians, as noted earlier. Their generous spirit would welcome weary travelers, giving them opportunities to share the gospel in their homes. They took seriously Hebrews 13:2 lest they fail to comfort and aid "angels unawares." In time, there were some guidelines set for entertaining strangers, such as those found in 2 John 10–11, but it is apparent that the Christians for the most part chose to err on the side of love for the stranger. In Third John, for example, Gaius is commended for his hospitality to "the brothers and strangers." Diotrephes is condemned, not only for a lack of hospitality, but also from prohibiting those who wished to give it to do so (3 Jn. 5–10). The result was that Christianity developed an Empire-wide network of Christian communities open to travelers, and provided an opportunity for the gospel to further spread as a result of Christian hospitality.

The flourishing of the Christian community and the emergence of its churches found precedence in the associations that were already in place in the Hellenistic world. The Roman imperial government left a large space in the life of its citizens that was not regulated by the government, nor did local administrations concern themselves with the social life of the people. Many of the significant societal infrastructures were left to the initiative of the people. Associations became the most important structural element in city life.[14] They played a role in the welfare and social care of their members.

The associations took on many forms. The dinner parties fostered symposia that were defined by shared interests such as "particular forms of worship, professional bonds, neighborhoods, inherited descent, or political interests."[15] These associations were critical to the social life of the people. Koester explains, "It is difficult to imagine how anyone could play a political, social, or professional role in society, or for that matter have any fun, without membership in an association."[16]

The Hellenistic period saw the greatest proliferation of associations. Most of them belonged to the middle class of the cities. There were gymnasiums, social clubs, professional guilds, and religious clubs dedicated to or named after a certain deity. Musical clubs, theater clubs, and dancing clubs were organized. There were a great variety of professional associations. Koester says, "These associations occupied privileged positions and in some places were organized under royal supervision. Their members served as teachers, so that these associations also functioned as schools for actors, dancers, and musicians."[17]

The model of the association was an important vehicle not only for social life within the Empire, but enabled the Christian community to function alongside the other associations of the time. According to Koester, "Religious associations were primarily founded for gods and cults that were not sponsored by the political community and so did not have publicly recognized sanctuaries."[18] These associations served as community structures for disseminating their faith. They would normally admit men regardless of their social class and would often admit slaves and women also. Koester indicates that any of the members, even women or slaves, were allowed to occupy positions of leadership. Therefore, when Christian meetings included slaves, the poor, middle-class persons, women, or any persons regardless of their social class, it was considered not unusual due to the large number of associations functioning within the culture. However, they were not entirely without suspicion. The Roman administration tried to regulate as many of the associations as they could, especially those they feared were seditious or for the purpose of drunken bouts. Koester illustrates: "Most suspicious were those that met at odd hours (Christians met early in the morning) and had leaders that were women and slaves."[19] But in spite of their suspicion, these associations functioned on a regular basis. Therefore, the presence of the association within the culture of the Empire contributed to the ability of the Christians to meet and to develop their associations into communities of faith. It is quite possible that established churches emerged out of many associations that met together for fellowship and support.

What may have begun at the local community association eventually extended outward via the universal fellowship of Christians, and to the edges of the Empire. According to Hinson, "No one can determine empirically, of course, how much the Empire-wide link of the individual churches enhanced the process of evangelism, but it must have been considerable."[20] The establishment of churches took Christianity a giant leap forward, far beyond what the individual missionary or community associations could accomplish. Christianity seems to have spread principally and normally through the planting of churches that may have arisen out of these associations of people. Hinson says, "These churches served as missionary communities which would evangelize and incorporate persons who were resident in their areas."[21] In time, they spread outward to the extent that hardly any corner of the Empire was without a witness.

The procedure of planting churches probably originated in Paul's missionary strategy. His strategy for taking the gospel to a province was not to preach in every city or town himself, but to establish churches as centers of Christian life. These would be places from which the knowledge of Christ might radiate.[22] Paul planted churches in towns and cities that were centers of Roman administration or of Greek or Jewish influence. Many were of commercial and military importance. Yet, how Paul established churches is a matter that needs to be examined.

The attraction of the faith was apparent. Hengel says:

The missionary effect of the Jewish synagogue worship, which had no sacrifices but rather with its prayer, hymn-singing, interpretation of scripture, and presentation of doctrine and ethical admonition in a sermon, was more like a philosophical assembly than the usual pagan worship involving a sacrifice, had an impact above all on members of the non-Jewish urban middle and upper classes.[23]

It was these pagan sympathizers whom Luke calls "god fearers" (Acts 10). They were Gentiles with leanings towards the synagogue. They faithfully attended synagogue worship and observed the law as best they could. They concerned themselves with good works and tried to stay away from idolatry. Hengel says, "Luke depicts such people in a very positive way in the person of the centurion of Capernaum, Cornelius, Lydia the purple trader in Philippi, Jason in Thessalonica or Titius Iustus in Corinth."[24] These were people among whom the formation of churches in the Hellenistic world was a possibility, to whom Paul preached and with whom he worked to establish formal congregations in the towns he visited.

As the Christians gathered together, first as a loose association of new friends, then into larger communities or associations, and as they began to meet outside of the synagogue in homes and other places, fertile ground was developed in which the zealot Paul could establish a church. According to Diogenes Allen, "Paul had by no means counted his work finished when he had preached and won a few converts. He took with utmost seriousness the task of church building, and the secret of his success lay in furnishing his converts as thoroughly as he could for their common life in Christ."[25] Paul's missionary method of building churches meant that he would visit a town with a group of Christians gathered together and stay with them for a period of time during which he would instruct them and equip them to function as an autonomous body. He would encourage their growth and expansion and when he left, often due to external circumstances, he would keep in touch with them by letter. Hinson explains, "During his residence, he reinforced his initial preaching with teaching according to the early *paradosis*,[26] with the observance of baptism (cf. 1 Cor. 1:13ff.) and eucharist (cf. 1 Cor. 11:23–25), and with the establishment of a suitable order."[27]

Paul was not satisfied simply to establish a church and to leave it to fend for itself with an occasional letter from him to offer support, encouragement, and guidance. Rather, he also thought of the churches in terms of a larger fellowship. Hinson says, "Fundamentally, he did not draw a sharp distinction between the church universal and the individual community, however large or small; rather, he designated now one and now the other with the word *ekklesia*."[28] He believed the churches in a province were part of a larger unity. He personally tried to forge bonds between them by encouraging the sharing of his letters and by personal visits to them. He desired a spiritual communion between the churches as well as practical help in times of need, such as the relief offerings that he devised. Hinson says, "For Paul the fulfillment of the Christian mission depended in large measure upon the actual unity of all churches within the one Body of Christ."[29]

What, then, does all this looking back on the early church's engagement in the mission of God to the world mean for us today? It means that we are not alone. We have the benefit of looking at some of the ways the early Christians interfaced with their world and we can be encouraged by what they did. It also means that some changes probably need to take place in the life of our churches today, which will enable them to become as missional as the early church, and it means to us that these changes need to be viewed as nothing short of what God desires if the communities around churches are ever to hear what the churches are saying. Some foundations need to be rediscovered.

First, the issue of the individual on mission needs to be rediscovered with new clarity in much the way that Latourette has illustrated. Given a culture that today is largely suspicious of religious organizations, it is more apparent than ever that individuals need reclaim a personal involvement in the mission of God. Unfortunately, the word *evangelism* has for many such a negative stereotype that they wish to stay clear of the concept all together. But *euanggelion* is a very important New Testament word. One could scarcely imagine the New Testament Christian as reluctant to tell what Christ meant to him personally. It is clear that the religious orientation of the world of the Empire placed religious inquiry on a high level. It is just as high today. People today are seeking spiritual fulfillment in many directions. Persons in churches must be equipped to speak of their faith through the maze of misunderstanding, suspicion, distrust of Christianity, political correctness, and a number of other filters imposed by the culture. Many churches give no help to members who wish to share their faith within today's context. Evangelism needs to be recast, away from the manipulative practices often including bait and switch methods, to the true nature of its calling. Evangelism is simply the holistic announcement of the good news of the kingdom of God. But that announcement is holistic in every way. It touches the whole of the person and the whole of his or her world. It is both word and deed. Its goal is to help people discover the joys of living according to the kingdom of God and God's righteousness.

Also, a church that is serious about interfacing with its community simply must focus on the spiritual dimension of the Christian life. Most Christians in churches today have never practiced the disciplines of a spiritual life. The teaching of spiritual formation in the churches may be of more importance than the traditional Sunday school classes, which only teach the facts of the biblical narrative with some commentary by way of application. But spiritual formation could be fostered in small groups within the church and focused on what it means to be a Christian in the context of the world today. The history of spiritual awakenings suggests that when persons are committed to fervent prayer and spiritual development, radical changes take place in their sense of mission and evangelism. An example can be observed in the Asbury College revivals of the 1970s, when fervent prayer, confession of sins, commitment to a recovery of spiritual passion, and personal discipleship led to an awakening that affected not only the college community but the town, state, and nation. The community of Wilmore, Kentucky, listened to what was happening at Asbury. It was caught up in the revival at the school. The witness of the students was authentic enough that the community observed, listened, and was impacted.

Another critical step toward a renewal of personal accountability for mission and evangelism that must be mentioned again is a serious and sober examination of the culture itself and the communities that surround the churches. One suspects that most churches know little of the culture around them. Ron Dempsey says, "The Christian church in the United States finds itself functioning within a society it no longer recognizes."[30] Robert Bellah, commenting on the modern church's societal perception wrote, "Our socially constructed conception of how things really are is seriously out of date."[31] If these observations are accurate, churches must become students of the culture and attempt to find creative ways to become important to the culture around them. Accountability to listen to the culture must be a commitment of the church. Every member of the church must be involved in dialogue with the culture of their communities. The agendas of the culture must be high on the list of priorities for the churches. The reason that government today is so involved in public benevolence issues is largely due to the fact that the churches have abandoned so many of the community's pleas for help. One is reminded that, in the wake of the great awakenings, schools, orphanages, aid societies, care for the poor, hospitals, and other benevolent ministries were established by the churches and by Christians who wished to see the gospel lived out not only in word, but also in deed. A recovery of the church's care for the culture is necessary if individual mission and evangelistic witness can ever take place with integrity.

Accountability for mission and evangelism has to be elevated in the church. Church members must be willing to be accountable to one another for the gospel they claim to believe. As it is now, a good church member is one who attends services on a regular basis and who tithes. Without accountability for personal involvement with the gospel, the church can never break outside the walls that enclose it from the culture. The apostle Paul often called for accountability among the members of the churches. Galatians and Ephesians are examples. The pagans of the Roman Empire were attracted to Christianity by the high moral standards and the love of the Christians for others. In today's culture it is not necessary to maintain high moral standards to be a member of a local church or, in some cases, to be its pastor! Those who think that the culture does not see the hypocrisy of such instances are avoiding reality. If the community around it really believed that a local church took the Christian life seriously, it might notice the same things critics of the early Christians noticed in the initial days of Christianity.

These steps are not exhaustive, of course. Much more must be done. But a recognition by the church that individual mission and evangelistic witness is possible in today's culture is vital. Many church members participate in the routine of worship as if personal mission involvement were not possible. The endless possibilities of being on mission must be held high in the life of the churches. Give church members the opportunity to dream and envision what might be done by a church that takes the mission of God seriously. Encourage every Christian to join God in what God is doing in the world.

There are evidences of spiritual movements happening across the world. A person does not have to look very far to engage others in conversations that illuminate this observation. An airplane flight might be an opportunity to meet someone from another country who is a Christian and who speaks of the advance of the gospel in his or her country. A meal with internationals might afford an opportunity to hear the stories. Richard Kew and Cyril Okorocha explain:

> It might be a "…Chilean talking passionately about his outreach among professionals in Santiago; across the table sits a woman from Sierra Leone, a bishop from Mozambique, or someone from Scotland. At the next meal your companions could be a Palestinian, a Sri Lankan, or a young man with a burning zeal for Christ from the Pacific island nation of Tonga."[32]

Certainly scholars such as Phillip Jenkins have reminded us that the gospel is on the move, especially in the Southern Hemisphere. We ought to pay attention to the reality that God is indeed engaged and on mission in the world. Experiences of this sort make it clear that the topic of Christianity is on the lips of people from nations all over the world. Kew and Okorocha prefer to illustrate such conversation by saying that the great spiritual depression is over.[33] People are indeed interested in spirituality. Instead of becoming depressed about the spiritual condition of America, we should recognize the reality that the communities around us are indeed talking among themselves about spiritual issues. Eugene Peterson writing of the situation in North America said:

> There is a ground-swell of recognition spreading through our culture that all life is at root spiritual; that everything we see is formed and sustained by what we cannot see. Those of us who grew up in the Great Spiritual Depression and who accustomed ourselves to an obscure life in the shadow of arrogant Rationalism and bullying Technology can hardly believe our eyes and ears. People all around us—neighbors and strangers, rich and poor, communists and capitalists—want to know God.[34]

If Peterson is correct, there is simply no excuse for our churches to satisfy themselves with business as usual, immersed in corporate religiosity, content to leave the gospel within the walls of the churches. There is simply no case that can be made to isolate our faith from the world and leave our communities hungry to hear while we remain mute and timid.

A further reason why the challenge to mission must be held high is the collapse of ideologies unfavorable to prophetic perceptions of the Christian gospel. Most persons, especially those who grew up in the period of the Cold War, could scarcely believe it when the Berlin Wall was torn down. I remember standing in Red Square and reflecting on my faith experience with other Russian Christians in front of Lenin's tomb. The personal impact was enormous, especially after living my whole life fearing the Russian threat and with the knowledge that the Soviet position toward Christianity was one of intolerance. Yet with the collapse of the Soviet Union came freedom for mission.

The same collapse is happening in many countries. While the People's Republic of China might be nominally communist, "even privileged Chinese insiders are prepared to admit that Maoism has been hollowed out."[35] The end of civil wars in Portuguese-speaking southern Africa, and the collapse of Apartheid in South Africa are evidences of the collapse of ideologies unfavorable to prophetic perceptions of the Christian gospel. Americans are waking up to the possibilities that the ideology of the assumed Christian nation they live in is distinctly more secular and that missionaries from Korea and Brazil now view America as a mission field. These realities open wide the door of opportunity for individual involvement in mission by Christians in all the churches.

Increasing opportunities through communication make mission more favorable. Technological advances, the Internet, chat rooms on the Web, and visual media are exploding. Kew and Okorocha aver:

> While "talking" through computers may seem horribly impersonal to older generations, people once felt that way about telephones. Yet online conversations could well become the starting point for many as they journey toward faith.[36]

More and more churches are focusing on seekers with little or no Christian memory and are providing learning opportunities for them to explore the attraction of the gospel. As the information age continues to unfold, the church must take every available opportunity to link to the culture and to answer the questions of those who are seeking spiritual knowledge.

Another implication that comes from New Testament history is that the culture today still fosters opportunities for small groups of Christians gathering together in associations. According to some estimates, more than 90 percent of Americans today are members of some kind of small group. It may be a golf group, a study group, a professional group, or some special interest group. There are significant opportunities for Christians to organize special interest groups in their homes to examine the issues of spirituality.

Persons who are seekers, like the Gentiles who attended the synagogue in the New Testament day, often welcome opportunities for fellowship and spiritual discussion outside the walls of the church.

Christians who wish to be on mission can take the opportunity to include friends and neighbors, coworkers, and even newcomers to the community in a small group in their home. Such a setting can allow those seeking to know about Christianity the opportunity to experiment with it in a small and intimate group. These groups offer perhaps the best opportunity to do evangelism in depth within the culture. Much of what is done in the name of evangelism in churches presupposes knowledge of Christianity and of Scripture, so that those who might be reached are frustrated with unanswered questions that the church is not prepared or equipped by way of its liturgy or programs to answer. Small groups or associations can offer opportunities to explore the concepts of Christianity in depth in the home of a Christian.

The New Testament church recognized that its mission was to reach those in a particular locale and to reach out to whomever it could regardless of their background. It was constantly hoping to draw into itself those who were seekers in the community. In each city in which Paul established a church there were problems that arose. Corinth is an example. The Corinthian community consisted predominantly of Gentiles. Not many were well-educated, as Paul says in 1 Corinthians 1:26. Evidence also suggests that some had been polytheistic (1 Cor. 8:5). Some of the people had come from backgrounds of immorality. Hinson says, "The larger agenda, however, was how the Corinthians should relate to their natural cultural backgrounds now that they were Christians."[37] Addressing such issues as those in Corinth was vital to proper contextualization of the gospel and provided the churches help in learning to interface with the general culture that surrounded them.

A church that is not sensitive to the culture around it will not easily become a kingdom-focused church. It is quite easy to develop a corporate model that appeals to one thin stratum of the culture. Yet, a kingdom-focused church will grapple with the imperfections of the culture as it seeks to be on mission. It will accept persons where they are and attempt to help them, as Paul did with the Corinthians, to live as Christians in their culture.

It is also important today for churches that are missional to recognize the importance of planting new congregations. The "America as melting pot" analogy no longer works (nor is desired). The United States is multicultural, multilinguistic, and multiracial. While it is assumed that there are plenty of churches in America to fill the spiritual needs of the nation, all of them added together would not be able to contain the population of this nation on any given Sunday should every person in America desire to attend at once. Further, most of the churches are locked in a cultural vacuum that does not reflect the multivariant nature of the larger community. Few churches, for example, are open to motorcycle clubs. These persons represent a culture vastly different from the churched culture. Their language, their lifestyle, and their mode of dress are abhorrent to many churched people. Yet a Methodist friend of mine has been called by one of the larger clubs in Atlanta as their pastor. They worship in an open area on a mountain. As one of the members of the club expressed, "I work construction, and I helped build some of those buildings in Atlanta with the points on top (churches with steeples), but I would not set foot in the damned place." While this may seem an extreme example, it is indicative of persons in the culture who wish to express their faith, but not in the context of the church as it now exists.

Many persons from other lifestyles–who might never be reached by established local churches–could become part of communities of faith, if different types of communities were to be established that will reach them. Church planting must become more contextualized and driven by needs of indigenous peoples. Church starting must emerge out of the context of the culture. It cannot be the object of the denominational agency's desire to begin a church in an area just because the area seems not to have a church within a few miles, or because they have the budget to begin one. Churches will be needed by the hundreds in many communities just to keep up with the demographic growth realities. Rather than insisting that the denomination be charged with church planting, local churches should take it upon themselves to plant congregations in areas of missional outreach. Churches must also be willing to be on mission to segments of the culture without a need to revise the cultural setting to be like the home church. Denominations must be willing to address problems, but also to let churches emerge with their own distinct understandings as Christian communities who can also be on mission.

History has much to teach the church on mission. The evolution of the Christian gospel is not complete; therefore, churches must see themselves as constantly evaluating their role in the Christian mission in terms of the precedent set by the New Testament. When missional Christians fully examine the context of the New Testament world in all its diversity and the churches that were established in it, they should be able to move beyond a Christendom mind-set that assumes a culture that is open to the gospel as Christians view it and toward the reality of a world that is pluralistic and diverse in its views of spirituality and faith.

A Final Word

The church of Jesus Christ has enormous potential to transform the world. Every expression of the body of Christ in communities has the potential of liberating persons from bondage, unhappiness, lack of purpose in their lives, and despair. The gospel changes lives. We who are absolutely committed to the work of Christ's body in the world want to join God in what God intends for the world. Nothing can become more important to our living than to be a part of God's great agenda. The *missio Dei* is redemptive. It is full of potential. It is life-giving in the here and now of everyday experience. Each church has been given a gift and an opportunity. The gift is the potential of a gathered group of people who have been transformed by the life of Christ. The opportunity is to live as transformed people in a way that will cause the community around our churches to observe us and to want to ask us about the hope that dwells within us. The community will never hear the gospel until we are willing to listen to them, to live along side them, to hurt when they hurt, to rejoice when they rejoice, and to dialogue with them in such a way that their deepest questions about God are freely explored. May God touch our lips, our hands, and our hearts so that we will be willing to bring healing to the deaf ears of the communities around us and with Jesus say, "*Ephphatha.*"[38]

Notes

Chapter 1: Becoming a Church for the Twenty-first Century

[1]To be discreet, I will refrain from mentioning specific congregations by name throughout this book.

[2]For further insights about the continual rediscovery of the church, see Darrell L. Guder, *The Continuing Conversion of the Church* (Grand Rapids: Eerdmans, 2000).

[3]I am indebted to Craig Van Gelder for the DNA metaphor. His article "From The Corporate Church to Missional Church: The Challenge Facing Congregations Today," *Review and Expositor* 101:3 (Summer 2004), p. 425–50 pointed out the importance of churches recognizing the reality of their genetic code.

[4]Schaller characterized the shift in American cultural lifestyle and religious life. He helped us to understand what was happening in mainline churches and among new congregations. His treatment also addressed the changing nature of families, the workplace, and other sociological shifts. Lyle Schaller, *It's a Different World: The Challenge for Today's Pastor* (Nashville: Abingdon Press, 1987).

[5]Americans do not speak with one voice about the influence of religion. While religion is a positive force in the world, the extent of religious war is troublesome to a majority. Nearly 65 percent of Americans believe that religion plays a significant role in most wars in the world. Pew Research Center, "Americans Struggle with Religion's Role at Home and Abroad" (March 20, 2002), available through http://people-press.org/reports/, accessed February 13, 2006.

[6]According to a Gallup poll, "In the last several years, there has been a gradual decline in the percentage of Americans satisfied with the degree of influence organized religion has on society–though this trend was temporarily interrupted by the Sept. 11 terror attacks. In January 2001, 64% of Americans said they were 'very' or 'somewhat' satisfied with the influence of organized religion on society. In January 2002, the first post-9/11 reading saw that the percentage satisfied was slightly higher, at 69%. A year later, in 2003, the percentage who said they were satisfied dropped to 59%, about where it was in 2004. In the most recent poll, conducted Jan. 3–5, 2005, 55% of Americans now say they are satisfied with religion's influence, and 41% are dissatisfied." Gallup Poll (February 01, 2005), available through www.gallup.com.

The uneasiness factor can be seen as especially prevalent in the lives of teens. According to the Gallup Poll, "Our nation's youth are apprehensive about the future, and believe the quality of life for children in the future will be worse than it is today. They are uneasy about a host of problems: the threat of AIDS; the availability of potentially deadly drugs; the ease of purchasing deadly assault weapons; random death and violence." Gallup Poll (April 27, 1999), available through www.gallup.com.

[7]See Paul Hiebert's foreword in Arthur F. Glasser, *Announcing the Kingdom* (Grand Rapids: Baker, 2003), 8.

[8]Michael Cassidy, *The Small Beginnings of Reconciliation in Port Elizabeth* (Port Elizabeth, South Africa: African Enterprise, 1997), 17–23.

[9]Robert Sellers. "A Baptist View of Mission for Postmodernity," *Review and Expositor* 100:4 (Fall 2003), 641–84.

[10]Darrell L. Guder, *Missional Church: A Vision for the Sending of the Church in North America* (Grand Rapids: Eerdmans, 1998).

[11]Van Gelder, "From Corporate Church to Missional Church."

[12]For a thorough examination of the kingdom of God and mission, see George Beasley-Murray, *Jesus and the Kingdom of God* (Grand Rapids: Eerdmans, 1986). Also see Glasser, *Announcing the Kingdom.*

[13]John Driver, *Images of the Church on Mission* (Scottdale, Pa.: Herald Press, 1997), 84.

[14]John Jonsson, *Crisis of Mission in the Bible* (Charlotte, N.C.: Nilses, 1987), 78.

[15]Jürgen Moltmann, *The Church in the Power of the Spirit* (New York: Harper and Row, 1975), 167.

[16]Ibid.

[17]Jonsson, *Crisis of Mission,* 80.

[18]Beasley-Murray, *Jesus and the Kingdom of God,* 145

[19]Glasser, *Announcing the Kingdom,* 225.

[20]John Fullenbach, *The Kingdom of God: The Message of Jesus Today* (Maryknoll, N.Y.: Orbis, 1998), 249.

[21]Peter Kuzmic, "The Church and the Kingdom of God," in *The Church: God's Agent for Change,* ed. Bruce Nicholls (Exeter, Australia: Paternoster, 1986), 49.

[22]Fullenbach, *Kingdom of God,* 249.

[23]Ibid., 252.

[24]Mortimer Arias, *Announcing the Reign of God: Evangelization and the Subversive Memory of Jesus* (Philadelphia: Fortress Press, 1984), 1–3.

[25]Fullenbach, *Kingdom of God,* 270.

[26]See Fred Craddock, *Overhearing the Gospel* (St. Louis: Chalice Press, 2002).

[27]Gabriel Fackre, as cited in Arias, *Announcing the Reign,* 70.

[28]Emilio Castro and Jacques Matthey, eds., *Your Kingdom Come: Mission Perspectives* (Geneva, Switz.: WCC, 1980), 93.

[29]Arias, *Announcing the Reign,* 70.

[30]See Walter Brueggemann for a treatment of the power of story in *Biblical Perspectives on Evangelism: Living in a Three-Storied Universe* (Nashville: Abingdon Press, 1993).

[31]Eduard Schillenbeeckx, *Church: The Human Story of God* (New York: Crossroad, 1990), 157.

[32]Gerhard Lohfink, *Jesus and Community* (London: SPCK, 1985), 150.

[33]Fullenbach, *Kingdom of God,* 270.

[34]Quoted in ibid., 271.

[35]Harold A. Snyder, *Models of the Kingdom* (Nashville: Abingdon Press, 1991), 154–155.

[36]David J. Bosch, *Transforming Mission: Paradigm Shifts in the Theology of Mission* (Maryknoll, N.Y.: Orbis, 1991), 10.

[37]Brueggemann, *Biblical Perspectives on Evangelism.*

[38]Bosch, *Transforming Mission,* 10.

[39]Paul F. Knitter, *Jesus and the Other Names* (Maryknoll, N.Y.: Orbis, 1996), 108.

[40]Alfred C. Krass, *Five Lanterns at Sundown: Evangelism in a Chastened Mood* (Grand Rapids: Eerdmans, 1978), 85.

[41]Henry H. Knight III, *A Future for Truth* (Nashville: Abingdon Press, 1997), 92.

[42]See my treatment of listening and ministry in evangelism in Ronald Johnson, *How Will They Hear If We Don't Listen?* (Nashville: Broadman and Holman, 1994).

[43]Krass, *Five Lanterns,* 127.

[44]Driver, *Images of the Church on Mission,* 188.

[45]George G. Hunter III, *Church for the Unchurched* (Nashville: Abingdon Press, 1996), 20.

[46]Knitter, *Jesus and the Other Names,* 109.

[47]Ibid.

[48]Ibid.

[49]Bosch, *Transforming Mission,* 378, quoting Howard Snyder, *Liberting the Church* (Downers Grove, Ill.: InterVarsity Press, 1983).

[50]Ibid., 519.

Chapter 2: Does Your Church Really Know Itself?

[1]Herb Miller, *Church Personality Matters: How to Build Positive Partners* (St. Louis: Chalice Press, 1999), 1.

[2]Joseph A. Litterer, *The Analysis of Organizations* (New York: John Wiley & Sons, 1973), 317.

[3]H. Wheeler Robinson, *Corporate Personality in Ancient Israel* (Philadelphia: Fortress Press, 1980), 25.

[4]Ibid.

[5]Paul Mundey, *Unlocking Church Doors: Ten Keys to Positive Change* (Nashville: Abingdon Press, 1997), 46.

[6]For additional help see Loren Mead, *The Once and Future Church* (Washington, D.C.: The Alban Institute, 1991), 8–29.

[7]Mary Tuomi Hammond, *The Church and the Dechurched: Mending a Damaged Faith* (St. Louis: Chalice Press, 2001), 74.

[8]Miller, *Church Personality Matters,* 128.

[9]Darrell L. Guder, *Missional Church: A Vision for the Sending of the Church in North America* (Grand Rapids: Eerdmans, 1998), 199.

[10]Ibid.

[11]Wilbert Shenk, *The Transfiguration of Mission: Biblical, Theological and Historical Foundations* (Scottdale, Pa.: Herald Press, 1993).

[12]Ronald W. Johnson, *How Will They Hear If We Don't Listen?* (Nashville: Broadman Press, 1994).

[13]Douglas Steere, as quoted in Johnson, *How Will They Hear…?,* 122.

Chapter 3: What Makes You Think the Community Cares about Your Message?

[1]C. Kirk Hadaway and P. L. Marker, "Did You Really Go to Church This Week? Behind the Poll Data," *The Christian Century* (May 6, 1988): 472–75, available at http://www.religion-online.org/showarticle.asp?title=237.

[2]Andrew Walsh, "Church, Lies, and Polling Data," *Religion in the News* 1:2 (Fall 1998). http://www.trincoll.edu/depts/csrpl/RIN%20Vol.1No.2/Church_lies_polling.htm.

[3]Penny Marler, Kirk Hadaway, and Mark Chaves, "Overreporting Church Attendance in America: Evidence that Demands the Same Verdict," *American Sociological Review* 63:1 (February 1998): 123–30.

[4]Walsh, "Church, Lies, and Polling Data.".

[5]Stanley Hauerwas and Wiliam H. Willimon, *Resident Aliens: A Provocative Christian Assessment of Culture and Ministry for People Who Know That Something Is Wrong* (Nashville: Abingdon Press, 1992), 15.

[6]Claude Geffre, "Christianity and Culture," *International Review of Missions* 84:332/333 (1995): 18.

[7]Ibid.

[8]Ibid., 19.

[9]Ibid.

[10]Ibid.

[11]Wilbert R. Shenk, "Missionary Encounter with Culture," *International Bulletin of Missionary Research* (July 1991): 104–9.

[12]Marva Dawn, *Reaching Out Without Dumbing Down: A Theology of Worship for This Urgent Time* (Grand Rapids: Eerdmans, 1995).

[13]Stephen Neill, *The Unfinished Task* (London: Edinburg House Press, 1958).

[14]Emilio Castro, "On Evangelism and Culture: Some Reflections," *International Review of Missions* 84 (1995): 365.

[15]Paul Russ Satari, "'Translatability' in the Missional Approach of Lamin Sanneh," in The *Church Between Gospel and Culture: The Emerging Mission in North America,* ed. George Hunsberger and Craig Van Gelder (Grand Rapids: Eerdmans, 1996), 273.

[16]Castro, "On Evangelism and Culture," 367.

[17]David J. Bosch, *Transforming Mission: Paradigm Shifts in the Theology of Mission* (Maryknoll, N.Y.: Orbis, 1991), 507.

[18]Hunsberger and Van Gelder, *The Church,* 32.

[19]Ibid., 34.

[20]George G. Hunter III, *Church for the Unchurched* (Nashville: Abingdon Press, 1996), 37–40.

[21]Bosch, *Transforming Mission,* 149.

[22]Ibid., 150.

[23]Ibid., 151.

[24]Kenneth M. Johnson and Calvin L. Beale, "The Rural Rebound," *American Demographics* (July 1995): 1–5.

[25]Ibid.

[26]Information from http://www.pepps.fsu.edu/safe/pdf/pop4.pdf

[27]Johnson and Beale, "The Rural Rebound."

[28]Ibid.

[29]Ron D. Dempsey, *Faith Outside the Walls: Why People Don't Come and Why the Church Must Listen* (Macon, Ga.: Smyth & Helwys, 1997), 43.

[30]David F. Wells, *God in the Wasteland: The Reality of Truth in a World of Fading Dreams* (Grand Rapids: Eerdmans, 1994), 13.

[31]"America's Heartland Turns to Hot Location for Melting Pot," *The Wall Street Journal,* 31 October 1995, 1a.

[32]Ibid.

[33]Calvin Beale, as quoted in Ibid.

[34]Phillip Jenkins, *The Next Christendom: The Coming of Global Christianity* (New York: Oxford, 2002), 100.

[35]Kevin E. Deardorff and Patricia Montgomery, "National Population Trends," *U.S. Census Bureau Report,* 1–4. http://www.census.gov/population/www/pop-profile/nattrend.html.

[36]Arlene F. Saluter, "Marital Status and Living Arrangements," *U.S. Census Bureau Report* (1998). http://www.census.gov/population/www/pop-profile/msla.html.

[37]Ibid.

[38]Oscar F. Blackwelder, "The Church and Our Time," *Theology Today* 5 (1948): 156–57.

[39]Robert Wuthnow, *The Restructuring of American Religion* (Princeton, N.J.: Princeton University Press, 1988), 66.

[40]Harry S. Truman, as quoted in Ibid.

[41]Dwight D. Eisenhower, as quoted in Ibid.

[42]Ibid, 67.

[43]Robert Bellah, as cited in Ron D. Dempsey, *Faith Outside the Walls: Why People Don't Come and Why the Church Must Listen* (Macon, Ga.: Smyth & Helwys, 1997), 75.

[44]Hunter, *Church for the Unchurched,* 20.

[45]Dempsey, *Faith Outside the Walls,* 74.

[46]Ibid., 22.

[47]Ibid.

[48]David A. Roozen and Kirk Hadaway, *Church & Denominational Growth* (Nashville: Broadman, 1993).

[49]Dempsey, *Faith Outside the Walls,* 46.

[50]Hunter, *Church for the Unchurched,* 20.

[51]Paul G. Hiebert, *Anthropological Reflections on Missiological Issues* (Grand Rapids: Baker, 1994), 19.

[52]Ibid, 31.

[53]Ibid, 33.

[54]Ibid.

[55]Alister McGrath, *Evangelicalism & the Future of Christianity* (Downers Grove, Ill.: InterVarsity, 1995), 161.

[56]Caleb Rosado, "The Nature of Society and the Challenge to the Mission of the Church," *International Review of Mission* 77 (1988): 22–23.

[57]Diogenes Allen, *Christian Belief in a Postmodern World* (Louisville: Westminster/John Knox Press, 1989), 8.

[58]Craig Van Gelder, "A Great New Fact of Our Day: America as Mission Field," *Missiology* 26 (1991): 412–17.

[59]Jean-Francois Lyotard, *The Postmodern Condition: A Report on Knowledge,* trans. Geoff Benningon and Brian Massumi (Minneapolis: Univ. of Minn. Press, 1984), as quoted in Lawrence Cahoone, *From Modernism to Postmodernism* (Cambridge: Blackwell, 1996), 481.

[60]Hans Kung, "The Reemergence of the Sacred: Transmitting Religious Traditions in a Postmodern World," *Conservative Judaism* 40 (Summer 1988): 8–18.

[61]Allen, *Christian Belief in a Postmodern World,* 6.

[62]Craig Van Gelder, "A Great New Fact," 412.

[63]Stanley Grenz, *A Primer on Postmodernism* (Grand Rapids: Eerdmans, 1996), 3.

[64]Thomas Oden, *After Modernity…What?: Agenda for Theology* (Grand Rapids: Zondervan, 1992), 44.

[65]Bosch, *Transforming Mission,* 350.

[66]Kung, "Reemergence of the Sacred," 10.

[67]Jacques Derrida, "The End of the Book and the Beginning of Writing," chapter 1 in *Of Grammatology,* trans. Gayatri Chakravorty Spivak (Baltimore: Johns Hopkins Univerity Press, 1974), 6–26, as quoted in Cahoone, *From Modernism to Postmodernism,* 336.

[68]Ibid., 337.

[69]Bosch, *Transforming Mission,* 263.

[70]Oden, *After Modernity.*

[71]Bosch, *Transforming Mission,* 263.

[72]Joe Holland, "The Postmodern Paradigm and Contemporary Catholicism," in *Varieties of Postmodern Theology,* ed. David Ray Griffin, William A. Beardslee, and Joe Holland (Albany: State University of New York Press, 1989), 10.

[73]Bosch, *Transforming Mission,* 263.

[74]Van Gelder, "A Great New Fact," 411.

[75]George G. Hunter, III, *How To Reach Secular People* (Nashville: Abingdon Press, 1992), 27–28.

[76]Alex Callinicos, *Against Postmodernism: A Marxist Critique* (New York: St. Martins, 1990), 32.

[77]Bosch, *Transforming Mission,* 264.

[78]Rick Gosnell, "The Postmodern Paradigm: Challenges to the Evangelistic Ministry of the Church" (Ph.D. diss., Southern Baptist Theological Seminary, 1993), 19.

[79]Huston Smith, *Beyond the Post-Modern Mind* (Wheaton, Ill.: Theosophical, 1989), 7.

[80]Lesslie Newbigin, *Foolishness to the Greeks* (Grand Rapids: Eerdmans, 1986), 25.

[81]Richard B. Cunningham, *The Christian Faith and Its Contemporary Rivals* (Nashville: Broadman, 1988), 77–78.

[82]Bosch, *Transforming Mission,* 263.

[83]Pauline M. Rosenau, *Post-Modernism and the Social Sciences: Insights, Inroads, and Intrusions* (Princeton, N.J.: Princeton University Press, 1992), 48.

[84]Sydney E. Ahlstrom, *A Religious History of the American People* (New Haven, Conn.: Yale University Press, 1972), 353–57.

[85]David Harvey, *The Condition of Postmodernity: An Enquiry into the Origins of Cultural Change* (Cambridge: Basil Blackwell, 1989), 12.

[86]Arnold E. Leon, *Secularization: Science without God?* (London: SCM, 1985), 7.

[87]Gosnell, *Postmodern Paradigm,* 35.

[88]James B. Miller, "The Emerging Postmodern World," in *Postmodern Theology: Christian Faith in a Pluralistic World,* ed. Frederic B. Burnham (San Francisco: Harper and Row, 1989), 9–10.

[89]Bosch, *Transforming Mission,*350.

[90]Van Gelder, "A Great New Fact," 411–12.

[91]Kenneth Scott Latourette, *The First Five Centuries* (Grand Rapids: Zondervan, 1970), 1351.

[92]Rosenau, *Post-Modernism and the Social Sciences,* 5.

[93]Kung, "Reemergence of the Sacred," 23.

[94]Gosnell, *Postmodern Paradigm,* 46.

[95]Irving Greenberg, "From Modernity to Postmodernity: Community and the Revitalization of Traditional Religion," *Religious Education* 73 (1978): 457.

[96]Kung, "Reemergence of the Sacred," 16.

[97]Wuthnow, *Restructuring of American Religion,* 15.

[98]Lesslie Newbigin, The Gospel in a Pluralistic Society (Grand Rapids: Eerdmans. 1989), 212.

[99]Ibid., 213.

[100]Gosnell, *Postmodern Paradigm,* 58.

[101]Rousenau, *Post-Modernism and the Social Sciences,* 4. See also: Diogenes Allen, "Christian Values in a Post-Christian Context," in *Postmodern Theology: Christian Faith in a Pluralist World,* (San Francisco: HarperCollins, 1989), 20–36.

[102]Thomas Kuhn, *The Structure of Scientific Revolutions* (Chicago: University of Chicago Press, 1970), 10–11.

[103]Brent Waters, "Ministry and the University in a Postmodern World," *Religion and Intellectual Life* 4 (Fall 1986): 113.

[104]Joel A. Barker, *Paradigms: The Business of Discovering the Future* (San Francisco: Harper, 1992).

[105]Kuhn, *Structure of Scientific Revolutions,* 111.

[106]Harry Lee Poe, *Christian Witness in a Postmodern World* (Nashville: Abingdon Press, 1991), 26.

[107]Jonathan Culler, *On Deconstruction: Theory and Criticism after Structuralism* (Ithaca, N.Y.: Cornell University Press, 1982), 22.

[108]Gosnell, *Postmodern Paradigm,* 66.

[109]Walter Truett Anderson, *Reality Isn't What It Used to Be: Theatrical Politics, Ready-to-Wear Religion, Global Myths, Primitive Chic, and Other Wonders of the Postmodern World* (San Francisco: Harper and Row, 1990), 8.

[110]Ibid., 183.

[111]Craig Van Gelder, "Postmodernism as an Emerging Worldview," *Calvin Theological Journal* 26 (1991): 415.

[112]Stanley Fish, *Doing What Comes Naturally* (Durham, N.C.: Duke University Press, 1989), 344.

[113]Gary B. Madison, *The Hermeneutics of Postmodernity: Figures and Themes* (Bloomington: Indiana University Press, 1990), 61.

[114]Michael W. Mesmer, "Making Sense of/with Postmodernism," *Soundings: An Interdisciplinary Journal* 68 (1985): 406.

[115]Tex Sample, *U.S. Lifestyles and Mainline Churches* (Louisville: Westminster/John Knox Press, 1990), 25.

[116]Anderson, *Reality Isn't What It Used to Be,* 9.

[117]Gosnell, *Postmodern Paradigm,* 87.

[118]Sample, *U.S. Lifestyles,* 25.

[119]Ibid., 11–17.

[120]Robert Bellah, et al., eds., *Habits of the Heart: Individualism and Commitment in American Life* (Berkeley: University of California Press, 1985), 226.

[121]George G. Hunter, III, *The Contagious Congregation: Frontiers in Evangelism and Church Growth* (Nashville: Abingdon Press, 1979), 26.

[122]Ben C. Johnson, *Rethinking Evangelism: A Theological Approach* (Louisville: Westminster/John Knox Press, 1987), 12.

[123]Richard Stoll Armstrong, *Service Evangelism* (Philadelphia: Westminster Press, 1979), 57–64.

[124]William J. Abraham, *The Logic of Evangelism* (Grand Rapids: Eerdmans, 1989), 13.

[125]Bosch, *Transforming Mission,* 420.

[126]Michael Green, *Evangelism Through the Local Church* (Grand Rapids: Eerdmans, 1970), 9.

[127]Carl F.H. Henry, *Twilight of a Great Civilization: The Drift Toward Neo-Paganism* (Westchester: Crossway, 1988).

[128]Henry H. Knight III, *A Future for Truth* (Nashville: Abingdon Press, 1997), 87.

[129]Carl F.H. Henry, *God, Revelation and Authority* 6 vols. (Waco: Word, 1976), 456.

[130]J. I. Packer, *"Fundamentalism" and the Word of God* (Grand Rapids: Eerdmans, 1958), 93.

[131]Knight, *A Future for Truth,* 89.

[132]Ibid.

[133]Henry, *God, Revelation and Authority,* 205.

[134]Knight, *A Future for Truth,* 90.

[135]Ibid., 91.

[136]Ibid.

[137]Ibid.

[138]McGrath, *Evangelicalism & the Future of Christianity,* 170.

[139]Thomas Torrance, *Reality and Evangelical Theology* (Philadelphia: Westminster Press, 1982), 17.

[140]Knight, *A Future for Truth,* 16.

[141]Ibid., 91.

[142]Clark Pinnock, *The Scripture Principle* (San Francisco: Harper and Row, 1984), 49.

[143]Grenz, *Primer on Postmodernism,* 114.

[144]Delos Miles, *Introduction to Evangelism* (Nashville: Baptist Sunday School Board, 1983).

[145]John R.W. Stott, *Christian Mission in the Modern World* (Downers Grove, Ill.: InterVarsity Press, 1975), 19.

[146]Mortimer Arias, *Announcing the Reign of God: Evangelization and the Subversive Memory of Jesus* (Philadelphia: Fortress Press, 1984), 15.

[147]Ibid.

[148]George G. Bosch III, *How to Reach Secular People* (Nashville: Abingdon Press. 1992).

[149]Hunter, *The Contagious Congregation,* 94.

[150]Sample, *U.S. Lifestyles,* 47.

[151]Green, *Evangelism Through the Local Church,* 91.

[152]Poe, *Christian Witness in a Postmodern World,* 139.

[153]Joel Barker discusses a similar approach when trying to imagine the future. His paradigm question relative to imagining the future is critical to new ways of thinking. Therefore, I have adapted his approach to challenge the church in new directions for the future. See his *Paradigms: The Business of Discovering the Future* (San Francisco: Harper, 1992).

Chapter 4: Using the Enneagram to Discover Who You Really Are

[1]Michael J. Goldberg, *The 9 Ways of Working: How to Use the Enneagram to Discover Your Natural Strengths and Work More Effectively,* quoted online at http://9waysofworking.com/qEnneaHistory2.html.

[2]Ibid.

[3]See http://www.ourladyswarriors.org/dissent/enneagram.htm, or Richard Rohr and Andreas Ebert, *Discovering the Enneagram: An Ancient Tool for a New Spiritual Journey* (New York: Crossroad, 1992), 5–13. Since the publication of Rohr and Ebert's book, a second book has provided further information. According to Ebert, "Since the first edition we have become convinced that the Enneagram does not derive from medieval Islamic (Sufi) sources, but can be traced back, at least in part, to the Christian desert monk Evagrius Ponticus (d. 399) and the Franciscan Blessed Ramon Lull (1236–1315)." Richard Rohr and Andreas Ebert, *The Enneagram: A Christian Perspective* (Crossroad: New York, 2004), ix.

[4]Rohr and Ebert, *Discovering the Enneagram,* 7.

[5]From the Lake Tahoe Wellness Institute Web site, http://www.tahoeinstitue.com?Hx%20of%20E.htm

[6]Other sources indicate that he was born in 1872; Patrick J. Aspell and Dee Dee Aspell, *The Enneagram Personality Portraits: Enhancing Professional Relationships* (San Francisco: Pfeiffer & Company, 1997), 20.

[7]Fr. Mitch Pacwa, "The Enneagram: Spirituality It Is Not," *Fidelity* (September, 1999): 33–36, available at http://www.catholicculture.org/docs/doc_view.cfm?recnum=2622.

[8]Rabbi Howard Addison, *The Enneagram and the Kabbalah: Reading Your Soul* (Woodstock: Jewish Lights Publishing, 1998), 19.

[9]Ibid.

[10]From the Enneagram Institute Web site, http://www.enneagraminstitute.com/articles/Ncontribute.asp.

[11]Rohr and Ebert, *Discovering the Enneagram,* 213–14.

[12]Ibid., 214.

[13]Ibid., 215–16.

[14]Ibid., 216–17.

[15]Ibid., 218–19.

[16]Ibid., 219–20.

[17]Ibid., 220–21.

[18]Ibid., 222.

[19]Ibid., 223–24.

[20]Ibid., 224–25.

[21]Http://www.digital-brilliance.com/kab/faq.htm. Kabbalah FAQ. Usenet/Internet newsgroup alt.magick. Copyright Colin Low 1993–1996 (*cal@hplb.hpl.hp.com*) Release Date: February 1996.

[22]Addison, *Enneagram and the Kabbalah,* 3–5.

[23]Ibid., 5–6.

[24]Ibid., 6.

[25]Rohr and Ebert, *Discovering the Enneagram*, 226.

[26]Ibid., 226.

[27]Aspell and Aspell, *Enneagram Personality Portraits*, 72.

[28]"A Mangled Angle on Personality," *Psychology Today* 28:3 (May/June 1995): 10. Web link: http://cms.psychologytoday.com/articles/pto-19950501–000005.html.

[29]Aspell and Aspell, *Enneagram Personality Portraits*, 2.

[30]Ibid., 71.

[31]Jean Seligmann, John Seligmann, and Joseph Seligmann, "To Find Self, Take a Number," *Newsweek* 124:11 (September 12, 1994).

[32]Helen Palmer, "Unraveling the Personality Puzzle," *Training and Development Journal* 43:9 (September 1989): 88.

Chapter 5: Exploring Your Church's Personality

[1]Renee Baron and Elizabeth Wagele, *The Enneagram Made Easy: Discover the 9 Types of People* (San Francisco: HarperSanFrancisco, 1994), 1.

[2]Aspell and Aspell, *The Enneagram Personality Portraits: Enhancing Professional Relationships* (San Francisco: Pfeiffer & Company, 1997), 99.

[3]Baron and Wagele, *Enneagram Made Easy*, 4.

[4]Aspell and Aspell, *Enneagram Personality Portraits*, 12.

[5]Ibid.

[6]For a more complete treatment of human personalities, see Howard A. Addison, *Cast in God's Image* (Woodstock: Jewish Lights Publishing, 2001), 19–21.

[7]Adapted from Addison, *Cast in God's Image*, 25.

[8]Ibid., 17.

[9]Discussion of these triads is adapted from Addison, *Cast in God's Image*.

[10]Ibid., 42.

Chapter 6: Facing the Obstacles: The Ones on the Inside

[1]Jim Collins, *Good to Great: Why Some Companies Make the Leap and Others Don't* (New York: Harper, 2001), 11.

[2]Herb Miller, *Church Personality Matters: How to Build Positive Partners* (St. Louis: Chalice Press, 1999), 75.

[3]Collins, *Good to Great*, 74.

[4]Mary Tuomi Hammond, *The Church and the Dechurched: Mending a Damaged Faith* (St. Louis: Chalice Press, 2001), 63.

[5]The Barna Group, "New Survey Examines the Impact of Gibson's *Passion* Movie," available on the Barna Web site, at http://www.barna.org/FlexPage.aspx?Page=BarnaUpdateNarrow&BarnaUpdateID=167.

[6]Ibid.

[7]Marva Dawn, *Reaching Out Without Dumbing Down: A Theology of Worship for This Urgent Time* (Grand Rapids: Eerdmans, 1995).

[8]Hammond, *The Church and the Dechurched*, 146.

[9]Ronald W. Johnson and Leonard Sanderson, *Evangelism for All God's People* (Nashville: Baptist Sunday School Board, 1990).

[10]Eduard Thurneysen, *A Theology of Pastoral Care* (Richmond, Va.: John Knox Press, 1962), 127.

[11]Thomas Kuhn, *The Structure of Scientific* (Chicago: University of Chicago Press, 1970).

[12]Joel A. Barker, *Paradigms: The Business of Discovering the Future* (San Francisco: Harper, 1992).

[13]Kuhn, *Structure of Scientific Revolutions*, 158.

Chapter 7: Facing the Obstacles: The Ones on the Outside

[1]Jim Collins, *Good to Great: Why Some Companies Make the Leap and Others Don't* (New York: Harper, 2001), 200.

[2]Harry Lee Poe, *Christian Witness in a Postmodern World* (Nashville: Abingdon Press, 1991), 37.

[3]Barna Poll, November 26, 2001, *http://www.atheists.org/flash.line/islam15.htm*. See also, Barna Poll, "How America's Faith Has Changed Since 9–11" Nov 26, 2001, http://www.barna.org/FlexPage.aspx?Page=BarnaUpdate&BarnaUpdateID=102.

[4]Poe, *Christian Witness in a Postmodern World,* 16.

[5]Joseph Fletcher, *Situation Ethics: The New Morality* (Philadelphia: Westminster Press, 1966).

[6]Ibid., 16.

Chapter 8: How to Listen to the World around You

[1]Mary Tuomi Hammond, *The Church and the Dechurched: Mending a Damaged Faith* (St. Louis: Chalice Press, 2001), 46.

[2]Ibid., 49.

[3]From http://www.rickcross.com/reference/gene_scott/scott4.html.

[4]From http://gonsalves.org/favorite/scott/scott.htm.

[5]From http://www.rickcross.com/reference/gene_scott/scott2.html.

[6]Ronald W. Johnson, *How Will They Hear If We Don't Listen?* (Nashville: Broadman, 1994), 111.

[7]Ibid., 155.

[8]Lyrics by Alison Krauss, from the film *Oh Brother, Where Art Thou?,* Touchstone Video, 2001.

[9]Johnson, *How Will They Hear,* 162

[10]E. Glenn Hinson, *The Evangelization of the Roman Empire* (Macon, Ga.: Mercer University Press, 1981), 52.

[11]Ibid., 53.

[12]Johnson, *How Will They Hear,* 163.

[13]Ibid.

[14]Ibid., 167.

[15]Need 2 Know Web site, http://www.need2know.com/FQ/needsite.cfm.

[16]Incisive Interactive Marketing site, http://www.nua.ie/surveys/how_many_online.

Chapter 9: Restructuring Your Church

[1]Gustavo Gutierrez, *A Theology of Liberation: History, Politics and Salvation* (Maryknoll, N.Y.: Orbis, 1988).

[2]Joseph A. Litterer, *The Analysis of Organizations* (New York: John Wiley and Sons, 1973), 48.

[3]Jim Collins, *Good to Great: Why Some Companies Make the Leap and Others Don't* (New York: Harper, 2001), 78.

Chapter 10: What Tomorrow Brings

[1]Kenneth Scott Latourette, *The First Five Centuries* (Grand Rapids: Zondervan, 1970), 116–20.

[2]Ibid., 116.

[3]Celsus, as quoted in ibid., 116.

[4]E. Glenn Hinson, *The Evangelization of the Roman Empire* (Macon, Ga.: Mercer University Press, 1981), 10.

[5]Ibid., 38.

[6]Ibid., 66.

[7]Martin Hengel and Anna Maria Schwemer, *Paul Between Damascus and Antioch* (Louisville: Westminster John Knox Press, 1997), 81.

[8]Ibid.

[9]Hinson, *Evangelization of the Roman Empire,* 49.

[10]Hengel and Schwemer, *Paul Between Damascus and Antioch,* 88.

[11]Hinson, *Evangelization of the Roman Empire,* 63.

[12]Ibid., 64.

[13]Hinson, *Evangelization of the Roman Empire*, 61.

[14]Helmut Koester, *History, Culture and Religion of the Hellenistic Age* (New York: Walter de Gruyter, 1995), 68.

[15]Ibid.

[16]Ibid.

[17]Ibid., 69.

[18]Ibid., 70.

[19]Ibid., 71.

[20]Hinson, *Evangelization of the Roman Empire*, 51.

[21]Ibid., 33.

[22]Diogenes Allen, *Christian Belief in a Postmodern World* (Louisville: Westminster/John Knox Press, 1989), 12–16.

[23]Hengel and Schwemer, *Paul Between Damascus and Antioch*, 61–62.

[24]Ibid., 62.

[25]Allen, *Christian Belief in a Postmodern World*, 81.

[26]A handing over of something, which is done by word of mouth or in writing or tradition.

[27]Hinson, *Evangelization of the Roman Empire*, 34.

[28]Ibid., 36.

[29]Hinson, *Evangelization of the Roman Empire*, 37.

[30]Ron D. Dempsey, *Faith Outside the Walls: Why People Don't Come and Why the Church Must Listen* (Macon, Ga.: Smyth & Helwys, 1997), 79.

[31]Robert Bellah et al., eds., *Habits of the Heart: Individualism and Commitment in American Life* (Berkeley: University of California, 1985), 77.

[32]Richard Kew and Cyril Okorocha, *Vision Bearers* (Harrisburg, Pa.: Morehouse, 1996), 33.

[33]Ibid., 32.

[34]Eugene Peterson, "Spirit Quest," *Christianity Today* (November 8, 1993): 27–28.

[35]Kew and Okorocha, *Vision Bearers*, 37.

[36]Ibid., 39–40.

[37]Hinson, *Evangelization of the Roman Empire*, 53.

[38]Mark 7:34.

Works Cited

Periodicals

Blackwelder, Oscar F. "The Church in Our Time." *Theology Today* 5 (1948): 156–57.

Bosch, David J. "Mission in Jesus' Way: A Perspective from Luke's Gospel." *Missionalia* 17 (1989): 3–21.

Bradley, Martin. "Churches and Church Membership in the United States, 1990." *Glenmary Research* (1990): 2–20.

Castro, Emilio. "On Evangelism and Culture: Some Reflections." *International Review of Missions* 84 (1995): 335.

Deardorff, Kevin E., and Patricia Montgomery. "National Population Trends." *U.S. Census Bureau Report* (1998): 1–4.

Fleming, Dean. "The Third Horizon: A Wesleyan Contribution to the Contextualization Debate." *Wesleyan Theological Journal* 30 (1995): 2.

Geffre, Claude. "Christianity and Culture." *International Review of Missions* 84 (1995): 332–33.

Greenberg, Irving. "From Modernity to Post-Modernity: Community and the Revitalization of Traditional Religion." *Religious Education* 73 (1978): 449–69.

Hiebert, Paul G. "Critical Contextualization." *International Bulletin of Missionary Research* (July 1987): 104–12.

Johnson, Kenneth M., and Calvin L. Beale. "The Rural Rebound." *American Demographics* (July 1995): 1–5.

Jonsson, John N. "An Elliptical Understanding of Mission and Its Roles." *Missionalia* 11 (1983): 3–10.

Küng, Hans. "The Reemergence of the Sacred: Transmitting Religious Traditions in a Postmodern World." *Conservative Judaism* 40 (1988): 8–19.

Mesmer, Michael W. "Making Sense of/with Postmodernism." *Soundings: An Interdisciplinary Journal* 68 (1985): 404–26.

Myers, Bryant L. "What Makes Development Christian? Recovering from the Impact of Modernity." *Missiology* 26 (1998): 143–53.

Peterson, Eugene. "Spirit Quest." *Christianity Today* (November 8, 1993): 26–30.

Rosado, Caleb. "The Nature of Society and the Challenge to the Mission of the Church." *International Review of Mission* 77 (1988): 22–37.

Saluter, Arlene F. "Marital Status and Living Arrangements." *U.S. Census Bureau Report* (1998): 1–3.

Shenk, Wilbert R. "Missionary Encounter with Culture." *International Bulletin of Missionary Research* (July 1991): 104–9.

Thomas, Norman E. "Evangelism Trends in the World Council of Churches." *Journal of the Academy for Evangelism in Theological Education* (1998): 43–58.

Van Gelder, Craig. "A Great New Fact of Our Day: America as Mission Field." *Missiology* 19 (1991): 409–18.

_____. "Postmodernism as an Emerging Worldview." *Calvin Theological Journal* 26 (1991): 412–17.

Books

Abraham, William J. *The Logic of Evangelism.* Grand Rapids: Eerdmans, 1989.

Addison, Howard A. *Cast In God's Image.* Woodstock, Vt.: Jewish Lights, 2001.

Ahlstrom, Sydney E. *A Religious History of the American People.* New Haven: Yale University, 1972.

Allen, Diogenes. *Christian Belief in a Postmodern World.* Louisville: Westminster/John Knox Press, 1989.

Anderson, Walter Truett. *Reality Isn't What It Used to Be: Theatrical Politics, Ready-to-Wear Religion, Global Myths, Primitive Chic, and Other Wonders of the Postmodern World.* San Francisco: Harper and Row, 1990.

Ariarajah, Wesley. *The Bible and People of Other Faiths.* Geneva: WCC, 1985.

Arias, Mortimer. *Announcing the Reign of God: Evangelization and the Subversive Memory of Jesus.* Philadelphia: Fortress Press, 1984.

Armstrong, Richard Stoll. *Service Evangelism.* Philadelphia: Westminster Press, 1979.

Atkinson, Donald A., and Charles L. Roesel. *Meeting Needs, Sharing Christ.* Nashville: LifeWay, 1995.

Barker, Joel A. *Paradigms: The Business of Discovering the Future.* San Francisco: Harper, 1992.

Barna, George. *Evangelism that Works.* Ventura: Regal, 1995.

Baum, Gregory, and Harold Wells. *The Reconciliation of Peoples: Challenge to the Churches.* Maryknoll, N.Y.: Orbis, 1997.

Beasley-Murray, G.R. *Jesus and the Kingdom of God.* Grand Rapids: Eerdmans, 1986.

Bellah, Robert, et al., eds. *Habits of the Heart: Individualism and Commitment in American Life.* Berkeley: University of California, 1985.

Bosch, David J. *Transforming Mission. Paradigm Shifts in Theology of Mission.* Maryknoll, N. Y.: Orbis, 1991.

Breech, James. *Jesus and Postmodernism.* Minneapolis: Fortress Press, 1989.

Brueggemann, Walter. *Biblical Perspectives on Evangelism: Living in a Three-Storied Universe.* Nashville: Abingdon Press, 1993.

Burnham, Frederic B. *Postmodern Theology.* San Francisco: Harper, 1989.

Buttry, Daniel L. *Christian Peacemaking: From Heritage to Hope.* Valley Forge, Pa.: Judson Press, 1994.

Cahoone, Lawrence, ed. *From Modernism to Postmodernism.* Cambridge, Mass.: Blackwell, 1996.

Callinicos, Alex. *Against Postmodernism: A Marxist Critique.* New York: St. Martins, 1990.

Carver, William Owen. *The Course of Christian Missions.* New York: Fleming Revell, 1934.

Cassidy, Michael. *The Small Beginnings of Reconciliation in Port Elizabeth.* Port Elizabeth, South Africa: African Enterprise, 1997.

Cobb, John B., Jr. *Reclaiming the Church: Where the Mainline Church Went Wrong and What to Do about It.* Louisville: Westminster John Knox Press, 1997.

Culler, Jonathan. *On Deconstruction: Theory and Criticism after Structuralism.* Ithaca, N.Y.: Cornell University, 1982.

Cunningham, Richard B. *The Christian Faith and Its Contemporary Rivals.* Nashville: Broadman, 1988.

Dempsey, Ron D. *Faith Outside the Walls: Why People Don't Come and Why the Church Must Listen.* Macon, Ga.: Smyth & Helwys, 1997.

De Gruchy, John, and Charles Villa-Vicencio. *Doing Theology in Context: South African Perspectives.* Maryknoll, N.Y.: Orbis, 1994.

DeYoung, Curtiss Paul. *Reconciliation: Our Greatest Challenge–Our Only Hope.* Valley Forge, Pa.: Judson Press, 1997.

Dorrien, Gary. *The Remaking of Evangelical Theology.* Louisville: Westminster/John Knox Press, 1998.

Driver, John. *Images of the Church in Mission.* Scottdale, Pa.: Herald Press, 1997.

Dyrness, William A. *Learning About Theology from the Third World.* Grand Rapids: Zondervan, 1990.

Eighmy, John Lee. *Churches in Cultural Captivity.* Knoxville: University of Tennessee, 1972.

Erickson, Millard J. *Postmodernizing the Faith.* Grand Rapids: Baker, 1998.

Estep, William R. *Whole Gospel–Whole World.* Nashville: Broadman, 1994.

Fackre, Gabriel. *The Christian Story.* Grand Rapids: Eerdmans, 1978.

Fuellenbach, John. *The Kingdom of God: The Message of Jesus Today.* Maryknoll, N.Y.: Orbis, 1998.

Gallup, George. *Religion in America.* Princeton, N.J.: Princeton Religion Research Center, 1984.

Gibbs, Eddie. *In Name Only.* Wheaton, Ill.: Bridgepoint, 1994.

Gill, Robin. *Readings in Modern Theology.* Nashville: Abingdon Press, 1995.

Glasser, Arthur F. *Announcing the Kingdom.* Grand Rapids: Baker Academic, 2003

Green, Michael. *Evangelism in the Early Church.* Grand Rapids: Eerdmans, 1970.

Grenz, Stanley J. *A Primer on Postmodernism.* Grand Rapids: Eerdmans, 1996.

Guder, Darrell L. *The Continuing Conversion of the Church.* Grand Rapids: Eerdmans, 2000.

_____. *Missional Church. A Vision for the Sending of the Church in North America.* Grand Rapids: Eerdmans, 1998.

Hadaway, C. Kirk. *Church Growth Principles.* Nashville: Broadman, 1991.

_____. *Church and Denominational Growth.* Nashville: Abingdon Press, 1993.

Hadaway, C. Kirk, and David A. Roozen. *Rerouting the Protestant Mainstream: Sources of Growth & Opportunities for Change.* Nashville: Abingdon Press, 1995.

Hall, Calvin S., Gardner Lindzey, and John B. Campbell. *Theories of Personality.* New York: John Wiley and Sons, 1978.

Hall, Douglas John. *The End of Christendom and the Future of Christianity.* Valley Forge, Pa. : Trinity, 1997.

Hammond, Mary Tuomi. *The Church and the Dechurched: Mending a Damaged Faith.* St. Louis: Chalice Press, 2001.

Harkness, Georgia. *The Ministry of Reconciliation.* Nashville: Abingdon Press, 1971.

Harvey, David. *The Condition of Postmodernity: An Enquiry into the Origins of Cultural Change.* Cambridge, Mass.: Basil Blackwell, 1989.

Hauerwas, Stanley, and William H. Willimon. *Resident Aliens: A Provocative Christian Assessment of Culture and Ministry for People Who Know That Something Is Wrong.* Nashville: Abingdon Press, 1992.

Hendricks, William D. *Exit Interviews.* Chicago: Moody, 1993.

Hengel, Martin, and Anna Maria Schwemer. *Paul Between Damascus and Antioch.* Louisville: Westminster John Knox Press, 1997.

Henry, Carl F.H. *God, Revelation, and Authority,* 6 vols. Waco, Tex.: Word, 1976.

_____. *Twilight of a Great Civilization: The Drift Toward Neo-Paganism.* Westchester, Ill.: Crossway, 1988.

Hiebert, Paul G. *Anthropological Reflections on Missiological Issues.* Grand Rapids: Baker, 1994.

Hinson, E. Glenn. *The Evangelization of the Roman Empire.* Macon, Ga.: Mercer University, 1981.

_____. *The Early Church.* Nashville: Abingdon Press, 1996.

Holland, Joe. "The Postmodern Paradigm and Contemporary Catholicism." In *Varieties of Postmodern Theology.* Edited by David Ray Griffin, William A. Beardslee, and Joe Holland. Albany: State University of New York, 1989.

Hudson, Winthrop S., and John Corrigan. *Religion in America.* Upper Saddle River, N.J.: Prentice Hall, 1992.

Hunsberger, George, and Craig Van Gelder. *Church: Between Gospel and Culture.* Grand Rapids: Eerdmans, 1996.

Hunter, George G., III. *The Contagious Congregation: Frontiers in Evangelism and Church Growth.* Nashville: Abingdon Press, 1979.

_____. *How To Reach Secular People.* Nashville: Abingdon Press, 1992.

_____. *Church for the Unchurched.* Nashville: Abingdon Press, 1996.

Jenkins, Philip. *The Next Christendom: The Coming of Global Christianity.* New York: Oxford Press, 2002.

Johnson, Ben C. *Rethinking Evangelism: A Theological Approach.* Louisville: Westminster/John Knox Press, 1987.

Johnson, Ronald W. *How Will They Hear if We Don't Listen?* Nashville: Broadman and Holman, 1994.

Jonsson, John N. *Crisis of Missions in the Bible.* Charlotte, N.C.: Nilses, 1987.

Kew, Richard, and Cyril Okorocha. *Vision Bearers.* Harrisburg, Pa.: Morehouse, 1996.

Klaas, Alan C. *In Search of the Unchurched.* New York: Alban, 1996.

Knight, Henry H., III. *A Future for Truth.* Nashville: Abingdon Press, 1997.

Knitter, Paul F. *Jesus and the Other Names.* Maryknoll, N.Y.: Orbis, 1996.

Koester, Helmut. *History, Culture, and Religion of the Hellenistic Age.* New York: Walter de Gruyter, 1995.

Kraft, Charles H. *Christianity in Culture.* Maryknoll, N.Y.: Orbis, 1981.

Krass, Alfred. *Evangelizing Neopagan North America.* Scottdale, Pa.: Herald Press, 1982.

Kraus, C. Norman. *An Intrusive Gospel?* Downers Grove, Ill.: InterVarsity, 1998.

Kroeber, Alfred and Clyde Kluckhohn. *Culture: A Critical Review of Concepts and Definitions.* New York: Vintage Books, 1952.

Kuhn, Thomas S. *The Structure of Scientific Revolutions.* Chicago: University of Chicago, 1970.

Kuzmic, Peter. *The Church: God's Agent for Change.* Exeter, U.K.: Paternoster, 1986.

Larkin, William J., and Joel F. Williams. *Mission in the New Testament.* Maryknoll, N.Y.: Orbis, 1998.

Latourette, Kenneth Scott. *The First Five Centuries.* Grand Rapids: Zondervan, 1970.

_____. *A History of Christianity: Reformation to the Present.* New York: Harper and Row, 1975.

Leon, Arnold E. *Secularization: Science without God?* London: SCM, 1985

Lindsell, Harold. *An Evangelical Theology of Missions.* Grand Rapids: Zondervan, 1970.

Lingenfelter, Sherwood. *Agents of Transformation: A Guide for Effective Cross-Cultural Ministry.* Grand Rapids: Baker. 1996.

Litterer, Joseph A. *The Analysis of Organizations.* New York: John Wiley and Sons, 1973.

Lochman, Jan Milic. *Reconciliation and Liberation: Challenging a One-Dimensional View of Salvation.* Philadelphia: Fortress Press, 1977.

Lohfink, Gerhard. *Jesus and Community.* London: SPCK, 1985.

Madison, Gary B. *The Hermeneutics of Postmodernity: Figures and Themes.* Bloomington: Indiana University, 1990.

Marsden, George M. *Fundamentalism and American Culture.* Oxford: Oxford Press, 1980.

Maynard-Reid, Pedrito U. *Complete Evangelism: The Luke-Acts Model.* Scottdale, Pa.: Herald Press, 1997.

McGavran, Donald A. *Understanding Church Growth.* Grand Rapids: Eerdmans, 1980.

McGrath, Alister. *Evangelicalism & the Future of Christianity.* Downers Grove, Ill. : InterVarsity, 1995.

McKinney, Duane Elmer, and Lois McKinney. *With an Eye on the Future.* Monrovia, Calif.: MARC, 1996.

Meade, Loren B. *The Once and Future Church: Reinventing the Congregation for a New Mission Frontier.* New York: Alban, 1991.

Miller, James B. "The Emerging Postmodern World." In *Postmodern Theology: Christian Faith in a Pluralist World,* 1–19. Edited by Frederic B. Burnham. San Francisco: Harper and Row, 1989.

Miller, Herb. *Church Personality Matters: How to Build Positive Patterns.* St. Louis: Chalice Press, 1999.

Moltmann, Jürgen. *The Church in the Power of the Spirit.* New York: Harper and Row, 1975.

_____, et al. *A Passion for God's Reign.* Grand Rapids: Eerdmans, 1998.

Mosher, Steve. *God's Power, Jesus' Faith, and World Mission.* Scottdale, Pa.: Herald Press, 1947.

Mundey, Paul. *Unlocking Church Doors: 10 Keys to Positive Change.* Nashville: Abingdon Press, 1997.

Newbigin, Lesslie. *The Open Secret: An Introduction to the Theology of Mission.* Grand Rapids: Eerdmans, 1978.

_____. *Foolishness to the Greeks.* Grand Rapids: Eerdmans, 1986.

_____. *The Gospel in a Pluralist Society.* Grand Rapids: Eerdmans, 1989.

_____. *Trinitarian Faith and Today's Mission.* Richmond, Va.: John Knox Press, 1963.

Noll, Mark A. *A History of Christianity in the United States and Canada.* Grand Rapids: Eerdmans, 1992.

_____. *Turning Points.* Grand Rapids: Baker, 1997.

Oden, Thomas. *After Modernity…What?: Agenda for Theology.* Grand Rapids: Zondervan, 1992.

Okholm, Dennis L. *The Gospel in Black & White: Theological Resources for Racial Reconciliation.* Downers Grove, Ill.: InterVarsity, 1997.

Orr, J. Edwin. *The Flaming Tongue.* Chicago: Moody, 1973.

Packer, J. I. *"Fundamentalism" and the Word of God.* Grand Rapids: Eerdmans, 1958.

Padilla, C. René. "The Unity of the Church and the Homogeneous Unit Principle." In *Exploring Church Growth.* Edited by Wilbert R. Shenk. Grand Rapids: Eerdmans, 1980.

_____. *Mission Between the Times: Essays on the Kingdom.* Grand Rapids: Eerdmans, 1985.

Phillips, James M., and Robert T. Coote. *Toward the 21ˢᵗ Century in Christian Mission.* Grand Rapids: Eerdmans, 1993.

Poe, Harry Lee. *The Gospel and Its Meaning.* Grand Rapids: Zondervan, 1996.

_____. *See No Evil: The Existence of Sin in an Age of Relativism.* Grand Rapids: Kregel, 2004.

_____. *Christian Witness in a Postmodern World.* Nashville: Abingdon Press, 2001.

Reid-Maynard, Pedrito U. *Complete Evangelism.* Scottdale, Pa.: Herald Press. 1997.

Robinson, H. Wheeler. *Corporate Personality in Ancient Israel.* Philadelphia: Fortress Press, 1964.

Rosenau, Pauline M. *Post-Modernism and the Social Sciences: Insights, Inroads, and Intrusions.* Princeton: Princeton University, 1992.

Roozen, David A., and Kirk Hadaway. *Church & Denominational Growth.* Nashville: Abingdon Press, 1993.

Saayman, Willem, and Klippies Kritzinger. *Mission in Bold Humility: David Bosch's Work Considered.* Maryknoll, N.Y.: Orbis, 1996.

Sample, Tex. *U.S. Lifestyles and Mainline Churches.* Louisville: Westminster/ John Knox Press, 1990.

Sampson, Philip, et al. *Faith and Modernity.* Oxford: Regnum, 1994.

Sanneh, Lamin. *Translating the Message.* Maryknoll, N.Y.: Orbis, 1992.

_____. *Religion and the Variety of Culture.* Valley Forge, Pa.: Trinity, 1996.

Schaller, Lyle E. *It's a Different World.* Nashville: Abingdon Press, 1987.

Scharpff, Paulus. *History of Evangelism.* Grand Rapids: Eerdmans, 1964.

Scherer, James A., and Stephen B. Bevans. *New Directions in Mission and Evangelization 1.* Maryknoll, N.Y.: Orbis, 1992.

Schreiter, Robert J. *Constructing Local Theologies.* Maryknoll, N.Y.: Orbis, 1986.

_____. *The Ministry of Reconciliation.* Maryknoll, N.Y.: Orbis, 1998.

Schillebeeckx, Eduard. *Church: The Human Story of God.* New York: Crossroad, 1990.

Senior, Donald, and Carroll Stuhlmueller. *The Biblical Foundations for Mission.* Maryknoll, N.Y.: Orbis, 1983.

Shenk, Wilbert R. *The Transfiguration of Mission: Biblical Theological and Historical Foundations.* Scottdale, Pa. : Herald Press, 1993.

Smith, Huston. *Beyond the Post-Modern Mind.* Wheaton: Theosophical, 1989.

Snyder, Howard. *Models of the Kingdom.* Nashville: Abingdon Press, 1991.

Southard, Samuel. *Pastoral Evangelism.* Nashville: Broadman, 1962.

Starkes, M. Thomas. *God's Commissioned People.* Nashville: Broadman, 1984.

Stott, John R. W. *Christian Mission in the Modern World.* Downers Grove, Ill.: InterVarsity, 1975.

Sweet, William Warren, ed. *Religion on the American Frontier: The Baptists 1783–1830.* New York: Cooper Square, 1964.

Thomas, Norman E. *Classic Texts in Mission & World Christianity.* Maryknoll, N.Y.: Orbis, 1995.

Van Kaam, Adrian. *Religion and Personality.* New York: Image Books, 1968.

Van Rheenen, Gailyn. *Missions: Biblical Foundations and Contemporary Strategies.* Grand Rapids: Zondervan, 1996.

Verkuyl, J. *Contemporary Missiology.* Grand Rapids: Eerdmans, 1978.

Verstraelen, F. J., et al., *Missiology: An Ecumenical Introduction, Texts and Contexts of Global Christianity.* Grand Rapids: Eerdmans, 1995.

Volf, Miroslav. *Exclusion & Embrace: A Theological Exploration of Identity, Otherness, and Reconciliation.* Nashville: Abingdon Press, 1996.

Wells, David F. *God in the Wasteland: The Reality of Truth in a World of Fading Dreams.* Grand Rapids: Eerdmans, 1994.

Wright, Tim. *Unfinished Evangelism: More Than Getting Them in the Door.* Minneapolis: Augsburg, 1995.

Wuthnow, Robert. *The Restructuring of American Religion.* Princeton: Princeton, 1988.

_____. *The Struggle for America's Soul: Evangelicals, Liberals, and Secularism.* Grand Rapids: Eerdmans, 1989.

Young, Pamela Dickey. *Christ in a Post-Christian World.* Minneapolis: Fortress Press, 1995.

Zorn, Raymond O. *Church and Kingdom.* Philadelphia: Presbyterian and Reformed Publishing Company, 1962.

Unpublished Dissertations

Bate, Stuart Clifton. *Inculturation and Healing: A Missiological Investigation into the Coping-Healing Ministry in South African Christianity.* Th.D. diss., University of South Africa, 1993.

Gosnell, Rick. *The Postmodern Paradigm: Challenges to the Evangelistic Ministry of the Church.* Ph.D. diss., Southern Baptist Theological Seminary, 1993.

Johnson, Ronald W. *An Evaluation of the Home Mission Board Programs of Evangelism in Local Churches.* D.Min. research project, The Southern Baptist Theological Seminary, 1988.

Johnson, Ronald W. *Paradigm Shift in Evangelism: A Study of the Need for Contextualization in the Mission of Southern Baptists.* Th.D. diss.,: University of South Africa, 1999.